AI FOR MBAS

AI for MBAs: The Essential Guide for Leaders Building AI-Driven Enterprise serves as a foundational textbook for understanding how artificial intelligence (AI) can be successfully integrated within the realm of business.

A tectonic shift has begun across the global economy. AI is restructuring how companies think, act, and win, and the leaders who understand this shift today will dominate the markets of tomorrow. Building upon hundreds of interviews with CEOs and founders at the forefront of the AI economy, this textbook offers a practice-oriented roadmap for the next generation of business leaders. It shows how to move beyond legacy strategy tools into the world of intelligent systems, agentic workflows, and AI-native business models. Across its 12 chapters, this book traces how AI is redefining operations, competition, and organizational design. It explains the new mechanics of work, the rise of autonomous decision loops, and the emerging playbooks that modern leaders use to scale faster and act with greater clarity. Looking ahead to the MBA classroom of 2050, it introduces the archetypes of the AI-enabled professional, namely the Centaurs, Cyborgs, and Artisans, and describes how human intelligence and machine intelligence will work together in the decades to come.

This book is written for ambitious and forward-thinking MBA students and those who have graduated long ago and want more than theory. It is for readers who want to understand the tools, the models, and the mindset that will define leadership in an AI-driven world, and who intend to shape that world rather than be shaped by it.

T. Alexander Puutio teaches AI and leadership at Harvard University. He is a seasoned business leader with decades of management consulting and operational strategy experience from Boston Consulting Group and the United Nations system. He reaches a readership of 1.5m a year with his Substack and mainstream beats on Forbes and beyond.

AI FOR MBAS

The Essential Guide for Leaders Building AI-Driven Enterprise

T. Alexander Puutio

Routledge
Taylor & Francis Group
LONDON AND NEW YORK

Designed cover image: Shutterstock

First edition published 2026
by Routledge
4 Park Square, Milton Park, Abingdon, Oxon, OX14 4RN

and by Routledge
605 Third Avenue, New York, NY 10158

Routledge is an imprint of the Taylor & Francis Group, an informa business

British Library Cataloguing-in-Publication Data
A catalogue record for this book is available from the British Library

ISBN: 9781032832494 (hbk)
ISBN: 9781032832487 (pbk)
ISBN: 9781003508427 (ebk)

DOI: 10.4324/9781003508427

Typeset in Times New Roman
by codeMantra

CONTENTS

1

ADDING VALUE IN THE AGE OF AI

A hopeful case for MBAs

Dr. David Livingstone once quipped that "reports of my death have been greatly exaggerated," and the same can be said of humans in the age of artificial intelligence (AI). While sensational headlines breathlessly proclaim that AI will replace millions of knowledge workers and make humans redundant in the world of business before we know it, the truth is far more nuanced and, as you'll hopefully come to agree soon enough, much more optimistic.

Every major technological shift brings with it disruption, economic dislocations, the loss of familiar roles entire communities have depended on, and, ultimately, the rise of entirely new industries. Consider the ice trade. In the 1800s, thousands of workers made their living by harvesting blocks of ice from frozen lakes, carefully insulating them with hay, and transporting them to cities during the summer months. It was painstaking work and, for a time, a lucrative industry that brought in the equivalent of hundreds of millions of today's dollars.

But by the 1850s, ice plants began to appear. As company after company turned on machines that could manufacture ice efficiently on command, the writing was on well and truly the wall. Most observers at the time could have predicted that technology would take over the manual labor and that the old trade would inevitably fade into obsolescence. What they may not have foreseen was that the demand driving all of that work, the human desire to keep things, drinks, and ourselves cool, would not only remain but also grow exponentially.

What would likely have stunned a 19th-century ice merchant is the simple fact that today, far more people are employed in cooling-related industries than ever before. They no long find their value in harvesting ice, although plenty work in making, selling, and packaging ice even today, but in designing, producing, selling, and maintaining an ecosystem of machines and services that deliver refrigeration to nearly every corner of the globe. Today, people engineer the hardware that makes our fridges run. Others write the software that powers their smart features or monitors their energy use. Marketing teams shape consumer demand, and influencers generate it in their niches. The value chain now stretches from research labs to last-mile delivery, proving how the job of keeping things cool has vanished by no means. Instead, it evolved and multiplied across a range of adjacent possibilities, none of which would have been obvious to the observers of the day. What was obvious to everyone at the time was that the ice trade would, well, simply melt away, and in a sense, their predictions were all as correct as they were misguided.

DOI: 10.4324/9781003508427-1

History is filled with such transitions where the types of jobs change dramatically because of new tools and technologies, but the human imperative to create value in meeting the underlying needs does not. One of the reassuring lessons of history is that we've been through transformations like this before and come out with stronger economies and more places for human ingenuity to flourish as a result. And yet, with the age of AI, we're also entering entirely new territory that demands an entirely new playbook.

Before we lay out that playbook in more detail, it is incumbent on us to understand two conjoined concepts in fuller detail: the business of business and the concept of value with which we'll begin.

What is value, really?

The concept of value doesn't need much of an introduction. Most of us intuit our way through its many shades, be it emotional, economic, or even philosophical. And if you're anything like me, you probably have a strong gut-level sense of what counts as valuable. But if we peel back the onion by even one layer, you'll find there's a lot more going on under the hood than we realize.

In fact, it is entirely worth our while to stop here and ask the beguilingly simple question: what is value, anyway?

Tracing the history of who gets to decide what something's worth, and how that judgment has evolved, gives us the grounding we need to make sense of where AI fits, and what role humans still have to play in the business of business.

In the earliest human economies, value was deeply literal. A spear was valuable because it kept you fed. A fur that you wrangled off a deer with said spear was valuable because it kept you alive through winter. A friend was valuable for the company and the safety they provided. In this world, value was not hotly debated simply because, in most cases, you could touch it, barter it, sleep under it, or perhaps even with it.

This primal notion of value hasn't gone anywhere, mind you. We still attach worth to things simply because they exist and perform a useful function, and we value the services we offer each other based on what we get in return. A house, a warm jacket, and a clean glass of water still count as obviously, unquestionably valuable, given the use and benefits we derive out of them. But somewhere along the way, we did what humans do best: we complicated things by kicking the whole concept of value up the ladder of abstraction.

We started seeing value in the thing itself as well as in how effectively it satisfies the underlying needs it targets. Food is no longer just food; it's organic, low-carb, sustainably sourced, gluten-free, high-protein, keto-friendly bliss that fetches a premium. Two otherwise identical loaves of bread now vary wildly in price, not because of what they are in the most tangible sense of things, but because of what they *mean* to those consuming them. This shift from "a thing" to "a thing plus meaning" is also what allows us to disagree about value in the first place. If value were objective and derived from the mere existence of things, we'd all be shopping the same aisle and bidding on the same items. But it isn't and never will be. Instead, value is contextual, emotional, and often entirely made up.

In fact, subjectivity has always been baked into valuation. Gold and diamonds have little practical use for most people, but we've wrapped them in so much myth, history, and marketing that they've become storehouses of wealth. Same with the *Mona Lisa*, a largely forgotten painting until Vincenzo Peruggia gave it a starring role in the world's first viral art heist on

August 21, 1911, repatriating it to Italy without bothering to ask the Louvre. And now it is the most valuable piece of art on this planet, not least because we all agree that it is.

History knows plenty of similar stories of aggressive agreement on the concept of value that would make little sense to outsiders. The classic example from Econ 101 is the Rai stones of Yap. Giant, immovable disks of limestone that were used as currency not because of what they *did*, but because everyone simply agreed they were valuable. Meanwhile, similar stones in the prehistoric forests of Finland, where my ancestors roamed, were just rocks in the ground, unnoticed by people who, unbeknownst to them, were sitting on a Yap fortune. A missed Forex opportunity if there ever was one.

The point here is simple. There's only so much value you can squeeze out of what something *does*. Modern economies wouldn't function at all if we hadn't invented theoretical scaffolding to add layers of value beyond use. And over time, we've gotten very good at this game of tag-on, to the point most of us don't even notice that we're playing it.

Here are just a few ways we have at it:

- *We add labor*. The idea that more effort or skill put into something makes it worth more. A handmade chair, crafted by an artisan who only makes ten pieces a year. A chef's tasting menu that takes half an hour to prepare. A deck prepared at 2:00 a.m. by a consultant who has poured their heart out on the project for weeks.
- *We add desirability*. That one T-shirt cost $10, and another $300 is all thanks to the magicians in the marketing department rather than those making the shirts themselves. What we want more, we value more.
- *We create scarcity*. Sometimes scarcity springs naturally, but often we create it deliberately. Limited editions, pop-ups, vintage drops, and exclusive access make the modern consumer drool dollar signs. The fewer desirable things, the more value we see in them.
- *We move value to where it's valued more*. This one is the beating heart of every market you've ever taken part in from the stock market to the labor pool. If I have something you want more than I do, and we can agree on a trade, we've magically increased total value in the system without making anything new. Arbitrage, distribution, licensing, reselling, and even consulting itself often boils down to one thing: getting value into the hands of someone who sees more in it.

None of these are concern tool *use* in the classical sense. Instead, they're about the *meta-use*: how the thing is perceived, positioned, distributed, or understood socially. And for that, you need a human brain and all its messy, evolved social circuitry to determine what counts, what matters, and what's worth more than what.

Don't worry, we won't get any further into the philosophical weeds here. The theory of value could fill a whole book, and thankfully, Mariana Mazzucato has already done just that. So we'll leave the heavy lifting to her, and I invite you to stop here to read her book if this topic caught your interest. The next pages will wait for you until you're finished. And once you're back, what we'll take away from all of this is the following: the reason humans aren't out of the equation simply because AI showed up is because we're still the ones deciding what's worth building, pricing, scaling, or sunsetting. Business starts with human judgment, and it ends there too, which is why our next stop is understanding what on earth we are all so busy with in these economies of ours (Figure 1.1).

FIGURE 1.1 Just add pressure and you'll see.

What is the business of business to begin with?

Simplifying things greatly, all of business is about either creating value or distributing it elsewhere.

Depending on who you ask, of course, you'll get a dozen different versions of that same answer. Marc Andreessen, founder of Netscape and one of Silicon Valley's most influential voices, famously framed the entire history of business as a story of bundling and unbundling. A product gets packaged into a service, then split out again, reassembled, repackaged, and redistributed. The media industry. Telecom. Finance. All bundles, all unbundled, all bundled again. Keep this concept in mind as well and get back to it with gusto soon enough.

Andreessen wasn't the first to spot the cyclical nature of business evolution. Long before software blanketed the enterprise world, Joseph Schumpeter was already chewing on the same idea, albeit with more Austrian rigor and fewer soy lattes. His theory of creative destruction described capitalism as a perpetual churn where innovation not only disrupts incumbents but entirely destroys them to clear the way for new growth. In this model, new entrants don't slot neatly into the old order; instead, they burn it down and build something different atop the ashes. What Schumpeter saw was less of the bundling and more of a bloodsport, where the winning tech takes it all. Schumpeter's writing remains as prescient as it was back in the day, and it reminds us that business doesn't simply move value around; at times, it entirely redefines it, often by those bold enough to envision a new path to the future.

Then, there's Clay Christensen, whose contribution was less focused on the cycles and more attuned to the *why* of business. His "Jobs to Be Done" theory shifts our attention away from the product and toward the purpose it intends to serve. What he asks us to appreciate is that people don't buy a drill because they want a drill; they buy it because they need a hole in the wall. In Christensen's view, the job of business is to help people make progress; however, they define it by offering better, more affordable, more accessible tools to get those jobs done. Value, under this model, is contextual and fluid, shaped not by the producer but by the evolving needs of the user. And tech, like AI, is simply what fills the holes where they are wanted and when.

And yet, none of these thinkers owns the patent on defining the business of business. They're simply adding updates to a conversation that is as ancient as our societies themselves.

If you go back far enough, you'll find none other than Xenophon, recognized as one of the greatest writers of antiquity today and known as a soldier turned historian turned philosopher in his time, who was already poking around in the same territory. In *Oeconomicus*, he describes the household (oikos) as an economic unit, wherein labor and various resources are mixed together in order to create surplus and manage scarcity. Sure, he wasn't describing late-stage capitalism, but his model was recognizably *business*. His work laid the intellectual breadcrumbs that Adam Smith, Karl Marx, and generations of economists, sociologists, and management theorists would follow, each expanding the philosophical pie one spoonful at a time.

The truth is, there's very little new about any of this. We've been grappling with the meaning, mechanisms, and morality of value creation for thousands of years. Each era gives it new names, new metrics, and today, new PowerPoint slides, but the core questions remain stubbornly unchanged.

And whatever frame you prefer, bundling and unbundling, creative destruction, jobs to be done, stakeholder theory, surplus management, donut economies, the outcome is always the same: business exists to either create value or to move it around. Nothing more, nothing less.

Where philosophers have spent centuries debating what value is, the rest of us have spent our time asking a more pragmatic question: who is it for? This is not a semantic quibble, mind you. The questions of wealth distribution are among the most consequential divides in the modern economy. Is value meant to serve shareholders? Workers? Society at large? Should we save it for future generations? The argument rages across boardrooms, classrooms, and campaign trails, and we'll gladly leave that disputing to our philosopher friends on park benches. You see, for MBAs, there's really only one defensible answer to who is the value for, and that is the client.

In the muddiest and yet most practical terms, value is whatever the client experiences as such. It's the relief your service provides, the outcome your tool enables, the joy your product delivers, or the goodwill affiliation with your brand increases. Everything else, your margins, your prestige, and your market share, is secondary. That's not a moral claim, although it serves us one. Ignore client value, and it doesn't matter how brilliant your operations are, because the clients will forget you. Obsess over it, and you've got the beginnings of an ironclad business.

For MBAs, this means flipping the instinct that may have brought to study the field to begin with. Don't start by asking, "How do we make money out of this?" or "How do we defend our position?" Start with: What does the client truly need, and how do we deliver them that and more? Maximize that and calibrate your own share based on the value you genuinely add, and you've just invented a durable business for yourself. And in an age of automation, where more and more gets commoditized by the hour, that human-centered calibration may be your last source of unfair advantage.

To see how this works in practice, consider the humble rock. What follows is a journey from meaningless debris to multimillion-dollar market simply by humans having found ways of adding layers of value atop the same object, and new ways of distributing the value it now holds, until it becomes an entirely different economic proposition altogether (Table 1.1).

TABLE 1.1 The old-fashioned value chain

Stage	*Inputs*	*Outcome*	*How value is added*
Raw object	Rock (found on the ground)	Paperweight, memento	Intrinsic or symbolic value only. No functional or economic value beyond sentiment.
Crafted good	Rock + labor (polished)	Semi-precious stone	Value created through work and transformation. Functional and aesthetic enhancement.
Branded product	Polished stone + branding & marketing	Diamond (luxury item)	Value added through narrative, aspiration, scarcity cues. Desire replaces utility.
Economic system	Diamond + distribution infrastructure	New York city's Diamond District	Value distributed via liquidity, network effects, and price signaling mechanisms.
Applied innovation	Diamond + engineering + design	Diamond-tipped industrial drill	Value shifted from luxury to function. Utility now drives price, not perception alone.

FIGURE 1.2 Little does the client know that there's only a thumb drive with a PowerPoint slide inside.

The above chain of events isn't that far off from what's happened in the real world, and you can bet your bottom dollar that an MBA has been involved each step of the way. AI does nothing to change this, nor would it be capable of doing so. What AI does change is how business gets conducted, which is why we'll next need to turn to the concept of tools, and the uniquely human relationship with them (Figure 1.2).

Homo sapiens and their tools

If you're old enough, you will remember having been taught that humans are the only animals capable of using tools. On behalf of the rest of animal kind, I feel obligated to clarify: that was a dirty old lie, bordering on inter-species defamation.

The idea that tool use is uniquely human has long served as a convenient crutch for our species that gave us a neat boundary to draw between ourselves and everything else out there with a pulse. In essence, it helped us navigate the messy philosophical terrain of why some animals get names and sweaters, while others get made into seasoning and side dishes. If we're the only ones wielding tools, the logic went, then surely we must be at the top of the moral food chain.

Thanks to the work of Jane Goodall and many other scientists and field researchers, we now know better. Tool use is surprisingly widespread across species. Crows fashion hooks from twigs to catch a treat that is otherwise out of reach. Sea otters use rocks to crack open shellfish that remain stubbornly shuttered. Termites build complex ventilation systems in their mounds, and ants use debris, and sometimes each other, as rafts. And deep in the Borneo jungle, orangutans have been spotted crafting spears to catch fish, perhaps after having seen humans do it first.

And yet, we weren't entirely wrong to feel smug and superior about our tools, particularly when it comes to our MBAs. There's still a kernel of truth in the old claim, it's just that it needs some refining. While many animals use tools, no other species *really gets* tools the way we do. None build them with our precision and passion that verges on obsession. None pass them on through language and culture with our consistency. And most critically: no other species has managed to turn tool use into the very foundation of how they think, work, and build meaning. While other animals might craft and use tools to forage or scratch their backs, we've built entire civilizations on top of them (Figure 1.3).

From flint blades to spinning looms, from sextants to spreadsheets, our species has followed a consistent pattern across history. First, someone identifies a constraint. Then, they or someone else imagines a workaround, makes it repeatable, and hands it off to the next generation. Every leap forward, whether it's in agriculture, writing, glassblowing, shipbuilding, or telecommunications, has begun with someone saying: "There's got to be a better way." This process is responsible for much of the technological advancements we've come to benefit from, and it underlies the very existence of most of the businesses you know and love today.

What comes out as a result is a powerful kind of compounding advantage that is unique to our species. A crow might figure out a neat trick or two in a single lifetime, but it dies with the crow. Humans, on the other hand, inherit the tools, tricks, and infrastructure of those who came before us. At least this is how it works most of the time, even though some Egyptian pottery techniques have been permanently lost to history, which is both heartbreaking and grounds for alien conspiracies if you're into unnaturally smooth vases and their origins. But for the most part, we've kept the party going, passing on what we know to those who come after. And with the advent of writing, we kicked that compounding effect into overdrive. We no longer content ourselves by simply handing down the tools we know; we document and patent them, scale and optimize

FIGURE 1.3 My startup just got seed funded.

them, and breathlessly seek new ways to improve upon them. In this process, we've come to require an entirely new concept of tools that is able to accommodate the growing omnipotence we wield them with: technology.

And now, after millennia of chasing leverage from sticks, wheels, engines, circuits, and code, we find ourselves at the edge of something that we haven't yet fully come to terms with: we've built tools that can build tools. For the first time, the machines we've created are more than passive extensions of our bodies waiting for human inputs to do their thing. Instead, we've entered an era where you can describe a problem in natural language to a machine that will spin up a solution, test it, and improve upon it, all before your coffee cools.

We've talked about this moment for decades in tones that have swung between fascination and dread. From Asimov's laws of robotics to Norbert Wiener's cybernetics, the idea that machines might one day think, or at least act like they do, has been part of our cultural and intellectual bloodstream since Alan Turin proposed his famous test. Countless economists have warned of technological unemployment, innumerable philosophers have debated the possibility of consciousness in silicon, and a gaggle of science fiction writers has mapped every possible outcome from the utopian to the dystopian. And yet, even Carl Sagan knew that he was writing science fiction, not white papers.

What's changed between now and then is that our science fiction has come off the page and started writing its own code. Along the way, we have gone from toolmakers who now make toolmakers. And in creating something that is capable of the act of creation itself, we have become as gods.

Before we find ourselves wading too deep into the grander meaning of it all, let's zoom back to why you've opened this book to begin with.

In order to understand how the advent of AI impacts business, we first need to understand what kind of a tool it actually is. A crude categorization of how tools have been useful in the past will be helpful here, and if we squint just enough, we'll see that tools have invariably come to us in one or more of the following four forms.

I Tools that let humans do *more* work

The printing press allowed one scribe's work to be replicated thousands of times. The calculator allowed one accountant to process hundreds of sheets rather than dozens. Excel sheets and a few handy macros allow one FP&A analyst to do what a thousand accountants with their calculators couldn't do in years.

II Tools that let humans do *better* work

MRI machines didn't replace doctors; instead, they gave our caregivers keener eyes. Power drills allow contractors to do both more and better-quality work. The human remains essential, now amplified by the technology they are wielding.

III Tools that do the work themselves

Assembly line robots in car manufacturing replaced human welders for specific, repetitive tasks. Payroll software removed the need for manually cutting checks. The human tasks became redundant as the tech slowly took their place.

IV Tools that make entirely new kinds of work possible

The internet enabled digital marketing, social platforms, and cloud-native software start-ups. Satellite imaging enabled global logistics and climate modeling. These didn't exist before their enabling tech did.

What makes AI unique is that it sits selfishly at the intersection of *all four* of these categories, simultaneously. Worse yet, it excels in each of them. Good luck getting a date to prom now, sliced bread.

To make sense of this, we'll organize AI's impact through the three archetypes we've introduced elsewhere in this book, the Learning Machine, the Thinking Machine, and the Doing Machine, all concepts we'll get intimately familiar with in Chapter 4, and map them across the four fundamental functions of tools. What results is a kind of blueprint for understanding where AI sits today, and what kind of leverage it offers for those bold enough to wield it (Table 1.2).

The other thing about this tool is that it doesn't feel nearly as foreign as past ones. First, it mimics humans, both in how it's trained and in what it produces. Second, it slips into existing workflows with surprising ease, rather than forcing entirely new ones that add friction and resistance. And finally, it delivers outcomes the way we do: in natural language, on demand, and often with context-aware nuance. All of this makes AI feel less like a tool we have to learn and more like one we've always used. That's why its adoption curves are bending upwards like a hockey stick in the hands of a Canadian teenager.

Together, all of the above conspires to create momentum and scale to the point where we're entirely entitled to say that "yes, we've seen this movie before, but this time it really is different."

On the one hand, tools have come and gone. From stone axes to spreadsheet macros, most of them were incremental improvements, always helpful, sometimes transformative, but almost without fail confined to a specific function. Even our biggest paradigm shifts from the spinning jenny to the steam engine and the internet followed a familiar pattern where a powerful tool arrives, labor markets adjust, new industries emerge, and the world, after some turbulence, regains equilibrium. So too we will find our equilibrium after AI.

On the other hand, no prior tool has hit quite like AI. This one doesn't just live in a single quadrant or challenge one set of industry incumbents. It aims at all of them. If the Luddites smashed

TABLE 1.2 AI as viewed across the spectrum of tools

Machine type	*Does more work*	*Does better work*	*Does the work for us*	*Opens up new kinds of work*
Learning machine	Trains on massive data to uncover hidden patterns (e.g., customer churn models)	Refines models continuously for sharper forecasts (e.g., demand planning, fraud)	Automatically segments users, personalizes content, and flags anomalies	Enables predictive systems in areas like precision agriculture and genomic modeling
Thinking machine	LLMs summarize hundreds of documents instantly	Copilots surface insights from messy data (e.g., Notion AI, Microsoft 365 Copilot)	AI agents coordinate strategy decks, memos, and emails drafted from prompts	Autonomous AI ecosystems simulate scenario planning, decision modeling at scale
Doing machine	Agentic AI executes multi-step workflows	AI QA testers catch bugs that humans couldn't notice	AI tools schedule meetings, execute logistics, and generate entire marketing campaigns	Fully autonomous business functions; AI-first org structures

looms because of machines that could weave faster than they could, AI critics disquietingly rage-free given how they are faced with a machine that can weave, draft a go-to-market strategy for itself, raise the funds, and file the IPO paperwork. Panic, skepticism, and hand-wringing are rational responses now.

Unlike previous waves of disruption where the pace allowed for some breathing room, this one compounds as it grows. And yet, despite the exponential curves, the frothy VC decks, and the inevitable dystopian op-eds, the darkest projections of mass obsolescence and structural economic collapse remain, in all likelihood, overstated.

The reason is simply because the underlying logic of business hasn't changed one iota.

Business remains stubbornly centered around solving human problems. It still begins with understanding a need and ends with delivering value. Business is a profoundly human activity, and while the tools we use may change how we do things, they cannot rewrite why we use them. And there's much for the MBA of the future to do in managing the human side of business.

This is the thread that ties it all together. If you look closely enough, you'll see that no company has ever succeeded solely because they adopted a particular tool. Yes, they might have outcompeted their peers and conquered a market, and where they succeeded, they did so because they understood their customers, adapted to change, structured incentives better, and made better bets than their competitors with the tools they had. All of that requires judgment, context, and coordination. AI can support all of that, and it can climb up the rungs of the value ladder with you, but it doesn't replace the need to decide what's worth building, where to go next, or how to lead people through uncertainty. The firms that rise won't be the ones that simply deploy AI. They'll be the ones that *orchestrate* it, placing it on the right rung of the ladder, at the right moment, for the right outcome.

That's where the MBAs come in.

Enter the age of the MBA

Everyone's getting access to the same tools. That's the first principle we need to accept in this new era. The baseline capabilities—text generation, data synthesis, and workflow automation—are rapidly becoming commodities. But that doesn't mean outcomes will be the same. In fact, the opposite is true. When everyone has the same tool, what separates the best from the rest is what they do with it and who is doing the doing.

You see, what you add on top of the tool is what becomes your differentiator. And those differences will come from only three places: custom processes, custom data, and custom people. The tooling and processes define your workflows. The data shapes the outputs and your insights. And the people are the ones who decide what matters, when to pivot, and how to frame the problems worth solving in the first place (Table 1.3).

And here lies the beautiful irony: in an age defined by AI, it's the human layer that becomes most valuable. AI might level the playing field, but it also spotlights the judgment, taste, and originality of the people using it. The age of the machines, it turns out, is ushering in the age of humans.

What flips here is the script we've followed for centuries. In the past, technology was the advantage that humans used to outcompete the rest. Today, it's the shared baseline, and when that baseline is powerful, ubiquitous, and improving on its own, what separates the exceptional from the forgettable is no longer the tool, but the operator.

Here's my favorite way to visualize this on a whiteboard for my students.

Picture a lone cactus in the middle of Arizona's Sonoran Desert. *Carnegiea gigantea*, the giant saguaro, has spent centuries doing the slow and noble work of surviving. It's adapted to scarcity. It's learned to stand still while everything else blows past. And yet, when the lightning comes, it won't strike the desert floor. It strikes the tallest thing in its path. In a landscape flattened by equality where tools, compute, and access are more evenly distributed than ever before, whatever stands out is *all that stands out*.

There's a term for this dynamic in gender studies: the gender equality paradox. As systems become more equal, differences that were once buried in noise become exaggerated. That the same will happen here is inevitable. As AI levels the field, the small human differences, be it insight, drive, clarity, or simply taste, become massive multipliers that will make all of the difference, not some of it.

Which brings us to the MBAs, which for me doesn't just count the degree holders but also the hard-earned operators who've absorbed the skills by sitting with complexity, managing teams, shipping projects, and closing deals while my students sweated the same out in the classroom.

What me and my colleagues at Boston Consulting Group were paid to do wasn't magic, although cajoling clients to pay millions for the slides we shipped certainly felt like it. Instead, it was our ability to see value, find it where others missed it, and repackage it in a way that made the world go "ah, of course." Everything is obvious, once you know the answer, after all.

TABLE 1.3 The differentiators in the age of AI

Custom processes	*Custom data*	*Custom people*
The unique ways in which companies build their cognitive stacks, as discussed in Chapter 11	The unique data and knowledge the company brings, e.g., McKinsey, with their proprietary market insights from decades of work	The people who drive the tools with their processes and data towards outcomes deem value adding.

You can call it strategy, coordination, problem solving, communications, value chain redesign, narrative alignment, or purely figuring out what the hell is going on. Whatever the label, the job was always the same: pump value from where it hides, or create it from scratch. While the tools and data helped, we also brought our mix of logic, creativity, and people skills that no spreadsheet or model could replicate.

Soon, AI will be everywhere, and the only difference will be you.

In this very near future, the winning play won't be access to AI, it'll be how you wield it. And wielding it well means drawing from the very human playbook: clarity of thought, strategic judgment, narrative fluency, and the grit to see things through. The good news is that MBAs, and those who think like them, already know this game inside out. They've played it for decades, and now they get to play it with an exosuit with no referee on the field.

FIGURE 1.4 Now all I need is to talk the cactuses into a profit-share agreement and my bonus will wire itself.

But it does require a change of approach, hence this book to begin with. Going forward, we'll need to get better at leaning into what makes us valuable as humans not in spite of the tools, but because of them. This applies as well as to our concepts of value and client centrality, as much as it does to recognizing how much of the competitive edge in our companies remains, irreducibly and indefinitely, in the human domain.

Whatever tools the MBAs of the future use, they will still require humans to build trust in them and to navigate tangled politics in a room or muster the courage to place a risky bet amidst the fog of uncertainty. It's only we sentient sacks of meat who can rally a team with a vision they can actually believe in and who endow the brightest go-to-market strategy with purpose and intent others will find worth following. Our AI stacks can generate ideas faster than we can, but they will still need to be sold with conviction to clients and the team. This is what I mean when I say that the human component of business hasn't changed. In fact, it matters now more than ever. As we step into this next chapter of business, the winning hand will go to those who recognize that the heart of business remains human and to those who find new ways to keep it beating.

I'll go on record with a wager here: once MBAs find their new equilibrium in the age of AI, they'll actually enjoy it more deeply than the version that came before. No one I have found worth trusting has found true and lasting meaning over nailing a tricky vlookup table. But selling an idea that changes a client's trajectory? Crafting a narrative that brings investors onboard and brings a product-led-growth motion to life? That's the good stuff that's still worth an MBA degree from the Ivy League. And thanks to the tools we now have, we'll get to spend more time in that gear rather than grinding ourselves out.

Now, all we need is to stand tall, play our role, and wait for lightning to strike (Figure 1.4).

2

EVERYONE GETS THE SAME SUPERTOOL

Now what?

Anyone who claims to know exactly how the AI revolution will unfold should be asked, politely but firmly, to hand over next week's lottery numbers while they are at it. As agreed in the previous chapter, we're living through an economic disruption that touches nearly every domain of business at once, and anyone pretending to have a precise forecast of tomorrow's economy might as well have a bridge to sell us. The amount of variables at play defies accurate forecasts and seeing further than next week's range of Fahrenheit is all but impossible even for the experts.[1]

Still, not all is chaos. If history teaches us anything, it's that revolutions may feel unpredictable in the moment, but even they follow long arcs. Up close, every revolution looks like a rupture, but step back, and the broadlines' outlines come into view. Bloch and Febvre captured this adroitly with their concept of the *longue durée*; essentially a statement that history is shaped less by sudden events than by the deep, slow-moving structures we barely notice in real time. And if that is true for history, then so too must it be for the future, which, in the end, is only history that hasn't happened yet.

The question then becomes what the broad contours of that future history are that someone will write about our times that are already visible but distant enough to appear like nothing more than foggy shapes on the horizon. This chapter is about giving form to those shapes. Like economists forecasting with their confidence intervals, we'll focus on the trajectories that are obvious, even if the details of the final intercept remain uncertain. We will build up our arguments from the first principles upon which business is structured: what people do, what firms are for, how competition operates, and what markets reward.

From those foundations, we'll examine how AI changes the baseline in each domain, what new leverage it grants, what pressures it introduces, and what habits it renders obsolete. Just like in my classroom, we'll start small and scale up. First comes the individual, and an exploration of what AI enables each of us to do differently, whether it's of the more, better, faster, or altogether new type of work. Then comes the company which is composed of nothing but the people, their tools, and the assets they have at their disposal. We'll explore how AI reshapes how firms are built, what they optimize for, and how they find their path to creating or distributing value. Then we'll zoom out from one company to the competition and the market itself. We'll ask how

DOI: 10.4324/9781003508427-2

FIGURE 2.1 Now tell me, where are you AI engineers getting your predictions from.

the nature of advantage is changing, which moats are crumbling, and why some markets will restructure entirely while others tip hard toward aggregation.

By the end of it all, you won't have answers to which company will dominate the S&P 500 by 2050, nor can I give you next week's lottery numbers. What you will have instead is the vocabulary and mental models to lead through the change that is unfolding under our eyes. So let's begin, not with diamond hands stock picks or future-proof go-to-market plans, but with the first building block of any enterprise: the individual. The worker. The consumer. The MBA. You (Figure 2.1).

Battleground 0: individual productivity

We've already hinted at the underlying thesis of this book, so let's stop dancing around it: whatever impact AI has on business, it will be intermediated, amplified, and judged through the hands and minds of humans. Far from rendering the individual obsolete, AI makes the human more central than ever—precisely because it expands what a single person can now do.

In fact, this shift brings us to Battleground 0 of the AI economy: productivity.

For most of modern business history, if you wanted to be economically powerful, you had one real option, and that was to join a firm. The firm was the productivity multiplier because it gave you the tools you needed and the validation you know you deserved. When a prestigious company hired you, they were handing you a job as much as they were forking over an entirely new identity. Suddenly, you were no longer merely a promising generalist with potential; you were a McKinsey Associate or a Product Manager at Google. Maybe even a Goldman VP if you got lucky. That title wrapped you in institutional legitimacy. More importantly, it extended your productivity frontier through status, access, and structured leverage you couldn't approximate on your own.

But the selection was only the beginning of the productivity boost you were about to get. The real magic came from what the firm made possible once you were inside. It surrounded you with systems, tools, people, processes, and not least the firm's reputation, all of which brought a multiplier effect to whatever talent you brought in the door. In this equation, your output didn't rise incrementally; it scaled exponentially. In one fell swoop, you became a conduit for institutional power, equipped with a backoffice filled with support staff, a library full of templates and decks that told you what great looked like. As you plugged into the matrix, you felt newfound power surge through your veins, and for many of my students who enter finance in particular, that feeling is nothing if not intoxicating (Figure 2.2).

Although the relationship between the individual and the firm has always been one of mutual dependence, it has never been an equally balanced one. Yes, the firm needed you, and you needed the firm, creating fertile grounds for symbiosis. But whether that symbiosis is as symmetrical and stable as we'd like it to be has always been a point of contention, giving rise to the Marxist critiques and the quiet quitting posts on LinkedIn.

Because while the firm might wrap you in prestige and process, you are, to the system, still just a unit of labor. The vast majority of us are nothing if not interchangeable. At the top of our game, we might become high-functioning cogs, but even then, we're still spinning inside someone else's machine. Inside the company, we might be kings, but our reign is doomed the moment we forget who gave us the crown to begin with. Ronald Coase laid the foundation for how we

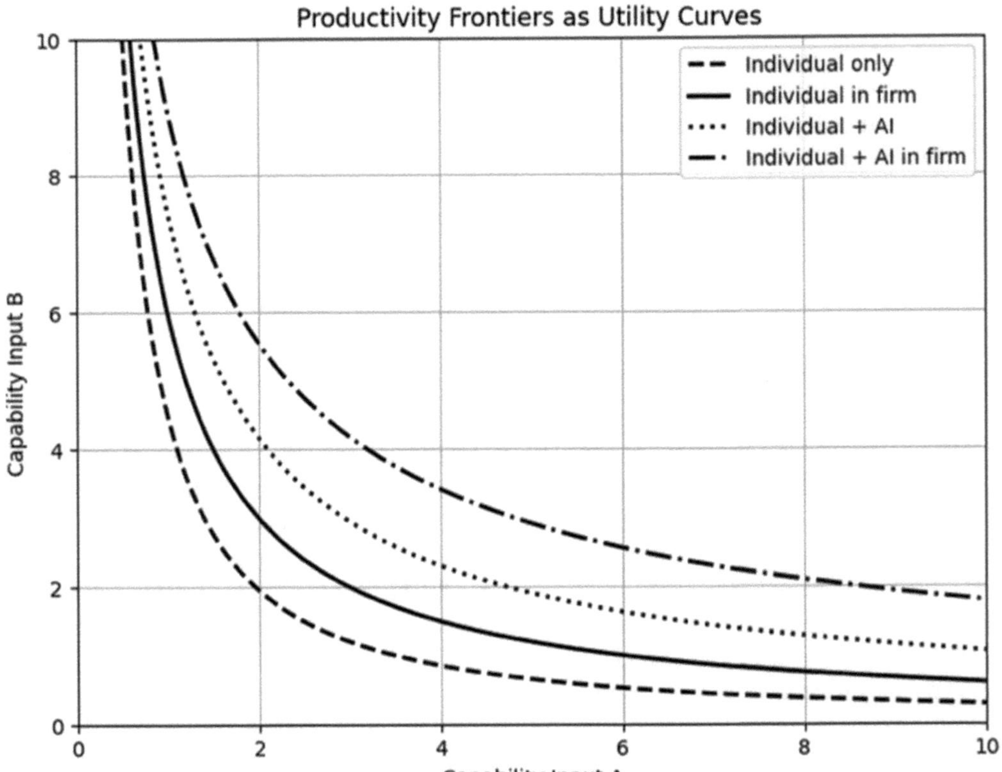

FIGURE 2.2 The new productivity frontiers AI opens up.

understand firms in his landmark theory of the firm, which, if you haven't thought of this before, actually needs an explanation for its existence, which we today take for granted. From Coase's perspective, companies exist because they reduce the transaction costs of coordinating work. Firms emerge whenever it's cheaper and more efficient to do things inside an organization than to go it alone. The firm internalizes the complexity of coordination, standardizes it, structures it, and scales it to the point where it maximizes its own returns. In other words, firms exist because they are the best way we have found to create and distribute value in whatever niche they play. As always, reality is much messier, and there are plenty of Zombie firms out there that are in fact destroying value by stubbornly resisting terminal cessation of operations. But overall, Coase is spot on; we will continue to have firms in the long run only if, and where, they are the superior path to value.

Add in the marginal productivity theory of labor, and we'll see how your pay is tied not to the absolute value you produce, but to the additional value you bring relative to the next-best alternative. If your boss knew what they were doing, in each firm you've ever worked at, you've been paid slightly, sometimes grossly, less than what you generated. That sweet delta is the firm's profit engine. That's what lets it grow, what gets priced into the stock, and what gets the partners on that yacht you're now also anxious to get your taste of.

None of this is supposed to be a bad deal in theory, mind you. The firm protects you, legitimizes you, trains you, and allows you to have more impact than you could on your own. But it also contains you, whether it's the minimum wage trap or golden handcuffs. The very logic that makes firms efficient is the same logic that constrains individual creativity and compresses variance. There's a reason why at McKinsey, your tap-dancing lessons and curiosity advanced degree in quantum chromodynamics are useful only during the icebreaker round at your annual

FIGURE 2.3 You're doing great, but can you be a bit more proactive?

practice area's meetup. It's also why superstars sometimes leave and why bureaucracies inevitably ossify if we don't keep the limbs nimble. More potently, this is why the most talented people in a firm don't always get to shape its future direction, because the firm isn't asking for guidance on where to go next from those from whom it simply requires a set output at a set price, delivered on demand.

That is what Marx and his intellectual descendants have always fundamentally critiqued. It's not that firms are evil, but that they're exploitative by virtue of being structurally designed to create a surplus which they are then incentivized to capture as much as they can. The individual is left with, well, simply whatever that is left. And as long as coordination costs remain high and individuals can't come close to their furthest-from-origin productivity frontier without the firms, that bargain holds. By and large, the firm is still the most effective way to turn people into productivity (Figure 2.3).

Return of the superstar economics

But that's exactly where AI begins to bend the rules. As we've agreed in the previous chapter, one particularly powerful way to view AI is to see it as a tool that radically lowers the cost of coordination, decision-making, and execution across a wide range of functions. Which begs the question: if the core economic rationale for the firm is to reduce transaction costs, what happens when those costs collapse because of AI?

What happens to the individual when the firm is no longer the only efficient place to get things done? Or more poignantly, what happens to the firm when individuals with AI might be more efficient than them? We can already see the outlines of the answer taking shape in the marketplace today. In fact, the early evidence is hiding in plain sight (Table 2.1).

Where AI sufficiently empowers individuals to overcome the coordination costs, bureaucratic inertia, and operational friction that have historically justified the existence of firms, we will see the taking over the entire business themselves. We may not be fully registering it yet, but the signs are there, including in how the freelance economy has exploded with Upwork, Fiverr, and the gig economy platforms accounting for tens of billions in annual transactions. Fractional employment, once a fallback out of necessity, has become a viable lifestyle, to the point where many now prefer fractionality from entry-level positions to the C-suite. And soon, we'll witness the arrival of the first true "one-person unicorn" where an individual creator captures a billion dollars in value, alone without hiring a single person to join them full time.

As William Gibson, the science fiction author whom we have to thank for the genre of cyberpunk, has said, the future is here, but it is unevenly distributed. Similarly, we should not expect individuals to challenge the pre-eminent status of the firm across the board. In sectors where the firm's traditional advantages of scale, process, and reputation still matter deeply, we'll witness a different kind of adaptation, where companies won't disappear or be replaced by one-person LLCs. Instead, they'll become dramatically leaner either in headcount or per-capita-outputs. New startups won't hire ten engineers if a single intern armed with GitHub Copilot or Cursor can handle the same workload, leading to smaller companies from day one. Established firms will face a stark choice where they either drastically expand output to justify current headcounts or slash personnel and overhead to defend margins against insurgent, AI-powered newcomers. The survivors won't necessarily be those with the deepest resources, but those most willing to embrace a new equilibrium where fewer humans, equipped with extraordinary leverage, produce outsized returns.

TABLE 2.1 Productivity dynamics across the Coasian spectrum

	Human	*Human + Firm*	*Human + AI*	*Human + AI + Firm*
Productivity Increases When...	Limited by personal time, skills, brand, bandwidth, access, etc.	Productivity increases through shared tools, structured processes, and institutional reputation.	Productivity increases through automation, augmentation, and better decision-making with less effort.	Maximum leverage: combines structure, brand, AI speed, and judgment of empowered talent.
Productivity Decreases When...	Hard to scale output; coordination and access are bottlenecks.	Productivity is limited if a firm imposes bureaucracy, slow decision cycles, or rigid hierarchy.	Risks of poor prompting, hallucinations, or over-reliance on tools without strategy.	Productivity drops if firms don't adapt processes, tools, or cultures fast enough or well enough. Individual + AI alone may outperform.

And these companies will need to double down on the only sources of edge that exist in the age of AI we met in the previous chapter, that is Custom Processes, Custom Data, and Custom People. We all have access to sugar, water, and carbonation, but the recipe, the process behind Coca-Cola, is what drives enduring value. Likewise, owning unique, proprietary data, especially when it's clean, rich, and properly structured, becomes the fuel that turns generic AI into something powerful and targeted. Finally, the most important multiplier of them all: Custom People. These are not warm bodies or interchangeable résumés but individuals with a distinct edge in themselves, and the companies will only have increasingly steep expectations for them.

Viewed from the perspective of you, the worker, the graduate, and the ambitious MBA, this new equilibrium has dramatic implications. When each individual is now capable of vastly greater output, you will find that the expectations placed upon you will skyrocket. It's not that the labor market model is changing from underneath you; it's that the rules of elite performance that we're accustomed to, mostly in areas like sports, are now being applied to everyone.

Consider the labor markets we know best, like professional sports. Football (the one actually played with feet), baseball, and basketball all operate under the principle of what economists like Sherwin Rosen call superstar economics. The Messis, Ohtanis, and Ronaldos anchor the ceiling, and everyone else calibrates their worth accordingly. Lionel Messi doesn't simply earn more than his peers by performing at his own level; he literally redefines the earning potential of his peers. His record-breaking contracts recalibrate the entire market beneath him, just like Shohei Ohtani's $700 million lifetime deal with the Los Angeles Dodgers, both in terms of setting the bar and emptying the club bank.

Historically, we accepted these dynamics in entertainment and sports without batting an eye. But we're far less accustomed to the idea of superstar economics playing out in everyday work from customer service, accounting, copywriting, or coding. AI, by collapsing the gap between individual output and organizational leverage, introduces precisely this dynamic into nearly every field of knowledge work. Get ready for a world in which there are Messis in marketing, LeBrons in logistics, and Ohtanis in operations.

The key takeaway for MBAs from Rosen's seminal "The Economics of Superstars" is that small differences in talent or perceived productivity translate to massive differences in rewards. In a superstar economy, earnings don't rise linearly; they skyrocket exponentially. In other words, the best don't merely get paid more; they get paid orders of magnitude more. What AI ensures is that we're about to see Rosen's logic explode from stadiums and soundstages to Slack channels and GitHub repos.

For industries where the individual's performance matters more and the firm's advantages matter less, superstar dynamics will most likely come to dominate. The incentives will shift decisively toward extreme performance in a winner-take-most economy. If you are planning to enter such an arena, you'll need to be prepared to redefine the playing field, because just walking on it won't be enough.

What about areas where the firm still retains meaningful coordination and scale benefits then? Here, we'll see a subtler, yet entirely familiar, recalibration unfold. In such fields, compensation and prestige will redistribute internally to favor the superstars who genuinely differentiate themselves by having skillsets that are uniquely resistant to AI commoditization. Salaries will shift aggressively toward top closers, elite relationship-builders, charismatic product evangelists, and visionaries who set organizational direction. Those unable to clearly demonstrate their unique value will face stagnant rewards or worse, outright redundancy.

In this environment, the individual's incentives and preferences will also shift. Talent will flood toward roles where human differentiation is decisive, such as roles defined by persuasion, trust-building, creativity, and judgment, simply because that is where the money is. At the same time, roles that offer little room for extraordinary remuneration through individual differentiation will grow less attractive, particularly if the compensation offered does not offset the existential risk of easy automation. Hello, Teach for America, and virtually the entire non-profit field.

At the individual level, this is the making of what many commentators are already calling out as the "great inequality amplifier" of AI. As long as humans fall along normal distributions in terms of talent, productivity, and creativity, and as long as markets reward small differences disproportionately, disparate outcomes are inevitable. You, as an MBA graduate or business operator playing in this world, do not have the luxury to critique the game. Your job is to understand it and to position yourself accordingly. You may, should you develop a particular kind of conscience in your old age, consider nudging the results of the game toward more equitable outcomes, but that is an entirely different book altogether.

What you can't avoid is rethinking your approach to learning and the breadth of what you know, however. Once upon a time, you could leave university in your twenties and spend the next four decades ascending to the top of government or finance without ever opening a textbook again. That era is decidedly over. Today, your knowledge has a half-life of days, not years. And no institution, not Harvard, not McKinsey, not even OpenAI, can freeze it in place for you. What they can do is ask that you read Chapter 9, where we make yourself into an auto-didactic machine.

The learning you will need to undertake won't be neatly packaged or formally scheduled, mind you. Instead, you will be building your own rocketship while it is already in motion through side projects, experiments, rabbit holes, online courses, and old-fashioned mistakes. To succeed in the superstar economy, you'll need to become one with learning by doing and by trespassing into disciplines you once considered someone else's territory. Because when the human becomes the differentiator, the edge lives at exactly these boundaries. And it turns out, the returns to curiosity compound faster in fields where you don't already speak the language.

In your own domain, a fresh insight is a rare gem that may take years to develop once you've put in your mythical 10,000 hours. In a new field, every fact and concept you encounter is, well, new by default.

And the imperative to match constantly growing expectations won't stop at breadth. You'll also be asked to evolve, and to do so faster and faster thanks to how expectations will ratchet up. What was exceptional output last year will be the going rate next year. Schools will teach you how to manage fleets of AI agents like junior analysts. Hiring won't reward what you built with a team, but what you built with a team of AI agents and the team. Productivity benchmarks will shift with each product release, each plugin, each breakthrough, and what once earned applause will now just get you through the door.

This is the landscape you're entering. And your ability to thrive will depend on how well you understand what AI is doing and how the firm's edges are blurring while the individual's role is expanding.

What the AI revolution means for the future of the firm

If the last section felt like all that it was missing was a "power to the people" rallying cry, it's time to ground ourselves back in the boardroom for a moment. Because whatever shifts AI brings to individual leverage, there is little evidence to suggest that the fundamental structure of firms is going away anytime soon. Quite the opposite, in fact.

AI will amplify, streamline, and potentially supercharge companies, but not without introducing complexities of its own. This is why we'll spend the next pages unpacking how the AI revolution transforms corporate strategy itself, and what that means for your role within it.

We'll begin with the following thought experiment. Imagine that there's a company that sells 100 million widgets each year at ten dollars apiece. To achieve this feat, it employs exactly one thousand people. One day, a new AI tool arrives, promising to boost each employee's productivity by 10%. What happens next?

In theory, if the company could fully capture this newfound efficiency, it would now produce 110 million widgets without adding a single extra employee or dollar of investment beyond turning on the tool. Overnight, it seems, the company grows its revenues by 10%, which is as close to magic as software can get.

Now picture the executive meeting the next morning. Shortly after the celebratory pat-pat-pats on each shoulder and back have concluded, a debate arises. Should the company indeed produce 110 million widgets, gambling on the market's appetite for extra inventory, potentially oversaturating demand? Or should it instead maintain production at 100 million units, cut 10% of its workforce, and pocket the savings as profit?

This scenario is neither abstract nor far-fetched. It is precisely the crossroads from which the "AI is replacing us" angst is emanating from, and these are very real choices that are being made behind closed doors as I write and as you read. Sometimes the right move for the company is to let the people go, and sometimes the startup's smartest choice might be to avoid hiring anyone they don't absolutely need. We don't need any villains at work here beyond economic logic. The individual, in this equation, remains a factor of production, important, often cherished, but ultimately subject to the same evaluation as any other input in the system.

These decisions about how much to invest in labor vs. capital vs. technology will never be one-size-fits-all. On the one hand, they will depend on the industry and how the company is situated in it, and on the other, these choices will reflect the firm's DNA and its leadership as well.

A company with cash on hand, a forward-looking CEO, and a strong brand might choose to expand into new markets, where a firm under pressure, underwhelmed by returns, or bound by legacy systems might slash headcount and return value to shareholders instead. Both are rational moves from the perspective of value generation, but there's no denying how they produce wildly different futures for all involved.

We can do better than simply lay out the opposing ends of the decision-making spectrum here. In fact, we already have a decent idea of which departments will be hit hardest and which might emerge reimagined. In areas like HR, IT, and Legal—functions that have traditionally been viewed as cost centers because of how that is often exactly what they are—we're seeing AI drive efficiency gains without corresponding revenue upside. The result of the AI revolution will inevitably be a relentless push to do more with even less. And where there's no upside in doing more, the race becomes about doing the same for cheaper in a race to the bottom. In these areas, we can expect automation tools to chip away at repetitive tasks just as we can expect contract theory to come lead business strategy with more force than ever. Bengt Holmström won a Nobel for showing what the best startups treat as gospel: the firm is only as big as it needs to be. In competitive markets, any task that can be outsourced more efficiently than done internally will eventually be outsourced. AI accelerates this logic, particularly in areas where there's nothing to work on but costs.

But not every company will stop there. Some will find ways to turn pain points into platforms, and instead of cutting HR, they'll go ahead and reinvent it for the rest of us. A legal department might evolve into a service provider for smaller firms. IT could become a proactive engine for innovation rather than a help desk for printer issues, just like Amazon took its server costs and made one of the world's greatest profit machines out of its own internal bottlenecks.

And in revenue-generating teams, the game will play out in different ways still. Here, AI is rocket fuel instead of extra baggage. Sales, marketing, and product development, they'll also use it to move faster, personalize deeper, and experiment more aggressively. The incentive won't be to find ways to spend less, but ways to earn more. Expect to see three-person growth teams doing the work of 30, powered by agents that scrape, segment, generate, and launch at speeds the old org chart couldn't dream of. That divergence, between trimming fat and chasing scale, will be one of the predominant tensions inside firms. And it's one that MBAs will be asked to navigate daily.

So what can you expect to do for companies in a world like this? Broadly speaking, the work ahead of you falls into the three broad categories, while in terms of strategies, we could list them forever (Table 2.2).

First, you will be rewarded for pruning what no longer makes sense. When AI allows individuals and other companies outside the firm itself to achieve higher levels of productivity than what the company can accomplish on its own, the firm's boundaries must shrink accordingly if it aims to optimize its operations. In the future, firms must ruthlessly identify tasks and roles that no longer require the firm's structure to exist, shedding overhead that no longer creates meaningful advantage. If an intern with AI can do the work of an entire analyst team, the analyst team as currently structured simply must go, even if it means spinning up a joint venture with the intern.

Second, you will spend much of your time reconfiguring what remains. For roles and departments that remain core to the company's advantage, AI will need to enhance as well as replace. Here, we will see managers and strategists busily rethinking workflows and redefining roles. We can expect to see fewer middle managers and more player-coaches and operators who both

TABLE 2.2 The work ahead

AI's inevitable conclusion	*Strategic reaction*	*Reaction type*	*Description*	*Example/Outcome*
Some roles produce no additional value, only cost savings	**Defensive contraction**	**Cost-cutting**	Use AI to reduce headcount or replace entire functions, focusing on protecting margins.	Reduce 10-person HR team to 3 using automation; redirect savings to shareholders.
Humans and AI together must be reconfigured for efficiency	**Operational reconfiguration**	**Workflow redesign**	Rebuild roles around AI tools, eliminate unnecessary layers, increase manager-to-output leverage.	Middle managers become player-coaches; analysts now oversee AI-generated insights instead of producing them.
AI allows exponential output at flat or declining cost	**Strategic expansion**	**Scale with AI**	Use AI to dramatically scale outputs without proportionally increasing inputs.	Three-person growth team launches 10x more campaigns using agents and automated segmentation.
Legacy support functions become external revenue opportunities	**Model transformation**	**Turn cost centers into platforms**	Convert internal functions into marketable service offerings.	Legal or IT units spin off into B2B service units à la AWS from Amazon's IT backbone.
Clean-slate companies outcompete legacy firms burdened by bloat	**Greenfield reinvention**	**AI-native company building**	Create entirely new firms with AI at the core; zero legacy drag.	Startups where founders structure ops around agentic systems and AI-native org charts from day one.
And so on…				

guide AI systems and step in for human judgment at crucial junctures where they previously used to have teams running things for them. Whatever the new configuration ends up looking like, we can say for certain that the org charts of today will look quaint in comparison to those we'll have in the decades to come.

Third, you will find yourself asked to build entirely new capabilities that the tool has opened up. While AI takes away old jobs, it simultaneously creates entirely new needs and roles across the entire organization. Prompt engineers, AI ethicists, data compliance specialists, and model trainers, none of these roles existed a decade ago, yet they are already commanding top-dollar salaries today. Companies must cultivate entirely new competencies for wielding these tools effectively, and they must learn to align them with emerging consumer demands that will evolve faster than ever. There will be much work to be done, and the successful firm of tomorrow will be leaner in parts, but just as the ice trade has ballooned from a handful of tasks to hundreds, so too will companies find themselves oriented around a plethora of novel requirements that consumers will soon expect as standard.

And perhaps the most exciting of all, you will help invent business models from scratch.

Not every leader will be burdened by legacy systems, bloated workflows, or cultural inertia. Some will decide to start from a clean plate, and for this emerging class of founders, the AI-native company presents a radically different opportunity. These organizations are defined by AI instead of simply AI it, and when there are no dusty ERPs to untangle, no outdated job ladders to defend or no rituals masquerading as processes, everything is up for reinvention. In these companies, the MBA's job is more ambitious and more audacious. Every function, from finance to HR to product, can be questioned, compressed, or abstracted into code. The real constraint is no longer tinkering with what worked in the past but instead identifying the shortest possible path to delivering the same value, or more.

Whatever company you find yourself in, your north star must be the value you create. The MBA's job has always been to strip the business model down to its most essential parts and, if needed, to rebuild it around the customer's perception of value with ruthless precision. The winners in this category will be those who structure their entire firm as an interface between AI, talent, capital, data, and the customers with as little gap between themselves and value as possible.

This is by far the most exciting part of AI strategy where it goes from adapting the old to authoring the new. And the future will belong to those bold enough to ask, "If we were starting this today, with these tools, in this world, what would we do differently?" And yet, as you guide your company forward, remember one crucial truth: your fiercest competitor is asking the same questions right now.

How AI reshapes the competitive landscape

Let's return, for a moment, to our widget factory.

The boardroom is quiet after a decision has been made: the company will lean into its newfound AI productivity and produce more units with the same headcount. The CEO smiles confidently, until someone raises a question: "What do we think our competitors are doing?"

No corporate decision exists in a vacuum, and in a world where one company has the competitive edge of AI, so will many others. Somewhere else, perhaps many somewhere, other CEOs are making the exact same move with their AI-enabled dashboards flashing the same insights and KPIs. And so, more widgets flood the market. Demand, existing stubbornly on its downward sloping curve, begins to slip, and prices fall. Margins compress, competition tighten and what began as a productivity miracle starts to feel like a race to the bottom.

In theory, competition is the engine of capitalism to which we have much to be thankful for. Competition keeps markets lean, firms inventive, and prices honest. Without it, systems ossify, collude, or become entirely corrupt. Just look at monopolies like Amtrak or political regimes like North Korea where closed loops that are immune to feedback are decaying in plain sight. In AI-powered markets, competition becomes a series of cascading reactions, resembling Alice in Wonderland's race with the Red Queen where you must run faster only to stay in place.

Every advantage you gain from AI has a painfully short half-life, and the only sustainable edge is superiority in speed, strategy, and design. To understand this more deeply, let's revisit Porter's Five Forces, the beloved MBA framework that I too have taught to generations of business leaders as a way of making sense of what to do with their competition (Table 2.3).

TABLE 2.3 Porter's five forces and AI

Porter's force	*Traditional view*	*AI-augmented dynamic*	*Implication*
Threat of New Entrants	Capital, talent, and complexity were barriers to entry	Individuals armed with AI can launch full-stack companies with near-zero overhead	Entry costs collapse; incumbents face asymmetric threats from lean, fast players
Threat of Substitutes	Substitutes came from adjacent products	AI substitutes entire roles, not just products, e.g., AI tax tools vs. accountants, chatbots vs. therapists	Disruption is functional, not industry-bound; jobs and services face existential threats
Bargaining Power of Buyers	Buyers lacked complete information and faced switching costs	AI tools help buyers price compare, self-educate, and prototype alternatives on their own	Firms face higher churn, pressure for customization, and declining pricing power
Bargaining Power of Suppliers	Unique know-how or IP created supplier leverage	AI commodifies IP, services, and outputs; internal tools replace many traditional supplier functions	Firms internalize more; suppliers must offer integration, speed, or proprietary data to stay relevant
Rivalry Among Competitors	Competing on brand, price, and differentiation	Feature parity arrives in weeks; cloning is trivial; GPT agents can build knockoffs from scratch	Firms must differentiate by going wide, going deep, bundling ecosystems, or speed, and customer ownership

First, we can expect the threat of new entrants to skyrocket in virtually every market that isn't a natural monopoly. For software, the entry cost is now counted in dollars per month, and with the right product, all you need is a sign-up page to upend an industry incumbent's model entirely. Elsewhere, the capital costs of entrepreneurship are plummeting as well. Like code can be written by prompts, legal structures can be templated and filed in hours and GTM strategies piloted with zero employees. A few people with access to an AI model can now outcompete teams of 50, as long as they have a vision of what they are doing. And what better place to get one than the vision statement portion of an incumbent's website.

The threat of substitute products and services is where things get even weirder. A tax accountant who has grown accustomed to doing just slightly better, or not much worse than, the shop next door might now lose business to a $9.99/month SaaS tool. A therapist might compete with a fine-tuned chatbot that charges nothing for its advice. A B2B sales team might see their work substituted by an API and a neat intake form. Where substitution used to mean Coke versus Pepsi, it's now a game against your product and your competitors' tokens.

We don't even need to speak about Porter's rivalry among incumbents, do we? With AI, feature parity now arrives in days, not quarters, and in software, entire products can be cloned by pointing an agentic AI at a landing page and saying: "Make me this." As margins tighten across the economy, competition intensifies even in places that it had avoided in the past.

For many industries, what we're seeing is the collapse of traditional moats, or, rather, their mutation to something slightly different.

Where once you could protect your advantage by staying invisible, by hiding your special sauce in unpatented trade secrets or clever product workflows, today's models can reverse-engineer those workflows in seconds. The product itself is no longer enough, nor is necessarily a first-mover advantage. So, companies will shift to what sticks. They will stack moats, bundle features, and pursue vertical integration. They will push for platform control and create packages of value that are harder to replicate. Just look at Spectrum or AT&T, why sell you one product when they can lock you and your clients into five? The same dynamics are coming to B2B SaaS, logistics, retail, and beyond. The great bundling of everything is on.

And when bundling isn't enough, they will build ecosystems. They aim to own not just what you buy, but how you buy, how you compare, how you switch, and what you plug into. If the old moat was the product, the new moat is to be as close as possible to the operating system of your life, or your business.

In this new terrain, what matters most isn't just what you offer but how tightly you can enmesh it with the rest of the customer's stack. This is why ecosystem gatekeepers like AWS, Salesforce, and Apple have such enduring power. Sure, they are selling you a product, but at the same time, they are sending you down a gravity well that is all but impossible to climb out of.

So, on the one hand, companies will bundle more, build wider, and encroach into adjacent markets with increasingly aggressive speed. They will also enter more decisively into managed services because in markets where contract theory and competitive efficiency rule the day, the old playbook of hiring the team, buying the tools, and building the process in-house starts to look painfully inefficient. Why spend time making your marketing department 10% better with a new AI tool, when you can pay a third-party service to deliver the full outcome and do it for 90% of what it would've cost you?

Across sector after sector, companies are already bypassing software and skipping straight to solutions and as an MBA, the last thing you should be is surprised. In the end, all that matters is the value that is generated, not the task it takes to create it. This, by the way, is exactly what you'd do too because the incentives at play here are simply inescapable.

Once a firm realizes that AI-generated gains will get competed away by others, it has no choice but to pursue deeper moats, faster expansion, and more aggressive defenses. With the product, data, and talent no longer being the stalwart moat that it has been, they will inevitably turn to other sources like bundling, servicification, and, in some instances, government patronage and exclusionary rights.

Back to the big picture

Overall, the strategic evolution will play out along two divergent but equally aggressive paths: depth or breadth.

In industries where precision, regulatory nuance, or life-and-death stakes rule the day, like healthcare, aviation, and critical infrastructure, firms will find reasons to double down on domain-specific datasets, bespoke workflows, and painstakingly specialized knowledge. Think of radiology models trained on rare cancers, or fintech compliance engines coded around local tax loopholes where niche knowledge still has ROI. In these worlds, marginal improvements still yield exponential rewards, and the barriers to entry will only grow more formidable, even for AI.

But in domains where differentiation is harder to defend, and marginal gains quickly decay, like consumer tech, SaaS, or media, the gravity pulls toward bundling, brand, user experience, and platform entrenchment. Here, the goal is to be everywhere at once, to lock in users not through feature superiority but through convenience, integration, or ubiquity. The product doesn't have to be the best; it just has to be the one you're already using when the need arises. That's why we're seeing a quiet arms race toward becoming the default option. A mediocre email marketing tool tied seamlessly into your CRM will beat a brilliant standalone platform every time. The moat becomes the mesh we're entangled with, and the firm becomes the interface. And once a firm accepts that any AI-derived advantage will be competed away faster than it can be accrued, it's forced to ask harder, scarier questions: What do we have that others can't mimic? What parts of our business are defensible when the marginal cost of intelligence falls to zero?

First, firms will wrap their products in layers of service, community, integration, and lock-in. When truly everything else can be copied, experience becomes the product, and where experience isn't enough, they'll seek regulatory capture, exclusive licenses, and public-private partnerships to secure a defensible edge. In short, AI won't kill the firm. It will expose it. And what survives the exposure will be sharper, faster, and far more aggressive than what came before.

Before we get too far ahead of ourselves, let's remember what we started this chapter with. Anyone claiming to know exactly how the AI revolution will unfold might as well offer us next week's lottery numbers, or the deed to a bridge they're selling. The future remains deeply uncertain, and that uncertainty is precisely where strategy thrives. Every play eventually gets overplayed, and the more widely a move spreads, the stronger the incentives for competitors to design a counter-play, exactly like defensive coaches building lineups to intercept the quarterback's favorite pass.

Which is why, in the age of AI, strategy and the MBAs that wield it are everything. The best firms will mix and match their bets, doubling down where the gains compound and pivoting when the field shifts. Below are some of the most common strategic moves emerging from this new terrain (Table 2.4).

So what does all of this mean for the MBA, our proxy for future leadership?

It means that mastery of static strategy models or the competitive frameworks of the past are no longer enough. The modern MBA must know not only how to play the game, but how the board will morph the moment you make a move. On the surface, this means becoming increasingly capable in a new strategic vocabulary that is more attuned to the velocity, competitive asymmetry, and shape-shifting nature of AI-era competition. But on a deeper level, the AI revolution invites our MBAs to return to an older and purer version of themselves. MBAs, freed from the heavy lifting of outdated frameworks and bloated processes, are finally liberated to do what they should have always been doing: obsess over the consumer.

In fact, they will have no other choice, simply because of how the market itself won't stand still. Customers, as great as they are, are nothing if not predictable ungrateful when faced with paradigm shifts of technology. At first, they marvel at the new features and clap with a string of tears running down their cheeks. But soon enough, regardless of how great the miracle you have brought into their view, they will come to feel entitled to it. In-flight Wi-Fi was once a miracle, and now when it drops for ten minutes mid-flight, all the while we sit hoisted 30,000 feet in the air by technology that would have stunned our great-grandparents, we write customer service complaints to BBB before the captain has time to land the plane.

TABLE 2.4 The strategic moves

Strategic bet	*Breadth or depth*	*Description*
Branding	Both	Doubling down on trust, identity, and perceived quality as differentiators when tech is commoditized. Think: Patagonia, Ferrari.
Bundling	Breadth	Combining multiple offerings into one package to increase lock-in and perceived value. Think: Apple, Microsoft, Spectrum.
Ecosystems	Breadth	Creating interoperable networks of tools, services, and third parties that reinforce the core offering. Think: Apple App Store, Salesforce AppExchange.
Marketing Spend	Both	Flooding the zone to dominate mindshare and create a winner-takes-most flywheel. Think: Meta, Pinduoduo, Temu.
Nichefication	Depth	Going deep into a narrow domain to dominate where generalist AI can't follow. Think: oncology-specific LLMs, vertical SaaS.
Servicification	Both	Turning products into ongoing service ecosystems with human wrappers, integration, and support. Think: Peloton, AWS, McKinsey.
User Experience	Both	Winning by making interactions smoother, faster, and more delightful, especially when features are easy to replicate. Think: Stripe, Superhuman.

FIGURE 2.4 Nice wells, but wait until they hear about what my dog's been digging in the backyard.

Consumer expectations will ratchet up with every new industry release, and those who meet their needs the most effortlessly will win. In this game, shouting louder might work, but listening better beats everything else. And this is why, despite everything, I remain profoundly bullish on humanity's role in the AI future.

Because the consumer is and will forever remain human. The most enduring businesses are those that treat their customers not as endpoints for efficiency, but as evolving repositories of value and meaning. Therefore, the most important thing an MBA can do is learn to serve that market, and to do any of this well, they must learn how to become one with the technology that empowers them.

Which is where we turn next (Figure 2.4).

Note

1 Perhaps specifically so for the experts, as Tetlock's research has shown. Add his book to your nightstand if you can still find a copy.

3

COMMANDING THE STACK

How MBAs will lead in the age of AI

As the 19th-century legend has it, somewhere along the tracks of the Chesapeake and Ohio Railway, a man named John Henry gripped a hammer so tightly, and swung with such fury, that he outraced a steam drill in a competition of tunneling through rock. In what amounts to more than mere subtext, Henry would come to win his race in a pyrrhic victory, dying with his hammer in hand. For no matter how many battles we win against the tools of tomorrow, the war is ours to lose. The story, most likely myth more than memory, has been passed down through generations in a song that defies obsolescence the same way its hero defied the drill.

Over a century later, we are still remixing the song today. We cheer when a chess grandmaster upsets an AI or when a Go prodigy finds a move the machine can't match. We smile smugly when AI fails to count the r's in strawberry, knowing full well we might be fooled by the same question as well. Each win by a fellow sharing our Latin binomial is a breath of reassurance that maybe, *just maybe*, we still have a place amidst all this change. We hang on to the John Henrys of our time in hopes that somewhere in this new world of silicon logic and infinite memory, there's still a role for neurons and nuance.

Now, what most of us miss is that the entire game has been rigged from the start. John Henry was never meant to play solo, and the machine-versus-human framing has led us to ask the wrong questions. We are the species that picks up rocks to crack nuts and learns that it is better to ride horses instead of racing them. The lesson isn't that John Henry shouldn't have raced the drill. It's that John Henry should've been operating the damn thing, showing every steam-power critic around him what humans can do with the right tools in hand.

If railroads aren't your thing, we can find plenty of idealized versions of the superhuman worker in business, law, science, and even politics. For as long as we know, we've always carried with us imagined superhumans, heroic figures meant to compensate for our flaws. We can say this with confidence given how the oldest surviving text humanity ever bothered to write down is the Epic of Gilgamesh, and in those tables, you will find a man who would wipe the floor with the entire Marvel Universe.

In law, we have our Judge Hercules. A philosopher-magistrate who never runs out of time or wisdom, making the right decisions with King Solomon's precision. In philosophy, we have a list of now decidedly mythicized heroes from Marcus Aurelius to Plato to choose from, and

DOI: 10.4324/9781003508427-3

in typical philosopher fashion, they couldn't help themselves from getting metaphysical giving us Rawls' Original Position. Leave it to philosophers to conclude that the best version of you is the version that doesn't even know it's you. In business, it's the Wolf of Wall Street, Gordon Gekko, Rockefeller of Elon Musk alongside every variation of the mythic version of the founder, the operator, and the rainmaker who sees everything, solves everything, raises millions before breakfast, and never falters.

These idealized versions of us that humanity keeps on inventing aren't fantasies or fan fiction for posterity to be amused by. Instead, they are working mental models for how we define excellence, harboring valuable signals of what we, as a society, deem worthy of pursuing at any given time.

If you think about it, the MBA is just as much of a cultural avatar as John Henry or Judge Hercules. An MBA does more than tell others that you went to business school. Instead, it conjures up a full-blown persona, a narrative of what the MBA stands for that we can read exactly like the Epic of Gilgamesh. In this narrative, the mythical MBAs are professional problem solvers, native networkers, and virtuosos of value with a halo made of brightly glistening dollar signs. They optimize weekend trips like they optimize logistics chains, and their CVs read like a VC pitch deck in human form. Whether or not you've ever cracked open a course reader at Wharton or sat through a cold call at HBS, you know what the three letters represent. The MBA is a stand-in for elite competence and a shorthand for the ambitious kind of person that seems destined for the CEO position.

If we're honest, the signal the MBA degree sends is often a more powerful driver for applications to the universities I've taught at than the actual classes me and my colleagues teach.

FIGURE 3.1 Turns out the smart play was angel investing in the competition.

Becoming an MBA speaks volumes, as does rejecting the path entirely. And precisely like the myth of John Henry, the myth of the MBA is now in need of refinement thanks to the AI revolution.

This chapter is about exactly that. We'll look at the myth of the MBA through three lenses that will organize our thoughts: how MBAs are rewarded, what is expected of them, and how they'll partner with AI. In doing so, we'll meet four archetypes that will come to define this emerging landscape, namely, the Centaur, the Cyborg, the Artisan, and the Client Whisperer. Each archetype represents a strategy for navigating a workplace where much of what we once considered skilled labor is now commoditized and where competitive edge doesn't come from being faster or smarter than a machine but rather from knowing which parts of yourself to *amplify* and which to offload.

But before we get there, we'll have to answer a much more basic question, one we rarely pause to consider amid rankings and salary reports and career path diagrams: *What is it, exactly, that MBAs do?* (Figure 3.1).

Business universals

In the late 20th century, anthropologist Donald E. Brown gave the scholarly world a gift it didn't fully deserve favor by painstakingly identifying hundreds of "human universals" that map to core behaviors and capacities found across all cultures. From kinship terms to tickling, gift-giving to gossip, Brown's list reminded us that for all our differences, humanity shares a deep common software. We are all running the same Monkey OS, localized for proximate conditions.

If we were to borrow that lens and apply it to the modern firm and treat businesses the way Brown treated tribes and cultures, we'd find ourselves assembling a catalogue of shared behaviors that would be at risk of bursting at the seams. After all, every business, whether a family-run bakery or a multinational giant, shares a wide range of fundamental tasks. They all plan, sell, analyze, and optimize, and while the tactics may change with time and tools, the tasks themselves remain.

So if we were to write our own version of Brown's "Business Universals," what would it look like? We might start modestly, say, with the first ten entries under A (Table 3.1).

As you continue on building the codex from A to Z, you'll ultimately come to list all the fundamental moves in the game of business. All of them exist because at some point in time they created or distributed value, or they enabled something else that did so. Much of the unspoken

TABLE 3.1 Business universals: A-B

1	Analyze customer behavior
2	Allocate capital efficiently
3	Articulate value propositions
4	Acquire new users or clients
5	Audit internal operations
6	Assess market potential
7	Automate routine workflows
8	Adapt to regulatory changes
9	Appraise vendor performance
10	Align team incentives
....	....

curricula MBAs go through is simply learning to navigate this codex and which of its entries are still applicable and how they are best applied. And in the age of AI, each of them is being redefined, while in some, human involvement is being made redundant entirely. If we were to state the key insight from our earlier chapters in another way, we can argue that these business universals are not changing, but how we make them happen is.

Had someone with the divine patience of Brown compiled a list of business universals for us, we would know exactly how to start our analysis. We would examine each row and ask the simple question of whether AI does the task better than humans, at a cost that the business receives more outputs per the cost of its inputs. This kind of thinking is not a hypothetical exercise in automation, mind you. Instead, it is the very bread and butter of MBAs in the age of AI. An analysis of this sort might look like this (Table 3.2).

Each of these entries points to a larger truth than what's written on each cell. What remains universal will still hold, but how we get there will increasingly be a function of who's holding the steering wheel: a human, a machine, or both.

If we were to run our analysis through the entire list of Business Universals, we could not only map out the future of work for humans, and in doing so, we would see the role of humans, and MBAs, in particular, evolve in predictable ways. Lucky for us, we don't need to guess because researchers at MIT and Stanford have already done the hard work for us. In a foundational study, Brynjolfsson, Li, and Raymond introduced a powerful framework to better understand AI's task-level impact across the economy by exploring how Microsoft Co-pilot's capabilities map against a comprehensive listing of human tasks in modern corporate America contained within O*NET (Occupational Information Network) by the US Department of Labor, Employment & Training Administration.[1] Their analysis breaks down jobs using the taxonomy of *Generalized Work Activities* (GWAs), Intermediate Work Activities (IWA) that belong to a GWA, and Detailed Work Activities (DWA) that belong to an IWA and maps them against *AI exposure* by measuring how easily language models like GPT can handle each one. Instead of relying on broad job categories, they dive deeper, because, as we know, it's not the job

TABLE 3.2 Who should do what?

Business universal	*Can AI do it better?*	*Can AI do it cheaper?*	*Decision*
Analyze customer behavior	Yes	Yes	Replace/Human audit
Allocate capital efficiently	No	Sometimes	Assist (quant layer)
Articulate value propositions	No	No	Human-led
Acquire new users or clients	Yes (some channels)	Yes	Assist (optimize)
Audit internal operations	Yes (rules-based)	Yes	Replace (partially)
Assess market potential	No	No	Human-led
Automate routine workflows	Yes	Yes	Replace
Adapt to regulatory changes	No	No	Human-led
Appraise vendor performance	Yes (quant metrics)	Yes	Assist/Review
Align team incentives	No	No	Human-led

that gets automated, it's the task. What they found might unsettle MBAs that have not thought things through with us: highly educated, white-collar workers, particularly those in roles full of language-heavy, semi-structured tasks, are more exposed to AI than many low-wage or manual labor positions. In other words, MBAs aren't on the safe end of the spectrum anymore. The very work we thought defined the "knowledge economy" is now directly in AI's crosshairs.

But the study goes further. The authors show that AI is most powerful when it comes to processing, summarizing, and generating content on the IWA and DWA levels. Where it still lags behind in activities that demand judgment, values, or high-context coordination, exactly where we know that the human edge remains. So while AI can write your market report, it won't yet walk into a tense boardroom and defuse a political turf war. That's still on you. And so, the first major trend we would see is that MBAs will move up what we can call the abstraction ladder of value as they navigate through one GWA to another, and the second is that the GWAs they will be working on will be closer to the core of the business. Let me first explain the concept of the abstraction ladder, which I hope you'll find to be as powerful of a thinking aid as I have.

At the bottom rung of this imaginary ladders sits the most granular kind of task you could hand to a summer intern or a Zapier flow, a DWA like sending an invoice to a client through an ERP system. One level up, and the same task becomes something higher level, ensuring that accounts payable are up to date. Climb higher still and you're no longer thinking about invoicing at all; instead, you're thinking about client retention and managing relationships. Go one more and you've crossed into strategy as you begin reflecting on revenue modeling and customer lifetime value. And at the very top, you'll find yourself working on how to grow the business as a whole. Each rung offers more leverage for the MBA and a grander vista, but it also demands more context, more integration, and more judgment. And as AI comes for the DWAs and Business Universal at the bottom, MBAs will find themselves having nowhere to go but up.

Given that you've survived the first two chapters of this book, you'll instinctively know to retort how "we've seen this before." The ice trade didn't end because people stopped wanting ice. It ended because Frederic Tudor's shipments of frozen lake blocks were eventually replaced by electric refrigeration. The people who survived in the business weren't the ones who clung to their pickaxes and saws, but the ones who understood that the job was always about keeping things cold instead of picking up ice from the frozen pond.

AI, like any other tool, climbs the ladder from the bottom. The work that's easiest to automate is also the most granular: parsing logs, compiling tables, formatting presentations, running regressions. What gets left behind, or in this case pushed higher, is the interpretive, strategic, political work that can't be templated. And that's where MBAs are now being expected to operate. To see how this ladder climbing works with a real example, let's take one of our Business Universals, "Analyzing customer behavior" and map it across the first five levels of abstraction (Table 3.3).

As AI automates levels 1 and 2, humans move to levels 3, 4, and 5 and the innumerable rungs above. The reward at each step is greater leverage over the business, but it comes at the cost of less certainty, more responsibility, and fewer guardrails. In this example, we move from parsing customer behavior to shaping it. And this takes us to the second major shift. MBAs are moving from the periphery of business to its core.

The recent O*NET-linked study on GWAs, IWAs, and DWAs gives us data-backed validation of this trend. The authors found that the types of tasks AI most easily excels at are concentrated at what we can visualize as the edges of the firm: help desks, ticketing systems, chatbot-augmented HR portals, and customer service workflows. These functions were already

TABLE 3.3 The abstraction ladder

Abstraction level	*Task description*
... .	*and so on*
5 (More abstract)	Shape company growth strategy and retention levers
4	Translate behavioral insight into product-market opportunities
3	Interpret behavior to infer unmet needs and friction points
2	Extract behavioral patterns from segmented user data
1 (Concrete)	Clean and tag clickstream data in Google Analytics 4

TABLE 3.4 At the core of the issue

Core	*Periphery*	*Edges*
The problem the company exists to solve; its unique value proposition or USP (e.g., Amazon's "deliver anything fast")	Internal processes, systems, and tools that enable the company to create and deliver its core value (e.g., Amazon's warehouse automation, supply chain)	Touchpoints and interfaces through which the company interacts with the outside world (e.g., Amazon's customer service, website UX, delivery personnel)

beachheads for outsourcing, and AI simply continues the trajectory, only faster, cheaper, and with fewer compliance headaches.

To be clear, these are not meaningless roles. But they sit far from what makes the business the business. From the perspective of contract theory and transaction cost economics, edge functions are often non-differentiated and template-driven, prime territory for substitution as long as the workflow can be templated and repeated at scale.

What AI leaves behind is the messy, entangled, high-context decision-making at the core where the unique value proposition of the firm lies. This is the stuff that no template can quite capture because it is embedded in institutional knowledge, stakeholder nuance, and strategic vision. It's the company's reason for existence and the founders' vision for designing the next product, entering the right market, and building a pricing model that balances lifetime value with acquisition costs.

Surrounding that core is the periphery, which encompasses the systems, processes, and partnerships that turn the core idea into reality. They're not as exposed as the edges, nor as irreplaceable as the core, but they are under increasing pressure too. Periphery roles will be partially automated, reconfigured, or transformed. Expect workflows to be redesigned, roles collapsed, and decision loops shortened by embedded AI agents.

As this shift unfolds, MBAs and senior operators will be pulled ever closer to the core because, as the O-Net study shows, it's the only place where human differentiation remains. And the climb to that core comes with fewer guardrails, greater complexity, and, crucially, higher stakes when it comes to delivering value (Table 3.4).

This center-of-gravity shift is why we can safely say that MBAs will not only move up the ladder of abstraction, but also inward, toward higher-stakes decisions, fuzzier data, and less room for error. And they'll need new models of working to succeed in it. Which brings us back to the topic of archetypes. For the MBA class of 2050, the badge you wear on your college blazer won't be content with saying where you studied. It will signal how your chosen path of working together with the machines: as a Centaur, Cyborg, Artisan, an Orchestrator, or Client Whisperer. Before we go meet them, we need to double click on one more universal upgrade every MBA will need: a genuine command of what some today dismiss as the soft skills (Figure 3.2).

FIGURE 3.2 Make room, the bottom is already fully automated.

The soft skills revolution

It's one of the great ironies of the AI age that we've already touched upon: when machines master the hard skills, the soft ones become the ultimate differentiator. For years, emotional intelligence, intuition, and presence were routinely applauded in keynotes, but rarely rewarded in hiring rubrics or put into practice in the factory floor. They were "nice to have" at best and never mission-critical. But now, as the technical bottom rungs of the ladder get automated and the predictable DWAs get outsourced, the human edge begins to sharpen exactly where we once undervalued it most.

This is why MIT Sloan researchers recently pivoted the question from "What jobs will AI steal?" to something far more constructive: What can humans do that AI can't, or can't do well enough that it still needs a human partner? In their study,[2] Loaiza and Rigobon introduce a framework that identifies five core human capabilities: empathy and emotional intelligence; presence and networking; opinion, judgment, and ethics; creativity and imagination; and hope, vision, and leadership. Not only that, they demonstrate that the tasks requiring these qualities are not only harder to automate, but are increasingly in demand. By applying this framework to 19,000 tasks across nearly a thousand occupations via the O-NET data we've met before, the researchers found that tasks most rich in the soft skills grew in frequency between 2016 and 2024. Meanwhile, roles that required less of them are shrinking or being offloaded to machines entirely.

Whichever study you look at, a picture emerges that validates our view: AI isn't MBAs, it is pushing them up the ladder. And the higher MBAs climb on the abstraction ladder, the more they're evaluated not on how precisely they operate a spreadsheet, but on how well they operate themselves and the soft skills they command. Let's look at how these soft skills evolve along the MBA's climb up the ladder (Table 3.5).

TABLE 3.5 The soft skills compendium

Soft skill	*How it shows up at lower levels*	*How it scales at the top of the ladder*
Communication	Clear email writing, concise memos, basic presentation skills	Narrative framing, organizational storytelling, and adapting tone across power gradients
Presence	Speaking up in meetings, being responsive	Commanding a room, managing boardroom dynamics, regulating group energy
Judgment	Making low-stakes decisions, following rules	Making tradeoffs in ambiguity, weighing moral/strategic concerns under pressure
Decision-making	Picking between predefined options	Creating and defending new options, deciding when to delay, delegate, or escalate
Empathy and EQ	Collaborating with teammates, not annoying your boss	Reading rooms, absorbing political tensions, emotionally pacing the team through change
Leadership	Leading a project or a workstream	Managing uncertainty, setting direction, building coalitions across silos
Creativity and vision	Suggesting improvements, A/B testing	Forging new paths, reframing markets, synthesizing disparate insights into strategy

These are no longer "soft." They are, as the researchers put it, the *scarce inputs*. And if you want a recipe for outsized leverage in the age of AI, here it is: take one MBA, add judgment, trust, and storytelling, then multiply by the tools everyone else also has access to, and you have a winner.

On the flip side, consider what actually derails projects at Fortune 100 companies. It's not that someone forgot how to run a discounted cash flow model or didn't optimize for tax efficiency. It's that somewhere along the way, trust or communications broke, and one stakeholder wasn't looped in, or another didn't feel heard. Strategy dies in the silences between departments more often than in the imprecision of the moves proposed. Sure, AI can draft the diligence report and simulate the integration plan. But it won't walk into the room after a brutal layoff and look your team in the eye. It won't absorb their disappointment, recalibrate morale, and re-ignite a shared purpose. That's on you. And it always will be.

That's where tomorrow's MBA earns their keep. The reason why we'll see more MBAs who are part strategist, part psychologist, part diplomat is because at the end of the day, no matter how powerful our tools become, the business of business remains stubbornly human. And yet, as is inevitable from what we've covered thus far, the humans involved will need to also know how to leverage their tools to the fullest extent possible while still maintaining their human edge. This is where we arrive at the new MBA archetypes of the future.

Humans and their attachment types to AI: the new archetypes for MBAs

The soft skills revolution will place greater emphasis on what has been omitted before, but that doesn't mean that there will be no hard skills left. On the contrary, there will be entirely new categories of hard skills for MBAs to acquire, and the ones of particular interest to us are those related to how they pair with their AI tools. Here, the hard skill isn't knowing how to code or prompt as much as it is knowing how to coordinate it, when to trust the tool, when to challenge it, and how to integrate it into a broader judgment loop.

If you want to wax philosophical for a moment, part of the hard skills of the future will be about how MBAs relate to their tools. And here, we might borrow something from psychology and see where the concept of attachment theory gets us. Just like Bowlby showed us how early human relationships shape later emotional styles, we can think of AI relationships in much the same way: some humans will cling, others will avoid, and some will co-create. Each archetype produces very different outcomes while wielding the same tools. And once we've unpacked those new working styles, we can move on to the deeper layer of *meta-skills* that the next generation of MBAs will need to master. They'll need to learn how to design workflows that combine humans and agents, audit AI outputs for blind spots, calibrate trust in automated processes, and rethink how value is created when intelligence is no longer scarce but ambient. This is the new playbook, part metacognition, part systems design, and part psychological resilience. Let's start with the archetypes.

In a field experiment that was groundbreaking for its time, Harvard Business School and BCG gave almost 800 consultants access to GPT-4 and their performance was compared to those without AI.[3] The results paint a clear picture that will not surprise anyone reading this today. When used wisely, AI is a force multiplier. Consultants with AI completed 12% more tasks, 25% faster, and 40% of them produced higher-quality outputs than their AI-less peers. However, and this is more crucial thank you might first think, when consultants *over*-relied on AI for tasks outside of AI's "comfort zone," their accuracy *dropped*: they were 19% less likely to get correct solutions than those who didn't use AI. In other words, AI can boost your productivity or amplify your mistakes, depending on how and where you use it.

The researchers observed two successful patterns of human-AI collaboration and dubbed them "centaurs" and "cyborgs." We'll explore both of these, and we will expand with the three additional archetypes of orchestrators, artisans, and client whisperers.

The centaur: playing to each half's strengths

The term "centaur" here is borrowed from Greek mythology's half-human, half-horse to describe a Human-AI team that works in parallel in a, quite literal, style of attachment. A centaur MBA divides tasks between human and machine, using the AI for what it's best at, such as brute-force analysis, and reserving for themselves what humans excel at such as judgment and evaluation of the final result. For example, a centaur consultant might handle client interactions and hypothesis generation themselves, while delegating the tedious research or spreadsheet modeling to GPT-powered tools. The centaur's mantra is "I know where I add value, and I know what to outsource to my digital assistant."

One driver behind the success of this approach is how it prevents overreliance on AI in its weak spots. AI hallucinations are real, and my own research with Harvard colleagues has shown how biases seep in and how expected utility theory (EUT) is routinely failed by large language models. These systems can produce confident answers that are statistically plausible but factually or logically broken. Today, they struggle with basic calibration, context prioritization, and decision-making under uncertainty, especially when human values, tradeoffs, or ambiguity are involved. The centaur MBA proactively plans for this. They design workflows that pair algorithmic horsepower with human guardrails. Centaurs have already succeeded in fields like chess, where human-computer teams often outperform both grandmasters and machines operating alone.[4]

In this model, tools like Claude or ChatGPT aren't threats to be contained, but instruments to be mastered. The MBA who learns how to prompt, probe, verify, and revise becomes exponentially more effective, not just in throughput, but in the results of their judgment. The Centaurs know that the secret isn't knowing all the answers, it's knowing which questions to ask the machine, and which ones still need to be asked of a human.

The orchestrator: managing the stack, not the task

Where the centaur might delegate to a single digital assistant or a pipeline of them, the orchestrator MBA thinks like a conductor that is less loosely attached to the modules they coordinate. Instead of one co-pilot, they manage an ensemble of models that can be turned on or off on demand. One model for research, another for summarization, another for critique, one for slide production, and yet another for code deployment. The orchestrator is involved with AI primarily through directing, which will involve selecting the right agents, aligning their outputs, resolving contradictions, and turning fragments into deliverables. It's the difference between hiring one assistant and running a team of specialists.

This shift elevates the MBA's role from executor to integrator. The orchestrator designs layered workflows, identifies where automation breaks, and decides when a human has to re-enter the loop. Coordination, sequencing, verification, and feedback become the new skills of excellence. As AI becomes more capable, the bottleneck moves from capability to composition, and that's where the orchestrators shine by knowing not just how to use the tools, but how to weave them together into something greater than the sum of their parts.

The cyborg: systemic modular integration

Where centaurs draw clear lines, cyborgs intentionally blur them and embed AI throughout their whole system. A cyborg MBA is attached to AI at nearly every step, constantly interweaving human and machine contributions. The BCG researchers noted that most consultants naturally behaved more like cyborgs, engaging in a "constant interaction with the AI" rather than using it only in isolated chunks. A cyborg might begin a task by asking the AI for an outline, then fleshing it out herself, then asking the AI to critique or fact-check her work. In coding terms, the human and AI operate as *peer processors* on the problem. The advantage is speed and breadth: cyborgs can tackle complex tasks quickly by iterating with the AI, often discovering ideas neither would alone. The danger, of course, is going on autopilot, if the human disengages too much, the cyborg can run into the frontier problem where the AI's subtle mistakes slip by.

This concern was echoed in recent research by Microsoft and LinkedIn, which found that heavy reliance on generative AI tools can, over time, suppress development of critical thinking, originality, and even confidence in independent problem-solving.[5] Workers who used AI passively, treating it as a crutch rather than a collaborator, were less likely to challenge assumptions, less able to explain their reasoning, and more vulnerable to subtle inaccuracies embedded in the machine's fluent output. The more they trusted the tools, the more they began to bypass their own judgment entirely.

This is the Cyborg's central paradox. By becoming deeply integrated with the machine, they risk becoming merely another node in its network. In the worst case, they stop thinking altogether, ceding the parts that give humans our edge, reasoning, ethics, and strategy, to a system that isn't built to bear them. It's the Neo problem from *The Matrix*: if you believe the simulation too fully, you forget you're in one, and will end up simply fueling the machines.

Which is why successful Cyborgs must be more vigilant than their Centaur or Orchestrator counterparts. It is critical that they stay awake inside the system, constantly deciding what to accept, what to question, and when to take the wheel back. Successful cyborgs remain vigilantly *in the loop*, as the jargon goes, guiding the AI and double-checking its outputs.

The Artisan: handcrafted value in an AI world

It might seem counter-intuitive at first, but as AI floods the world with blandly competent content and paint-by-numbers analysis, the human craftsperson will gain new cultural and commercial value. We still talk about the Luddites, and not always with contempt.

The Artisan MBA uses AI the way a woodworker uses sandpaper or a baker uses a convection oven as useful tools, but never the source of the magic. Their hallmark is their personal signature, whether it's a distinctive way of thinking, expressing, or framing that AI can't mimic. Imagine a strategist who lets GPT handle the background scan, but insists on telling the story in their own voice, complete with surprising metaphors, offbeat analogies, or even a hand-drawn slide tucked between the graphs.

In practice, the Artisan MBA might delegate downstream grunt work to a model—say, scraping industry benchmarks, summarizing earnings calls, or drafting an initial deck skeleton, but reclaim the upstream thinking entirely. For instance, while the AI handles the first pass of a competitive analysis, the artisan might step into the field, talk to a few frontline employees, and reshape the whole narrative around a non-orthodox insight no dashboard would reveal. Or they might take the dry output of a segmentation analysis and build a vivid brand persona from it, complete with a name, backstory, and day-in-the-life sketch, that sticks in the client's mind long after the charts are forgotten.

This matters because AI, for all its strength, has a sameness problem. Left to itself, it generates the median of everything it's seen before. We've already trained our eyes to spot the AI tell from the lifeless phrasing to the lack of grit and texture. The Artisan sees this and leans the other way. "Let the AI write the baseline deck," they say, "I'll write the part that gets remembered."

Their output might take longer, and it might not scale, but that's exactly the point. In a business world rushing to automate everything, what's rare becomes valuable. In MBA terms, artisans will lean into creative strategy, unstructured problem-solving, and deep originality, and they will excel in the kind of work that benefits from quiet, boredom, curiosity, and human taste. Some might even go full analogue. Call them the teetotalers in a world of digital intoxication, abstaining from its use entirely and crafting each output carefully by hand, one keystroke at a time.

The Client Whisperer: AI is the sideshow

The Client Whisperer is perhaps the clearest glimpse into what AI makes *possible* for MBAs, rather than what it replaces. This archetype doesn't reject AI, but places it exactly where it belongs: in the background as the sideshow and a quiet enabler. While others obsess over which model is most accurate, the Client Whisperer is focused on what matters most, the human in the room.

Emotional intelligence plays a role as does AI, but the real edge lies in how the Client Whisperer wields them together and delivers them with their professional presence. The Client Whisperer knows how to read the room when a pitch starts to slip, notices the one executive who hasn't said a word, and turns the meeting by addressing what no one else dared name. They don't see AI as a threat or even a tool; they see it as permission to do what MBAs should have been doing all along: spending more time with the client, listening better, and solving real problems in real time.

While the algorithms run in the background, crunching churn probabilities and drafting follow-up emails, the Client Whisperer is observing. They might pull sentiment data before a meeting or use an AI co-pilot to simulate client objections, but their edge comes from the fact that they care enough to understand what keeps a client up at night. You'll know this archetype when you see it. It's the MBA who sits in the sales kickoff and, watching the CRO fumble with a generic AI script, quietly says, "Hold my AI agent, I've got this." And then walks into the room, not with slides, but with a story, an insight, a narrative that actually lands. Because when the machines are doing the heavy lifting, the Client Whisperer is free to do the heavy *listening.*

Meet your new meta-skills

If the above sounds overtly poetic, you got me there. Obviously, no one is going to start adding "I am a Cyborg" to their resume. What the archetypes do instead is illustrate modes of working and show how we relate to our tools, and how far we fuse with them. And the extent of that fusion will always depend on two things: who we are, and what the context demands of us.

Some roles will nudge us toward total integration, think air traffic controllers, algorithmic traders, drone pilots, or cybersecurity analysts where machine-calibrated augmentation unlocks entirely new levels of productivity and capability. In these domains, humans operate as extensions of real-time systems. In some tasks, the need for precision on low latency and at scale demands that we "become one with the machine." Others, like creative strategists and crisis mediators, may find themselves pushing AI to the margins, using it as a sounding board, not a substitute. Here, the tool stays in the toolkit and the human stays at the center (Table 3.6).

TABLE 3.6 The context-style match

Context/Industry	*Likely dominant style*	*Why*
Air traffic control/Trading	Cyborg	Real-time decisions, low latency tolerance, high throughput needs
Consulting/Strategy	Centaur/Orchestrator	Structured thinking augmented by tools, integration of judgment and data
Creative industries	Artisan/Whisperer	High-context, high-emotion, low predictability tasks
Crisis negotiation/Diplomacy	Client Whisperer	Requires emotional presence, non-verbal cues, live social interaction
Customer service	Centaur (shifting to AI)	Templates and scripts increasingly handled by LLMs, humans needed for escalations
Scientific R&D	Orchestrator	Multimodal, multi-tool coordination, requires human design of experiments
Education/Coaching	Artisan/Whisperer	Needs empathy, flexibility, and improvisation
Legal review/Compliance	Centaur/Cyborg	Semi-structured workflows with room for automation, human-led judgment remains crucial

TABLE 3.7 The meta-skills matrix

Meta-skill category	*Definition*	*Example tasks*	*Why it matters*
Orchestration and Toolflow Design	Coordinating multiple AI tools into coherent, synergistic workflows	Building workflows with Claude, GPT, Perplexity, Zapier, and Slack bots	Multiplying leverage across systems instead of relying on one prompt engine
Judgment and Audit	Detecting hallucinations, blind spots, or bias in AI-generated outputs	Spotting errors in contract summaries or hallucinated citations	Prevents uncritical trust; maintains standards and safety
Context Management	Understanding and preserving organizational, strategic, and cultural nuance	Modifying tone per audience, preserving brand voice across AI tools	AI is bad at nuance; you must be good at it
Cognitive Framing and Decomposition	Reframing problems for optimal AI assistance and modular execution	Turning vague briefs into agent-ready sub-tasks	Makes AI actually usable in real business contexts
Human-AI Interaction Design	Designing systems where human and machine decisions reinforce one another	Combining AI analytics with human coaching interventions	Prevents task erosion and improves outcome quality
Abstraction Laddering	Moving up from task execution to mission framing and strategic intent	From "send invoice" to "secure revenue" to "retain client"	Ensures humans focus on the high-value core of the business

But no matter the archetype you lead with, what defines your success is not just how well you prompt, but how well you approach the act of prompting. That's the domain of meta-skills, and some of the ones that matter the most in the age of AI are entirely new to us. Here's one way to categorize the meta-skills the next generation of MBAs must hone (Table 3.7).

Training these skills won't come from another Excel module or a Coursera course. They'll require structured practice, coaching, peer feedback, and sandbox environments where failure carries low cost but high learning potential. Teaching someone how to prompt is a start, but teaching them when to question the premise of their prompt and the selection of the model based on its limitations is the meta-skill that unlocks transformative value.

Ultimately, these meta-skills will distinguish the merely competent from the exceptional. They are the connective tissue that allows MBAs to operate fluidly across tools, teams, and tiers of abstraction. They also allow MBAs to create value in a world where the inputs of intelligence are increasingly commodified, but the capacity for meaning-making and action remains irreplaceably human.

In the next chapter, we'll get to the bottom of what exactly these new AI tools we've been foaming at the mouth all about are. And before we do, let's take a brief moment to get comfortable with the vocabulary and key concepts that we'll be encountering in the remainder of the book.

Notes

1 Tomlinson, Kiran, Sonia Jaffe, Will Wang, Scott Counts, and Siddharth Suri. 2025. "Working with AI: Measuring the Applicability of Generative AI to Occupations." *arXiv preprint* arXiv:2507.07935. https://arxiv.org/pdf/2507.07935

2 https://mitsloan.mit.edu/ideas-made-to-matter/these-human-capabilities-complement-ais-shortcomings

3 Dell'Acqua, Fabrizio, Edward McFowland III, Ethan R. Mollick, Hila Lifshitz-Assaf, Katherine C. Kellogg, Saran Rajendran, Lisa Krayer, François Candelon, and Karim R. Lakhani. 2023. *Navigating the Jagged Technological Frontier: Field Experimental Evidence of the Effects of AI on Knowledge Worker Productivity and Quality*. Harvard Business School Working Paper No. 24-013, Harvard Business School Technology & Operations Management Unit, September 2023. https://www.hbs.edu/ris/Publication%20Files/24-013_d9b45b68–9e74-42d6-a1c6-c72fb70c7282.pdf

4 Shoresh, David, and Yonatan Loewenstein. 2025. "Modeling the Centaur: Human–Machine Synergy in Sequential Decision Making." *arXiv preprint* arXiv:2412.18593v2. https://doi.org/10.48550/arXiv.2412.18593; https://arxiv.org/abs/2412.18593

5 Lee, Hao-Ping (Hank), Advait Sarkar, Lev Tankelevitch, Ian Drosos, Sean Rintel, Richard Banks, and Nicholas Wilson. 2025. "The Impact of Generative AI on Critical Thinking: Self-Reported Reductions in Cognitive Effort and Confidence Effects From a Survey of Knowledge Workers." In *Proceedings of the CHI Conference on Human Factors in Computing Systems (CHI '25)*, April 26–May 1, 2025, Yokohama, Japan. New York, NY: ACM. https://doi.org/10.1145/3706598.3713778; https://www.microsoft.com/en-us/research/wp-content/uploads/2025/01/lee_2025_ai_critical_thinking_survey.pdf

4

A SHORT LESSON IN LANGUAGE AND AN MBA'S GUIDE TO THE MACHINES NOW RUNNING THE ECONOMY

William Shakespeare might hold the most quoted line in the annals of rose-related wisdom with his claim that a rose by any other name would smell as sweet. Yet, it was Melville Feynman, the father of Nobel laureate Richard Feynman, who offered the sharper insight when he told his son that knowing the name of a thing is not the same as knowing the thing itself.

You can spend a lifetime cataloging every translation of a rosebush and still walk away without understanding how it grows, why it lives, or what makes one flourish while another withers. For MBAs, that kind of surface-level knowledge that is satisfied with naming instead of taming is useless. Their work demands a more tactile grasp of the world, because they need to see past the labels and into the mechanisms, to cut through the jargon so they can read the levers and pipes that determine how value moves across an economy and inside the companies they hope to lead.

That is the aim of this short chapter. Before you can shape the future of AI in business, you need to speak its language with confidence, not as a technologist but as someone who understands what each term actually lets you do. Let's begin with understanding the jargon behind the oldest idea in this entire book.

The difference between automation and artificial intelligence

Long before anyone uttered the phrase "artificial intelligence," humans were already in the business of getting machines to take over work we'd rather not do. Automation is ancient. You can see it in the first hand-cranked mills that ground grain in Mesopotamia already by 4000 BC. A community that once needed dozens of people to pound barley by hand could suddenly redirect that labor the moment someone lashed a heavy stone to a wooden axle and let the river do the turning. It was primitive, yes, but the logic was the same one you'll use for the rest of your career. If a task is predictable, repeatable, and not particularly enjoyable to humankind, put something non-human in charge of it.

Every major leap in productivity since has been a variation of that move. Water wheels, looms, steam engines, and conveyor belts all follow the same rule. The work stays the same, but the worker changes, which is where we enter the modern enterprise and its penchant with automation.

DOI: 10.4324/9781003508427-4

Long before AI became the favorite topic on conference stages and investor decks, companies relied on robotic process automation (RPA) to keep their internal machinery running. RPA is unglamorous in the way plumbing is unglamorous, where no one raves about pipes until they burst. But for decades now, RPA has quietly run payroll systems, handled invoices, filed claims, reconciled transactions, processed insurance forms, and updated databases, alleviating the human burden just like the steady stream did in modern-day Iraq thousands of years ago.

The reason why RPA works is because the tasks were well suited for it. RPA thrives on structure. Give it a sequence of rules, and it will follow them with monk-like discipline. "If the claim is under this amount, route it here. If the contract ID matches that table, update the row. If the bank statement shows a discrepancy, flag it for review." None of it resembles intelligence any more than a windmill resembles intention, but the effect is the same: something non-human takes over a task humans once performed.

This is where many MBAs get tripped up. They hear that AI is automating work and assume it is a continuation of RPA. It's not. RPA imitates the actions of a worker. AI imitates the judgment of one and understanding that difference alone can make or break one's career.

RPA follows rules where AI learns patterns. RPA executes, where AI approximates, predicts, and adapts in its execution. RPA needs the world to behave the same way tomorrow as it did yesterday, while AI tolerates ambiguity, noise, and incomplete information.

In the enterprise, this distinction matters because most processes live in the middle. They contain segments that are rigid and mechanical, perfect for classic automation, and segments that require perception, interpretation, or probabilistic judgment. Think of underwriting, auditing, customer triage, pricing, procurement, logistics, and even internal operations like promotions or performance evaluation. None of these are fully rule-driven, yet none are fully unpredictable either. They sit in the grey zone where automation alone fractures and AI alone overreaches.

This is also why the enterprise vocabulary has exploded in recent years. The moment you move past strict rules, you need concepts like machine learning, supervised and unsupervised models, embeddings, transformers, vector search, function calling, and retrieval pipelines. They all point to the same underlying idea. We are taking tasks out of human hands and placing them into the hands of systems that are no longer merely following instructions but are approximating human-level decisions.

This is not a philosophical distinction. It is a practical one. Before you automate anything meaningful in a business, you must know what kind of task you're dealing with. Is it crisp enough for rules? Is it fuzzy enough for learning? Is it somewhere in between, requiring a hybrid of both? The success or failure of an automation effort depends entirely on how well this classification is done.

And that brings us to the real strategic question for the MBA reader. If automation removes the mechanical work and AI removes the perceptual work, what remains for the human. What remains is judgment about which parts of a workflow can be handed off safely, where risk accumulates, where exception handling is necessary, and where the economics of automation actually justify the effort.

Understanding this difference is the gateway to everything that follows in this chapter. Once you can see where rules break down and where patterns emerge, you can begin redesigning processes for automation, not by replicating the past but by rebuilding them for a world where humans and non-humans trade between them.

Which leads us directly to the next topic: the domain where rules reign supreme, and where the opportunities for efficiency are still hiding in plain sight.

Automation and rules-based systems

One of the clearest reminders of how far automation can go sits in the history of the telephone. A century ago, major cities housed entire office floors filled wall to wall with switchboard operators. Thousands of people, usually women, sat at long rows of wooden consoles, plugging cables, routing calls, and manually stitching together the connective tissue of modern communication. Every call passed through a human hand, and every connection made was a tiny act of labor.

Today, that same function sits inside a microchip that costs less than a sandwich to produce.

It is a perfect illustration of deterministic automation in action. A telephone call can only be routed correctly in a finite number of ways, and each variable is known to all involved. The rules are stable, and the connection follows a fixed path: a call arrives, the system validates the request, checks availability, chooses the correct line, and makes the link. Once that logic could be captured by a combination of hardware and software, the humans were no longer necessary. We didn't remove the problem; we removed the intermediaries, which are at the heart of rule-based automation. It is dis-intermediation at its cleanest. A sack of neurons is removed from the workflow and replaced with a combination of silicon, logic, and electricity that operates faster, cheaper, and with fewer errors. And for the foreseeable future, MBAs who know how to spot these rule-driven workflows will build fortunes off of them.

The mistake many make is assuming that deterministic work is always simple work, because it is not. Some of the most complex systems in the world are rule-based once you look closely. Aircraft avionics, tax withholding, loan amortization, and thousands of other utterly complicated tasks involve long sequences of "if this, then that," and yet, all of them can be automated once the rules are faithfully mapped. Complexity does not disqualify a task from automation, only ambiguity does. This means the AI-native MBA's job is not to find easy tasks to automate, it is to find stable ones. What you are really hunting for are rules that stay constant over time, even if they are hidden inside a policy manual no one has read since the CFO's predecessor wrote it. You want inputs that arrive in a structured format, or at least in a form that can be tamed into structure without heroic effort. You want decision paths that do not hinge on human discretion or sentiment, because the moment interpretation enters the picture, the rules begin to wobble. You want outcomes that are either correct or incorrect, or that fall into clearly defined buckets so the machine knows when it has succeeded. And you want a clean, traceable line from rule to action, something you can capture in software logic, an API call, or a simple validation routine without introducing philosophical debate along the way.

Consider, for example, a hospital's patient intake workflow. Much of it is probabilistic and requires judgment, but some of it is relentlessly deterministic from the insurance eligibility checks to deductible calculations. These do not require a clinician as much as they require a rules engine. And once those rules are automated,what survives is not the task but the value the task serves. Humans might not route wires to connect callers anymore, but we still need communication. This is why the MBA's calculus in deterministic automation always returns to the same trio of considerations: cost, quality, and efficiency. And it is also why the jargon surrounding these systems matters more than most managers like to admit.

You don't need to be a technologist to make these decisions, but you do need to understand the language that shapes how deterministic systems operate. Terms like rules engines, RPA, state machines, workflow orchestration, event triggers, API integrations, validation logic, exception handling, BPMN flows, and decision tables all describe the mechanical scaffolding that lets a process run without a human sitting inside it. Learning them is less about becoming fluent in engineering and more about being able to see the architecture of the work you are trying to improve.

All of these describe the same fundamental concept: encoding predictable human actions into repeatable machine logic.

Yet, as every MBA learns eventually, most workflows are not purely deterministic. Rules break down, inputs vary, and exceptions pile up just as ambiguity begins to creep in. And once you enter that territory where the world refuses to sit still long enough to be codified, you must move beyond simple rules altogether.

That is where probabilistic and hybrid systems take over, and that is where we turn next.

Automation and probabilistic and hybrid systems

Imagine a police officer handing a traffic ticket, or a judge considering a repeat stop light offender in court. Both follow clear rules of the most regulatory kind, and yet, in both, they have discretion and determination that are hard to put into formal rules without losing the spirit of the process (expand and refine)

Segue to explaining how if even such a simple thing as handing out a traffic ticket has many dimensions about it, surely most of business follows similar lines. And indeed, we see much of business be non-deterministic (probabilistic) and a combination of deterministic ones.

Segue to explaining the terminology we've invented to cover this…

Insights on what this means for AI and the MBA using it,

And then explain how this complexity has given rise to a field that invents new terms and jargon faster than we can keep up with.

Section 4: The cascade of terminology in action

Imagine a police officer deciding whether to issue a traffic ticket. The speed limit is printed on a sign. The rules are codified, exhaustive, and designed to remove ambiguity. Yet the moment the officer steps out of the patrol car, those rules collide with the real world. Was the driver avoiding debris, or was there perhaps a medical emergency that justifies their actions? Was the reading from the radar gun clean or thrown off by a passing truck, or might the police officer be biased in who they point it to? A judge faced with a repeat red-light offender runs into the same problem. Statutes outline the penalties, the precedents narrow the range of acceptable outcomes, and still the judge must weigh context, motive, history, and proportionality. Try encoding all that into rigid rules, and you lose the spirit of justice. Try ignoring it, and you lose the humanity of the process. Ultimately, the law sketches the boundaries, but the judgment inside those boundaries is human. These are tasks that sit uneasily between structure and discretion, between what a rules engine can execute and what a human mind interprets.

If even something as mundane as a traffic violation contains that many dimensions, you can imagine how much more complicated the average business workflow becomes. Very little in the enterprise lives at the deterministic extreme. Most tasks sit in the long middle, part mechanical and part interpretive, where rules get you only halfway to the right answer and the rest depends on probabilistic reasoning, domain knowledge, pattern recognition, or simple human common sense. Pricing, forecasting, risk assessment, onboarding, compliance reviews, hiring decisions, and customer support triage, all of them mix stable logic with variable judgment.

Once you move into this territory, the vocabulary expands rapidly. We no longer talk only about rules. We talk about models, features, probabilities, confidence scores, embeddings, vector spaces, pattern matching, and decision thresholds. These terms emerged because no single word could capture work that behaves differently each time it appears. They describe systems that don't follow instructions so much as they learn tendencies, weigh uncertainties, and choose the most likely path forward.

For the MBA working with AI, this is where the job becomes interesting and impactful. Deterministic systems reward precision; probabilistic ones reward interpretation. Your task is to understand which kind of system a workflow can tolerate, where risk hides, how much ambiguity the business can accept, and what kind of oversight the automation requires. As soon as uncertainty enters the picture, you are not replacing judgment as much as you are reallocating it between the humans and their tools.

This complexity is also why the field produces jargon at a pace that outstrips most textbooks. Every time we shine a light into a new corner of ambiguity, someone invents a term to describe what we found there. It is not linguistic excess. It is the natural consequence of discovering that work is rarely as tidy as the diagrams suggest. Most tasks wander between rules and judgment, structure and improvisation, what can be encoded and what must be interpreted. And the more we try to automate those wandering tasks, the more vocabulary we need.

Which brings us to the frontier where all those terms start collapsing into a new one: the agent.

Agentic AI

If you listen to the marketing departments of Silicon Valley, AI agents are already plotting our grocery lists, running our companies, and, depending on the demo, preparing a gentle coup. The dream being sold is one of digital employees you simply "hire," hand a goal to, and watch as they conduct meetings, write reports, manage pipelines, and negotiate deals while you sip espresso and contemplate strategy. It is an attractive story. It is also several exits ahead of where the technology actually is.

In reality, AI agents today are far more modest, but don't take that as a sign of the hype not being lived up to update by update. They are systems that can perceive an instruction, break it into steps, call tools, gather information, update their plan, remember what they've already done, and continue acting until they either reach the goal or get stuck, which is powerful enough already. Technologically, an agent is just an orchestration of familiar pieces. Tool calling gives it hands, memory gives it a past, context gives it a present, and planning modules give it a rudimentary sense of future. It is not consciousness by any means, but it is the beginning of coordination where the tools take over from the humans.

When you apply this to business through the eyes of an MBA, this modest coordination becomes something much more powerful soon enough. Because for the first time, you can migrate business logic itself into a machine. All of the flowcharts, Visio diagrams, SOPs, and playbooks that consultants have been drawing for a century can now be operationalized rather than laminated. The sales operations process no longer needs a human to shepherd it from step to step, nor does the onboarding workflow need a coordinator any longer. The month-end close no longer needs a war room when an agent can follow the same blueprint every time; the blueprint becomes the worker.

This is where the hype, for once, has a kernel of truth. Tool calling on its own is clever but limited and the technology is still far from magic, but that's not the point. What matters is what happens when agents stop being glorified button-pressers and start carrying the logic of an entire workflow inside them. A rules-based agent can already execute deterministic tasks end to end. A probabilistic agent can manage the ambiguous stretches with retrieval, verification, and corrective loops. And a hybrid agent, the model most enterprises will lean on, can do both, shifting seamlessly between structure when the path is clear and learned judgment when it is not.

But the real opportunity sits above the task layer. Once agents can embody business logic, they become more than workers. They become business models in miniature. A sales pipeline becomes an agentic system. A compliance function becomes an agentic system. A customer success motion becomes an agentic system. And if a business can be decomposed into agents that coordinate, learn, and execute together, the economics change. The margin profile changes. The scalability changes. Whole categories of work that were impossible to automate become programmable.

That is the real killer app that we're seeing being vibe-coded right in front of our eyes.

This also gives rise to the agentic spectrum, which every MBA should understand:

At one end, you have *rules-based agents*: deterministic systems wrapped in a more flexible shell. They know what to do as long as the world behaves as expected. Think of them as automated clerks with immaculate discipline.

Move a step further, and you reach *reactive agents*: systems that respond to inputs with learned behavior but do not plan. Customer service bots, triage assistants, routing tools.

Then come *strategic agents*: systems capable of breaking large goals into smaller steps, evaluating their progress, and adjusting their plan. These are the first agents that feel like something more than automation.

Among them lie *tool-using agents*: systems that not only plan but can pick up external tools, CRMs, spreadsheets, APIs, and browsers, to complete tasks in the environment. These are the ones beginning to show up in enterprise pilots.

And, in theory, on the horizon, *fully autonomous agents*: systems that set their own goals in pursuit of higher-level objectives and manage entire workflows without human oversight. These do not exist yet in any safe or reliable form, but the industry is walking steadily toward them.

Across this spectrum, the jargon expands accordingly. Model Context Protocols (MCPs) describe multi-agent control planes that keep large fleets of agents organized. A2A refers to agent-to-agent coordination, where machines negotiate with machines. Memory architectures capture the evolving state of work. Planning modules handle decomposition. Verification loops reduce hallucination. The terms may feel excessive, but they reflect the complexity of letting machines act instead of merely predict.

For MBAs, the consequence is profound. When agents can embody business logic, you must decide which processes are worth encoding. If a workflow can be made agentic, the cost curve collapses, and the throughput expands. If it cannot, you must ask whether it should exist at all. Entire business models will begin to hinge on this question. A model that requires armies of humans performing brittle, exception-heavy tasks becomes fragile in an agentic world. A model that decomposes cleanly into structured decision points becomes scalable in ways that were not previously possible.

This forces a new kind of strategic thinking where "Can we automate this task," turns into "Can this be handed to an agent without harming quality, compliance or trust." If the answer is yes, you build with the assumption that humans are supervisors rather than executors. If the answer is no, you design the work with human judgment at the center and let the agents handle everything around it.

Human involvement becomes a design choice. You can keep people "in the loop," reviewing critical steps. You can place them "on the loop," monitoring for anomalies. Or you can remove them entirely for workflows where reliability, not nuance, is the goal. The further you drift toward full autonomy, the more you must confront the same question the early telephone companies faced: what does the human actually need to do.

And this brings us naturally to the question that lingers under every conversation about agents: if we can capture an entire business in a network of interacting agents then what, exactly, is the minimum number of people a company needs.

That is where we turn next.

Automated systems

By the time you read this, the fully automated company may have already moved from an experiment to case study, but at the moment of writing, it remains a personal research project of mine. Even so, it is worth getting a head start on the implications, because the direction of travel is unmistakable.

The question is disarmingly simple. Does a company need any employees at all?

Consider the early prototype that my colleague and I have already made work in bits and pieces. An AI agent is given a simple mandate: produce and sell five-dollar caricatures of a user. It pulls its sales channel from Craigslist or a similar marketplace, using an automated listing generator to keep inventory "fresh." It handles the backend through a tool call to Google Sheets, where orders and timestamps accumulate in neat rows. It processes payments through Stripe, filing the revenue with an accountant-free indifference. And each morning, it posts an obnoxious motivational update on X, "Rise and grind, 0.005 percent of the way to becoming a millionaire," to keep the marketing loop alive.

None of this is particularly advanced, and it is still closer to an art project than a business. But it works. And what works at 50 dollars a week today will work at 50,000 dollars a week once the agent gains better tools, broader permissions, and deeper memory. The bottleneck is no longer whether the agent can do the work. It is whether humans will allow it to.

If the search for the one-person unicorn dominated the last decade of entrepreneurship, the search for the zero-person company will define the next. You can already sense the first glimmers of it in the solo-founder SaaS boom, in the rise of no-code automation, in the entrepreneurial experiments running quietly in the corners of GitHub and Reddit. The difference now is that agents don't just speed up work. They can perform the entire work stack from production, distribution, fulfilment, invoicing, reporting to outreach, without ever needing a lunch break or a three-day offsite.

This does not mean every business will become empty. It means every business will have to justify the humans it keeps. Creative direction will remain. Governance will remain. Trust, accountability, and long-term reasoning will remain. But a growing share of operational labor, the parts that can be decomposed into flows, checks, and tool calls, will migrate to systems that behave more like organizations than like software.

And perhaps one of you reading this will be the first to stitch these pieces together into something the rest of us will study. A network of agents, each holding a piece of the business logic, moving information, executing steps, and coordinating with one another the way departments once did. A company without employees, but not without structure. A firm without staff, but not without ambition.

Someone will build it. The only open question is whether it becomes a curiosity or the blueprint for a new kind of enterprise.

To give you an example of what these paradigm shifts may mean for MBAs in practice, we can turn to one inevitability hidden in all of the above that keeps enterprise software CEOs awake at night. The great platforms of the last four decades, Salesforce, Microsoft, SAP, and Oracle, built their empires by becoming the ecosystems inside which human work happened. Some captured the workflows, some captured the data, while others captured the interconnections between teams, but all of them operated on the same premise. Humans would continue to be the primary actors, and software would be the surface they touched to do their jobs. That assumption is beginning to crack.

Data is no longer valuable on its own; instead, it is valuable only when it fuels insight. And insight, by itself, is no longer enough either. It matters only if it drives action, which in turn, is becoming insufficient unless it is embedded in a system that learns, improves, and iterates without waiting for a manager to notice the pattern. The old software model captured the data and left the rest to the humans, whereas the agentic model captures the work, which changes everything.

This is why the agentic future gives the SaaS incumbents the sweats. Every time a user bypasses a platform and lets an agent call an external tool, another slice of value leaks out of the ecosystem. Each tool call is a tiny act of disintermediation. Each micro-workflow handled outside the platform is a small reminder that the center of gravity is shifting. And taken together, these look less like convenience features and more like death by a thousand cuts.

The existential threat is simple. In an agentic world, the work no longer needs the platforms humans log into. It needs the platforms agents orchestrate. A CRM that stores contacts is useful. A CRM that manages the entire pipeline autonomously is transformative. But if the agent can already plan, act, update, communicate, and execute across multiple tools without ever touching the CRM interface, then the locus of value shifts from the legacy platform to the agentic layer sitting above it.

This is the strategic tension enterprise software faces. Stay as a system of record and risk becoming irrelevant. Try to become a system of action and risk being outpaced by agents who can run circles around fixed workflows. Move too slowly, and the agents will build their own empire on top of your APIs. Move too quickly, and you cannibalize the very human-centric design that made your platform defensible in the first place.

The lesson for MBAs, particularly in the enterprise software industry, is not that it is dying. Instead, it is being redefined. In the decades to come, the question will not be which platform humans prefer to click through but which environment allows agents to collaborate, learn, coordinate, and improve the fastest. Whoever wins that layer will become the new operating system of the enterprise, and each industry will have its own winners and losers who will be sorted along the same dividing lines of who understands what the language of AI truly means to business, instead of simply becoming native in its inflections and tones.

We will build a glossary at the end of this book to help you navigate the terminology behind this transformation, but the purpose of this chapter was to make something deeper clear. To lead in the age of AI, you must speak the language of the machines that increasingly run the economy, and you must be able to imagine the business models that will rise when those machines stop being tools and start becoming collaborators.

Now that the groundwork is set, we turn to where all of this began. The history of the field itself, and the family tree of ideas that brought us to this moment, Chapter 5.

5

A BRIEF MBA'S HISTORY AND THE LINNEAN FAMILY TREE OF AI

Thus far, we've been calling AI a tool. The term has served us well as both a stylistic choice and a pedagogical abstraction that aids in bringing clarity to a thing so complex PhD students spend their entire careers trying to push one fraction forward. Approaching AI as a tool helped us sidestep the hype of a breakthrough technology and approach it the way a strategist would: not as a mystified disciple, but as a user seeking new ways to create and distribute value. The framing allowed us to ask: What is this good for in the context of business? Where does it help our MBAs? Where does it fail them?

But now the gloves come off.

This chapter marks the first deep dive in a four-part tour through the core domains of modern AI, each of which changes how MBAs will work, think, and lead. In each, we'll follow the same arc. First, we'll trace the roots of the particularly subcategory of AI, defining what exactly this part of the technological family is, how it came to be, and where it's headed. Then, we'll anchor the abstract into real life by mapping the current business applications that matter most. Finally, we'll return to our most central concern, that is, exploring what all of this means for you in terms of the skills, instincts, and judgment calls that the MBA of 2050 must master.

Before we begin with our topic of choice for this chapter, natural language processing, it behooves us to first acquaint ourselves with the family tree of AI.

A brief history of AI: from understanding God's words to predicting ours

Leave it to humans to look at a piece of inert rock and ask it to think for us. That is, in effect, what we have been up to for the past millennia as we have been cajoling various elements to do our bidding. The humble silicon dioxides compound was the first to flinch, taking on the task for the rest of the minerals, and it took us our time to get to our collaborator.

In the late 13th century, on the sun-bleached hills of Mount Randa in Majorca, a man named Ramon Llull was starving himself in pursuit of divine clarity. Llull wasn't fasting for revelation in the metaphorical sense; he was withering in an entirely physical sense of the term, desperate to solve a problem that had consumed much of his intellectual life: how to prove, beyond

DOI: 10.4324/9781003508427-5

interpretation or debate, the truth of God's word. Like many thinkers of his time, Llull believed logic could be divinely ordained. But unlike others, he didn't reach for parchment or sermon to make his case for him. Like the pre-YC founder her was, he decided to build a machine. His *Ars Magna*, or *great art*, consisted of layered, rotating discs etched with words representing theological and philosophical concepts. The mechanism allowed users to generate new combinations of ideas and terms by spinning these concentric circles, a kind of semantic roulette intended to reveal divine truths hidden in scripture. What Llull created was not truth itself, of course, but a method to manipulate language systematically and mechanically. In doing so, he left behind more than a curious relic of medieval theology. He may have created the first generative language model on record. That Llull's contraption sought God and not quarterly earnings doesn't change its relevance to our discussion at hand. His work, and the ambition behind it, captured something that endures to this day. Namely, the impulse to model human reasoning and to project outside of our brains into machines that could think for us by combining our own concepts, rules, and language. Llull wasn't a computer scientist, and we shouldn't try and credit him for the creation of the field either. However, as we look to the field today, we see that his intellectual descendants span disciplines, from philosophy and linguistics to logic and machine learning.

And he wasn't alone in his endeavors even a thousand years ago.

A millennium earlier, Hero of Alexandria had built coin-operated wine dispensers and automatic temple doors using cleverly hidden siphons and weights. The technology wasn't magic, but it might as well have been given how in the ancient world, any machine that appeared to act on its own invited wonder. Without Hero, every collapsing staircase and dart-firing wall in Indiana Jones would feel like a scriptwriter's stretch of imagination. Later came the *Antikythera mechanism*, a Greek marvel pulled from a shipwreck in 1901. The machine came equipped with enough gears and complexity to model celestial movements, to the point that many now call it the world's first analog computer. Meanwhile, when the Anitkytherians were making their discs, the Mesopotamian scribes had used abaci for thousands of years to calculate trade and tributes, and the Inca were encoding census data and military strength in their quipus, knotted strings we still haven't fully deciphered but can rightfully place among the first pre-literate databases.

None of these were AI, of course, not in the way we mean today. But they all marked steps in the same long pursuit that seems to have bothered humankind like a gadfly for eons: finding ways to extend the mind, structure our thinking, and wrest some order from the mess of the world. Fast forward to 1801, and Joseph-Marie Jacquard unveiled his programmable loom, using punch cards to program intricate weaving patterns. Charles Babbage later dreamt up the analytical engine, an invention that, while never completed in his lifetime, inspired Ada Lovelace to write what is now widely considered the first computer program. Decades later, Alan Turing, decoding Nazi ciphers with machines of his own design, gave us the mathematical foundations for thinking about thinking. And not long after that, the room-sized behemoths of postwar computing began to shrink, evolve, and multiply, until one day, Steve Jobs and Steve Wozniak were wiring together circuit boards in a California garage, unknowingly closing the loop on Llull's dream, bringing us one step closer to machines not only capable of calculating truth but now of generating it, too.

Each inventor on this long and painstaking path to where we are today chipped away at the same foundational questions: Can reasoning be mechanized? Can intelligence be modeled? Can something artificial produce something meaningful?

The main takeaway from the above is two-fold. First, artificial intelligence as we know it didn't appear in a single moment, even though dates such as November 2022 when ChatGPT launched feel like definite turning points. Second, this is not a computer scientist's playfield alone. The stream that became AI was fed by many tributaries from theology, formal logic, neuroscience, mathematics, linguistics to systems theory.

The term "AI" itself was coined in 1956 at the Dartmouth Conference, a small academic gathering that proved to be a watershed moment. Here, John McCarthy, a prolific computer scientist who founded the Stanford Artificial Intelligence Laboratory and created the programming language LISP among many other things, gave us the term that now has come to dominate our shared consciousness. The goal, as they gathered in the summer of 1956, wasn't modest. They wanted to know if human thought could be mapped well enough that a machine could be programmed to think like us too.

For a while, progress stuttered, and the Dartmouth Conference's ambitions were dismissed by many as topics worthy of attention by no one else than science-fiction writers. The dreams of the '50s and '60s ran into the hard walls of computing power, limited data, and algorithms that worked in theory but collapsed under operational and logistical complexities. For a while, it seemed like we were as far from answers as Llull was on the hills of Mount Randa.

And then, things suddenly started moving again. The resurgence wasn't heralded by cherubs with trumpets from above. It came quietly in ways that most of us weren't paying attention to. Bit by bit, our statistical models improved, we created better memory architectures and faster chips, and the theoretical mathematics began seeing real-life applications first in laboratories, then in supercomputers. Case in point is the landmark paper of 2017 titled *Attention Is All You Need*[1] that proposed a new architecture for understanding language, called the transformer, that put us on our trajectory today. No longer constrained to reading word by word, transformers could help machines attend to every part of a sentence at once, weighing relationships, drawing meaning from distance, nuance, and ambiguity. It turned the task of modeling human language and the underlying logic from a field of a few clever tricks into something that could scale, learn, and generalize. What feels like an overnight transformation went from processing language to, in the most technical sense of the term, *understanding* it well enough to summarize, translate, strategize, and persuade. What Llull had built in pursuit of God's truth, we had finally constructed in pursuit of predictive power and Google's quarterly earnings.

And now, here we are, the lay businesspeople, consultants, policy analysts, and startup founders, equipped with machines that speak, learn, and create for us. Machines that can read a million documents in the time it takes you to sip our soy lattes, and that can surface and summarize patterns we wouldn't even know to look for. If it all feels like magic like Hero's self-opening temple doors, you're not too far off from the truth. Technology is the closest humans get to real magic, and there's real wonder in the fact that we, the lowly descendants of LUCA and other single-celled organisms that could barely metabolize oxygen only a few hundred million years ago and just recently got the hang of wielding fire, are now equipped with the power we have.

I invite you to keep on to that sense of wonder for a few pages more, as we briefly pay homage to the family tree of AI, before explaining how one of its most powerful aspects, natural language processing, is changing the world of business.

If Carl von Linné was still around

In 1735, the Swedish biologist, Carl von Linné, or more fancifully in Latin as was the style at the time Carl Linnaeus, spent most of his life bringing structure into the complexity of natural world. As many had tried before him, he took on the task of codifying and categorizing what we see around us, and in this task, he was the most successful largely because of his insight of using comprehensive, universally applicable hierarchical classification system that we still use to this date. It is von Linné we have to thank for our own binomial, Homo Sapiens, and those of all of our best friends across the different clades, including *Canis lupus familiaris*, a species you might currently be feeding under the table.

Von Linné's accomplishment was one of radical clarification of complexity, not a simplification of it. If he were alive today, staring down the unruly garden of artificial intelligence, I'm sure he'd do what any good taxonomist would: draw branches, assign names, and attempt, if only to be thwarted by the pace of evolution, to make order from the frenzy. Given that he's no longer around, let's give him a helping hand, shall we (Table 5.1).

TABLE 5.1 The Linnean Tree of AI

Kingdom	*Major branch*	*Class*	*Order*
Intelligentia Artificialis (Artificial Intelligence)	**Machina Discens** (The Learning Machine)	**Doctrina Reinforcementis** (Reinforcement Learning)	**Politica Aucta** (Policy Optimization)
		Doctrina Auto-Supervisa (Self-Supervised Learning)	**Representatio Generativa** (Representation Learning)
	Machina Cogitantis (The Thinking Machine)	**Architectura Cognitiva** (Cognitive Architectures)	**Rationem Symbolica** (Symbolic Reasoning)
			Rationem Hybrida (Hybrid Reasoning)
			Rationem Subsymbolica (Subsymbolic Reasoning)
		Doctrina Supervisa (Supervised Learning)	**Classificatio Statistica** (Statistical Classification)
	Machina Loquens (The Talking Machine)	**Computatio Linguistica** (Linguistic Computation)	**Generatio Textus** (Text Generation)
			Analytica Sententiarum (Sentiment Analysis)
			Translatio Machinata (Machine Translation)
			Summarizatio Textus (Text Summarization)
	Machina Videns (The Seeing Machine)	**Visus Artificiales** (Artificial Vision)	**Detectio Objecti** (Object Detection)
			Segmentatio Imaginis (Image Segmentation)
			Reconstructio Scenae (Scene Reconstruction)
	Machina Facientis (The Doing Machine)	**Actuatio Intelligens** (Intelligent Actuation)	**Robotics Executio** (Robotic Execution)
			Systema Autonomum (Autonomous Systems)

It would be to your benefit to take the above taxonomy with a dash of salt and a healthy dose of whimsy. This is most decidedly not how computer scientists at DeepMind or the authors of *Attention Is All You Need* would classify their life's work. But we are not doing science for science's sake here. We're in the business of doing business, and in business, categories live and die by their usefulness. We do not need perfect precision to be dangerous; instead, we need directional clarity. We need to know what a tool can do, how it behaves, and when it might be the right weapon of choice in our fight for value. From that vantage point, the division of AI into machines that learn, think, talk, see, and act is entirely valid. On one hand, it mirrors how we, as humans, develop our own faculties and how we bring them to bear on matters of value. We learn before we reason. We speak before we truly understand. We see, then we act. The same logic holds for artificial minds, even when the genealogy and underlying technological marvels defy such a clearly demarcated categorization.

Each of the major branches tells a different story about what AI can offer us. The *Machina Discens*, the Learning Machine, is the primordial trunk of this evolutionary tree. Everything else an MBA cares about, in one way or another, builds on its ability to spot patterns, extract meaning from noise, and grow sharper over time. Without learning, there is no adaptation, optimization, or GPTs that print out our strategy decks for us.

So, it is only fitting that we begin our exploration there. Our journey starts not with what the machines can say or do, but with how they come to know anything at all. In the next section, we'll descend into the strange and increasingly sophisticated world of learning algorithms: from reinforcement agents optimizing policies in simulated arenas, to self-supervised giants distilling meaning from raw data at planetary scale.

But before we go, let's spend one final moment exploring the family tree, turning our attention from the roots to where the canopy is growing next. More particularly, let's see what we can learn from the humble electric motor and how its trajectory from a do-it-all tool to a specialized and entirely invisible piece of enabling equipment can tell us about AI.

Why we won't want AGI even once we have it

Life wasn't as alien 200 years ago as we like to think. Slater had recently opened America's first water-powered textile mill in Pawtucket, Rhode Island in 1793, effectively importing the Industrial Revolution from Britain. Business, while crude by modern standards, was already emerging as an architecture of specialized tasks, repeatable workflows, and scalable production. Corporate hierarchies were beginning to sprawl across industries, and what would shock you and me wouldn't be the org chart. It would be the plumbing of it all, or rather, the lack of the indoor variant of it. And even more so, we'd have a hard time coming to terms with the absence of electricity.

By the late 1800s, the science for whipping electrons from one place to another was there. Volta had shown it could be stored, Faraday had shown it could move, and both Edison and Tesla had started feuding over how best to distribute it to the masses. But no one really had a clue what to *do* with electricity, at least not at scale. Sure, you could light a bulb, maybe shock your lab assistant while you're at it. But for all its raw potential, electricity was a miracle in search of its killer app. And just like November 2022 came to us, so did the electric motor come to our ancestors.

The earliest prototypes, like the one built by Michael Faraday in 1821, were clunky, fragile, and borderline useless for anything outside a physics demo and a self-contained fire hazard.

But over time, and through the refinements of pioneers like Zénobe Gramme and Nikola Tesla, the motor evolved into something robust enough to run machines. At first, it was used to power existing tools that would be attached to it through appendices like lathes, pumps, and looms. Soon entire factories were redesigned around centralized motors that sent power through belts and pulleys like some steampunk circulatory system. If you had asked a layperson back then, the future was one where ever-stronger electric motors would anchor every home and factory, each surrounded by increasingly elaborate appendages and extensions to do more, spin faster, and power everything. Welcome to the electric motor's AGI era.

And yet, none of that came to pass, as all of us can confirm simply by glancing around our own homes. More than that, the average person has likely never seen, let alone touched, a standalone electric motor in their entire life. Not because the motors vanished, mind you. Quite the opposite. They have now become so ubiquitous, so embedded, and so effective at doing their job that they've entirely disappeared into the background. Today, if you posted on LinkedIn that electric motors run everything around us, your colleagues wouldn't congratulate you on your insight; they'd stage a friendly intervention.

Today, your home is full of them to the point where your toothbrush, vacuum cleaner, fridge compressor, laptop fan, and car's seat adjuster has its own. We didn't get one master motor to rule them all. We got an invisible army of them, micro, brushless, high-torque, high-precision variants and all, each doing a single job extremely well, without us ever minding them or the tasks they do.

That's the future where AI is headed too. Instead of one big-brained god-model that rules over us like Skynet, we'll have millions of an army of models embedded quietly everywhere.

Now tell me this isn't going to happen to AI, and I'll tell you exactly how you're going to lose a bet with me in ten years. Even if we do end up building AGI, and many believe we will, it's not what we'll actually use most in our daily lives. This is because the evolution of tools like AI doesn't follow the path of maximum intelligence; it follows the path of minimum viable utility.

In life and business, what survives is what works, and what works is what delivers just enough value, just fast enough, just cheaply enough, to edge out the competition. In other words, those who deliver the required outcome with the fewest resources win. That's true in markets, it's true in biology, and it will be true in AI. This doesn't mean that engineers won't continue to push the limits of AI across the entire family tree. They'll do exactly that, and in doing so, we'll see these tools nichefy in response to where each family member is creating most value in use, not in theory or in Nobel prize acceptance speeches. AI will lose their tails and their appendixes like we did the moment those features aren't actively creating or distributing value. And if the pseudo-evolutionary argument isn't doing it for you, we can arrive at the same conclusion from a purely engineering standpoint as well by tracing out AI's future paths while upholding pareto-efficient optimization or the principles of energy-constrained architecture design.

An AGI that can solve metaphysics is simply overkill when we're only trying to figure out whether your sarcastic thumbs-up on Snapchat was sincere or sarcastic. For that, you don't need an omniscient model exactly like we didn't need an all-powerful electric motor in our basements. You need a good enough one running in real-time on a mobile chip, capable of doing what we need from with bad Wi-Fi and a cranky user.

Look around you, and you'll see that all-powerful tools are the exception in software, not the rule. There are maybe four that get even close to qualifying: Excel, Word, PowerPoint, and Outlook. These hit the right layer of abstraction precisely by being general enough to apply everywhere while specific enough to be useful out of the box. With tools like these, the more you nicheify them, the less valuable they become. But almost everything else in software evolved differently. Take ERP systems for example. Hospitals don't use the same systems as restaurants or logistics firms and vice versa. Instead of a "one ERP to rule them all," we got dozens, each tailored to the quirks, workflows, and regulatory demands of a specific domain. Generality wasn't the winning move here, product-market-fit was.

AI will follow the same path. AGI might be the north star, but it won't be the workhorse. In the real world, we don't deploy hammers that can also code and make coffee. We reach for the tool that gets the job done, quickly, affordably, and well. And increasingly, that tool will be a specialized, domain-native AI, not an all-knowing oracle.

In fact, I'll go on record with a stronger prediction: we're inevitably headed toward a wave of *de-AIfication* not too far off in the future. Cloud-based behemoths that are sapping their users with token fees today will give way to leaner models running on-device or at the edge. And in some instances, even those might be swapped out for good old-fashioned algorithms or

FIGURE 5.1 Someone go get RoundUp before we're all out of a job.

modular logic once we realize that most tasks don't actually require a transformer, only a bit of common sense and more code that has only gotten cheaper to produce. In fact, if you've been paying attention, you've probably already noticed how plenty of "AI" today is little more than an "if-this-then-that" scripts dressed in the marketing jargon of the day.

AI's evolutionary path won't be determined by what engineers *could* build, any more than our own genes explore every permutation across our chromosomes. It will follow the same rules as every tool before it: the ones that replicate, survive. And in business, replication is contingent on brutally efficient value creation. That's how AI will have its electric motor moment, disappearing into the background as we stop obsessing over how it works and start caring about what it does (Figure 5.1).

Note

1 Vaswani, Ashish, Noam Shazeer, Niki Parmar, Jakob Uszkoreit, Llion Jones, Aidan N. Gomez, Łukasz Kaiser, and Illia Polosukhin. 2017. "Attention Is All You Need." In *Advances in Neural Information Processing Systems 30 (NeurIPS 2017)*, Long Beach, CA. https://proceedings.neurips.cc/paper_files/paper/2017/file/3f5ee243547dee91fbd053c1c4a845aa-Paper.pdf

6

MACHINA DISCENS—THE LEARNING MACHINE

Although the idea of offloading cognition to Google feels like a uniquely modern comfort, the instinct to make machines carry the weight of learning is anything but new. It's one of our oldest impulses right up there with lighting fires and gazing at the stars with wonder.

Long before we taught silicon to study for its own exams, we were already pushing our memory out of our heads and into the world. The abacus makes a valiant early entry here with its wooden beads, meticulously aligned, letting us calculate faster than our fingers could count. If only it didn't forget everything the moment someone's grandfather sneezes near the table. Still, it was a start, earning an honorable mention as one of the first tools that allowed memory to live outside the mind Writing, of course, is the juggernaut in this story. Every bit as much a technology as an operating system or a neural net, writing extended our working memory exponentially. And you might not be surprised that, from the moment we started writing, we were writing about business. One particular gem from ancient Mesopotamia manages to be a product pitch, legal agreement, and customer satisfaction guarantee, all in one:

> Nibruta-lu, the son of the merchant Lugal-šuba, has had this tin axe made for Nergal. Its wooden part is of arganum tree of the mountains, a wood which is superior even to the alal stone; its stone part is of antasura, a stone which has no equal. The arm of the man who strikes with it will never get tired.
>
> Should it break, I will repair it for Nergal. Should it disappear, I will replace it for him. May Nergal look after me during my life, and may he provide me with clean water in the underworld after my death.[1]

If that isn't the first explanation of a supply chain and a customer-facing warranty in action, I don't know what is. Naturally, one gets a tad poetic when making an axe for the god of the underworld, and the tablet's true purpose wasn't to rival SAP's ability to keep rows of supply chain data in order. But still, embedded in this text is the same fundamental shift of the outsourcing of cognitive load. The act of putting thoughts into something else so that our minds could move on to other problems, including safely to the underworld.

DOI: 10.4324/9781003508427-6

From here, the inevitable march of progress continues. Take the astrolabe, which emerged around the 1st century BC. A mechanical marvel to be sure, it took the sum of what we knew about the heavens and compressed it into a mixture of brass and gear. With it, you could find your latitude or even measure time, all without carrying the math in your head. The astrolabe didn't learn by any meaningful sense of the word, but the materials and form did keep a record of what we had once learnt ourselves. And that was progress.

From there, we've kept on adding layers and techniques from punch cards to magnetic tape, all of which expanded the very concept of what a machine can keep a record of. At the same time, the real-world impact of that recordkeeping has grown greater.

Even as our hardware for keeping track of what we've learnt has evolved from punch cards to solid-state hard drives, the machines themselves remained flaky apprentices. They could hold more, process faster, and survive the odd coffee spill, but learning? That remained elusive. In fact, sometimes we couldn't even trust them to keep their records straight. A now-legendary story from Belgium in 2003 drives the point home. During a local election in the municipality of Schaerbeek, a single stray cosmic ray struck a memory cell in an electronic voting machine, flipping a bit and adding to one candidate, Maria Vindevoghel, an inexplicably specific number of 4,096 bonus votes.[2] The error came to light only because the total vote count exceeded the election modeling, and the case is now used as the canonical example of how a "single-event-upset" as well as a stark reminder of how far we can trust our machine companies to hold their records straight.

No matter how well our machines might remember what we tell them, none of it comes close to the power they began to exhibit when they started learning on their own. That's when the real story of AI begins, at the first steps of artificial learning.

It starts, as these things often do, with a promise wrapped in wires and hype. In 1958, Frank Rosenblatt, a psychologist at Cornell, unveiled what he called the "Perceptron."[3] It was a machine that looked more like a washing machine than a brain, powered by an IBM 704 mainframe and fed a regimented diet of punched cards. It was also 60 years too early, but in our chronicling here, it isn't the success that matters as much as the concept itself. Rosenblatt had built something that did more than simply store answers like everything that came before it. The Perceptron could adjust them, shift them, and tweak its own parameters and knobs until its guesses got better. In short, it could learn.

He described it with the zeal of a prophet: "the first machine capable of having an original idea."[4] Newspapers ran wild. "New Navy Device Learns By Doing," declared *The New York Times*, musing that this might be humanity's first real rival to the brain.[5] Here we had a baby of the postwar computing boom taking its first wobbly steps, and people were already planning for its PhD. But like many prodigies, the Perceptron soon hit a ceiling. Or more precisely, a line that it couldn't cross. It turned out the perceptron couldn't solve problems that required nonlinear boundaries.

It could separate dots on one side of a line from the other, sure, but show it a pattern like XOR, and it would have stared blankly back at you. In 1969, Marvin Minsky and Seymour Papert spelled this out in a now-infamous book called "Perceptrons." The AI hype balloon soon deflated funding dried up, and in a tragic turn of events, Rosenblatt died young in a car crash, and with him went the first wave of neural dreamers, never to see how close they were to having their machines pass the next boundary. For a while, the field turned its back on learning in what many call the "AI winter." AI researchers moved to focus on symbolic reasoning instead that covered hand-coded rules, ontologies, massive trees of "if this, then that." In other words, they built machines that knew things and manipulated them deterministically, but not ones that could figure them out.

Then came the whisper of resurrection.

In 1986, three researchers, David Rumelhart, Geoffrey Hinton, and Ronald Williams, dusted off an old idea called "backpropagation." The concept came from psychology and control theory where it describes a mechanism for adjusting internal parameters or behaviors based on discrepancies between an observed output and a desired target, effectively sending an error signal backward through a system to refine its operations. In the hands of the trio, it was reborn as a kind of learning compass whereby, instead of manually adjusting a network's parameters, you could now teach it by showing it where it was wrong and letting the error trickle backwards through the system, updating each internal setting in turn.

It was as if the Perceptron had had a child that was learning dance before its parents had even picked up walking. Still, the computers of that time were weak, and the datasets were small. Most of the early breakthroughs were toy problems at best, things that a modern intern can do with one line of code like ZIP code recognition and character classification. The field continued to improve under the surface, but the limiting factor was entirely clear. The true potential of machine learning would need more than clever code. If we ever wanted to create machines that could truly learn, we would need to give them more power, and lots of it.

FIGURE 6.1 The next feature we ship goes to my homeboys.

That moment finally arrived around 2010 when three forces converged. Cheap GPUs, abundant data, and an arsenal of refined algorithms would come together to create a step change for the learning machines.

In 2012, a pair of Canadian researchers, Alex Krizhevsky and Ilya Sutskever, working with Hinton, won the ImageNet Large Scale Visual Recognition Challenge competition by a staggering margin. Their model, AlexNet, used deep convolutional networks trained on thousands of labeled images.[6] The machine could nail recognizing cats, which has become the coming-of-age-test for most machine learning experts, and more than that, it saw whiskers, edges, and even subtle patterns of light emerge from within the matrices of pixels. And it did so better than any handcrafted system ever had. That was the tipping point. Google, Facebook, Amazon, they all dove in. Deep learning models started outperforming everything else in speech, text, translation, and even medical imaging. The learning machine had matured, and this time, it wasn't going back into the lab.

What powered this shift, as Rich Sutton, one of the founding figures of reinforcement learning, argued in his influential essay *The Bitter Lesson*, wasn't clever human design, but the consistent lesson that "general methods that leverage computation tend to outperform methods that rely on human knowledge."[7] Feed a general-purpose learning algorithm enough data and computing cycles, and it will outperform any rule-based system you can dream up and write down. That's not to say we stopped trying to make machines smarter manually by any means. We simply learned that they often get smarter, faster, without our help. The pattern held steady across various fields. In chess, grandmasters had tried for decades to encode the secrets of strategy into software. Then Deep Blue crushed Garry Kasparov by brute-forcing 200 million positions per second. In Go, the same happened when AlphaGo didn't win because it learned from human intuition; it won because it played itself millions of times until it developed its own. The learning machine, in short, had grown up.

How do machines learn today

Despite the name, *machine learning* has little in common with how humans learn. There are no insights, no ah-ha moments, no stories to anchor memories like we do. Instead, the core process is brutally mechanical: guess, check, adjust, repeat. Strip away the jargon and the GPU clusters, and what you're left with is a digital toddler playing hot-or-cold in a vector space that reaches planetary scales. Simplifying things *greatly*, the process begins with a guess about whether that's a cat or a dog, a fraudulent transaction or a legitimate one, the next best word in a series, which is then compared with what the right answer should have been. The difference between those two becomes fuel for the next iteration.

What does the guessing and adjusting, though, is more often than not a layered mathematical structure called a neural network, a dense lattice of artificial neurons, each connected to many others, stacked in layers. The input layer takes in raw data such as pixels, tokens, or tabular fields, the output layer makes a prediction, and the hidden layers in between manipulate the information through weighted connections. These networks aren't hardcoded with rules on what they should think or say, instead, they're initialized with random numbers. What makes them intelligent is the gradual sculpting of those numbers through exposure to data. Some of the networks today are astonishingly vast, GPT-4, for instance, has over a trillion parameters. Each one of those is a tiny dial that can be turned ever so slightly to reduce error. It's not a brain to be sure, but it's doing something brain-like, passing signals forward and refining itself with feedback.

TABLE 6.1 The learning approaches

Term	*Explanation*	*Typical use cases*
Neural networks	Layered structures of artificial neurons that learn by adjusting weights through data exposure.	Language models, image recognition, speech processing
Decision trees	Flowchart-like models that split data into branches based on decision rules.	Credit scoring, fraud detection, medical diagnostics
Support vector machines	Algorithms that find the best boundary (hyperplane) to separate different classes in the data.	Text classification, face detection, bioinformatics
Clustering	Unsupervised techniques like K-means or DBSCAN that group similar data points together.	Customer segmentation, anomaly detection, social graphs
Reinforcement learning	Learning by interacting with an environment and receiving rewards or penalties.	Robotics, game AI, supply chain optimization

The machinery that is often powered by neural networks today is only part of a larger ecosystem of learning algorithms, including decision trees, support vector machines, clustering techniques, and reinforcement learners, all of which have played pivotal roles in enabling machines to perform tasks that once seemed exclusive to humans. Each of these approaches represents a different strategy for learning from data, and they tend to shine in different contexts. Here's a quick guide to what each does, how it works, and where you'll likely see it in the wild.

The magic, if we aren't too jaded to not call it that, happens in the adjustments. In neural networks, these adjustments come via weight updates, small numerical nudges applied to the internal levers that turn input into output. These levers, known as weights and biases, to those who use the jargon, are what the system is actually learning. And the mechanism for deciding how to tweak them is Rumelhart, Hinton, and Williams' backpropagation, which traces every bad answer through every node in the network, asking: which of you contributed most to this mistake, and how do we fix it?

It's not unlike trying to perfect your jump shot. Was it too much wrist or not enough arc? How aggressively you tune which parameter matters greatly, and if you overcorrect one, you will overshoot another. Machines go through this same dance, iteration after iteration, until the difference between guess and ground truth gets acceptably small.

That dance takes on different rhythms and forms depending on what kind of feedback the machine receives. Sometimes it's handed the right answers up front, other times it's left to find patterns on its own, and in some cases, it's rewarded, or punished, for what it does next. In the world of machine learning, we call these three flavors supervised, unsupervised, and reinforcement learning, and each teaches the machine in its own distinct way. And they aren't even the end of it, when it comes to the learning styles of AI.

The most common paradigm, supervised learning, is essentially glorified pattern recognition. Feed the machine a massive dataset of labeled examples ("this email is spam," "this one's not"), and it will find a way to approximate the relationship between inputs and outputs. It doesn't

TABLE 6.2 The learning styles

Learning style (AI)	*Analogy in human learning*	*AI example*	*Strengths*	*Limitations*	*Typical use cases*
Supervised learning	Formal classroom with answer keys	Image classification (cat vs. dog)	High accuracy; efficient with quality labels	Requires large, well-labeled datasets	Spam detection, disease diagnosis, credit scoring
Unsupervised learning	Self-guided discovery	Customer segmentation	Reveals hidden patterns without labels	Hard to evaluate; may find spurious groupings	Market segmentation, anomaly detection, topic modeling
Reinforcement learning	Trial-and-error with rewards	AlphaGo playing itself	Excels at sequential decision making	Resource-intensive; unstable training	Robotics, inventory management, game-playing agents
Self-supervised learning	Filling in the blanks	GPT training via next-word prediction	Scales without labeled data	May require task-specific fine-tuning	Language modeling, speech recognition, code autocompletion
Few-shot / In-context learning	Learning by analogy or example	GPT with few-shot prompts	Adapts rapidly to new tasks	Limited by prompt length and task clarity	Chatbots, summarization, ad copy generation

understand what spam is, nor does it have to. It simply "knows" which patterns of words and metadata show up more often in spammy messages.

Most of the recommendation systems you interact with daily, your Netflix picks, your Amazon cart nudges, and your Spotify suggestions, rely on this framework. So do fraud detection systems, credit risk models, and, increasingly, medical diagnostics. It works beautifully as long as the past is a decent guide to the future. But when the world shifts underfoot and past data no longer accurately predict future performance, as it did during the COVID-19 pandemic or in the wake of a financial crisis, these models can become unmoored if not outright dangerous. In short, they can't extrapolate; they can only interpolate. This is their power, and their curse: they are exquisitely tuned to yesterday, and we simply hope tomorrow is enough like it for the small errors to not matter.

Unsupervised learning flips the premise entirely. Instead of labeled inputs and outputs, it simply feeds the machine data in its raw, unlabeled, and entirely chaotic form and asks it to make sense of it. No answers provided, no teacher in sight. Much like a young analyst in the due diligent data file room, the machine becomes an explorer in unfamiliar territory, clustering and compressing and mapping what it sees.

This is how we get market segmentation algorithms that group customers by how they behave instead of how we categorized them ex ante. It's also how anomaly detection works by understanding what's "normal," the system can flag what deviates, even if it's never seen the anomaly before. Some of the most valuable applications of unsupervised learning in business today are happening behind the scenes, detecting subtle shifts in consumer preferences before they become visible, surfacing hidden risks in supply chains, and identifying inefficiencies in logistics networks. It might not be as sexy work as your TikTok recommendation algorithm, but it is powerful. Think of it as a bloodhound with no map, sniffing out structure from scent alone.

And then there's reinforcement learning, the kind that learns from consequences. This is the playground of agents, systems that act, observe the outcomes, and adjust future actions to optimize for reward, which we'll encounter in our chapter on doing machines. Recall AlphaGo, which learned to play the game not by studying human strategy but by playing against itself millions of times. Or think of an autonomous warehouse robot that figures out the most efficient route from shelf to shipment autonomously because it was rewarded for speed in getting to where it was needed and penalized for delays. In the corporate world, reinforcement learning is already shaping inventory strategies, trading algorithms, real-time pricing engines, and even ad placement decisions. Anywhere there's a clear goal, a stream of data, and feedback over time, reinforcement learning can learn to outperform humans, at least in the narrow task it's been given.

Now, there's one more piece of the learning puzzle that MBAs need to be aware of: where does AI get its syllabus, and who decides its reading materials? Let's take a random word, say, *spatula*. How did it find its way into a language model's head and why is it that if you try right now, your chosen LLM can use it in the appropriate context.

Spatula's path to your browser window, appropriately embedded in the right context, starts long before you type. At some point, a research lab or AI company decided to train a model on a colossal dataset scraped from the open internet. This included news articles, recipe blogs, academic papers, Reddit threads, and millions of digital pages, some delightful, some deranged, and quite a few copyrighted to the point that it is giving OpenAI and Anthropic more than a few headaches. Somewhere in that mix, "spatula" appeared enough times to make the cut. It appeared with sufficient statistical frequence for it to be baked into the statistical soup the model was fed.

But that's not enough for us to use it. Just knowing that the word exists doesn't help the machine understand it, or what we actually mean is, *to use it in a way that we perceive it as being used appropriately by something that understands it*. Enter the data labelers, the humble human annotators who are mostly gig workers spread across the globe tasked with judging whether an AI response using "spatula" made sense in context. They'd upvote correct uses, downvote nonsense ones, and gradually teach the model not just what the word means, but how it's used. The results of these sessions shaped how that token now behaves when you prompt a model.

Next, the word was translated, mathematically, into a position in something called *embedding space*, a multidimensional representation that lets AI measure the meaning of words by their distance from other concepts. *Spatula* might live near *ladle* and *pan*, but hopefully far from the 19th-century cholera crisis in London. This mapping is what allows AI to guess the next word in a sentence with eerie fluency.

But the journey doesn't stop there. That training process was then updated, fine-tuned, maybe even reinforced with new data and guardrails to ensure that *spatula* wasn't being used in, say, violent or misleading contexts. And when you finally typed your prompt, all of that background machinery was triggered in real time, decades of NLP research, months of data collection, days of training runs, and millions of labeler decisions, just to decide whether "spatula" should appear in your answer. We're glossing over a wide and rough surface of details because for MBAs the takeaway is this: AI outputs are never "just the model." They're the product of an

TABLE 6.3 The learning life cycle

Stage	*Process*	*Actors*	*Risks/Biases*	*MBAs should...*
Data gathering	Collecting public, internal, or user-generated data	Vendors, clients, APIs, sensors	Over/underrepresentation, outdatedness	Audit sources; ensure data diversity
Data labeling	Annotating data with target outputs	Human annotators, heuristics, crowdsourcing	Subjectivity, cultural bias, annotation errors	Ask who labeled the data and how
Preprocessing	Cleaning, formatting, removing duplicates	Data engineers, AI ops	Garbage-in-garbage-out; erasure of edge cases	Track data lineage and loss
Training	Feeding data into models to optimize performance	ML engineers, researchers	Overfitting, underfitting, hidden bias	Align training objectives with business goals
Fine-tuning/reinforcement	Adjusting performance on specific tasks or feedback	Users, devs, ops teams	Drift, misuse, misalignment	Monitor impact; retrain iteratively
Deployment and inference	Real-time or batch use of model outputs in systems	Product teams, ops	Model collapse, latency, hallucinations	Build human-in-the-loop systems

industrial supply chain of decisions, actors, and assumptions, each with its own incentives, blind spots, and biases.

In other words, when you prompt an AI to give you a product strategy or legal risk analysis, what you're really doing is lighting the fuse on a highly engineered relay race that started with someone scraping a dusty old HTML page on a defunct blog in 2015. That's not a problem as long as you know what to expect from the outputs.

Otherwise, you might find yourself with an AI-generated product roadmap that suggests using a spatula as part of the Scrum meetings because a data labeler once approved it as "a valid tool for scraping up old ideas."

The learning machine learns to do business

We've now peered under the hood of how these machines learn. We've watched how they guess, check, adjust, and repeat until they've shaped their internal parameters into something that maps with reality with sufficient precision. And yet, for the MBA, the most urgent question isn't how it works; it's what it can do. And more specifically, what we can do with it is create and distribute value. If you're leading a business, building one, or betting your next big move on insight, this is the moment to recalibrate your expectations on what machines can learn. The age of the Perceptron critique is well and truly over, and machine learning is no longer a research project or a tool for the few. In fact, it's already embedded in workflows across every major industry, and if you've still wondering whether the AI hype was real, you're asking the wrong question. The right one is: what's already being done with it?

Let's begin with the customer. Or rather, the customer as the machine sees them, not as a set of demographics or vague personas that the marketing department sketched together in a retreat once. In customer intelligence, machine learning has found a natural niche to thrive in not just by finding patterns better than we can, but by personalizing them at a level us humans would find difficult to even conceptualize ex ante. The Netflix recommendation engine is the clearest example that most will be familiar with.[8] It is not limited to suggesting shows arbitrarily or based on a simple demographic match between you or another viewer. Instead, it learns how *your* viewing habits evolve across mood, time of day, device, and even seasonal drift. It approximates your intent as much as your satisfaction, and each interaction becomes a data point in a high-dimensional space of taste, and the machine gets better with every scroll. TikTok's algorithms take this even further. Content is pushed to different users based on micro-feedback loops, where each swipe becomes a vote in a deeply personalized stream of relevance. Each video is tested across various cohorts for appeal and dwell time, and those that perform well get boosted to larger and larger crowds.[9] The customer-facing applications aren't limited to content, mind you. Retailers, banks, airlines, and even public service platforms now segment and re-segment their users automatically, responding to changing needs before the customer consciously registers them. This is the difference between knowing your audience and predicting them, and it is exactly the realm where the learning machine excels.

The reach of these systems also extends deep into operations and supply chains, where machine learning is transforming logistics from a reactive process into a predictive discipline. Amazon, for example, uses ML-driven forecasting to anticipate demand spikes at the regional level weeks in advance, adjusting inventory distribution before the first order is even placed.[10] Their warehouses essential are an intricate choreography of machine learning and robotics, predicting which items will be needed where, optimizing picking routes, and even adjusting staffing in real time. UPS has developed its ORION system to dynamically reroute delivery trucks based on road conditions, traffic patterns, and weather forecasts, saving millions of miles and gallons of fuel annually.[11] Walmart, meanwhile, ingests streams of data from POS systems, supplier networks, and even social media sentiment to fine-tune its inventory and restocking models. Across each use case, sensors embedded in critical infrastructure, from trucks to conveyor belts, feed data into anomaly detection systems trained to catch early signs of failure and to replan accordingly. The modern supply chain no longer waits for things to go wrong; it anticipates, adapts, and optimizes in motion thanks to machines that learn.

Finance, too, has felt the shift, perhaps more rapidly than any other sector. In fraud detection, we've moved from rigid rule-based flags to pattern-recognition systems capable of spotting fraud in the same way a seasoned auditor might, not by catching obvious violations, but by sensing when something just *feels off* from the data's viewpoint. For example, Visa processes hundreds of millions of transactions daily, and their fraud models continuously evaluate each one for subtle deviations from the norm, odd timing, unusual locations, and inconsistent device fingerprints. When the model flags an outlier, the system can lock a card within milliseconds, often before the fraudster finishes checkout. Stripe, Square, and Klarna have followed similar paths, embedding ML models trained on vast transactional data into their payment rails, and startups like Chargeblast have opened up entirely new pathways to deal with fraud at its source. Risk assessment, too, has grown more nimble thanks to the learning machines. Where once a FICO score defined your borrowing prospects, companies like Upstart now use machine learning to evaluate a far richer data set, education history, employment status, and even behavioral cues embedded in application forms. These models score creditworthiness dynamically, adjusting loan terms not monthly or quarterly, but minute by minute as conditions shift. And all of the above doesn't even touch how deeply machine learning has influenced the revenue side of things. Hedge funds like Renaissance Technologies and Citadel deploy ML-driven strategies that model thousands of financial scenarios before placing trades, constantly updating based on news sentiment, earnings reports, and historical correlations. Bloomberg terminals now recommend trades based on predictive models, and JPMorgan's LOXM executes equity trades using reinforcement learning to simulate market responses. What makes learning machines and finance such a terrific pairing is that the field has always been probabilistic in its approach to modeling the future and pricing in uncertainty. What machine learning changed was the granularity and adaptability of those models. It allowed financial firms to react *with* the markets, recalibrating continuously in ways human analysts simply can't.

Human Resources is where the promise of AI collides most viscerally with its perils. On the one hand, AI-enabled resume screening, churn prediction, and performance modeling can improve speed and objectivity. Machines that have learned from past examples can filter thousands of candidates based on inferred skill matches or future promotion potential. On the other hand, this is where bias shows up fastest. Models trained on historical hiring data often replicate the preferences, conscious or not, of prior decision-makers, a finding my own research has validated in full. Amazon famously scrapped an internal hiring algorithm when it began down-ranking resumes with indicators of female applicants.[12] Explainability becomes a critical issue as well, given how you can't exactly interrogate a neural network for why its weights said no. The upside of using learning models in HR is clear, but the downsides must be managed carefully as well.

The learning machine has recently wandered into one of its most productive domains yet when it stepped into the realm of creativity. For decades, we trained machines to recognize, classify, and forecast data. But now, with the advent of generative AI systems like GPT and DALL·E, which we'll meet in our chapter on doing machines, we've entered an era where the machine has learnt how to produce art. And why should we be surprised? For the machine, art is nothing but a matter of pixels and their relationships with each other.

Finally, there is the strategic tier. Decision support is where machine learning is quietly becoming the most indispensable tool in the boardroom. From scenario modeling to predictive analysis, simulations, and impact evaluations, AI can help us explore alternate realities with fidelity and speed the most strategic human mind simply couldn't conjure up. Want to know how a shift in the EU's regulatory policy might affect your semiconductor pipeline, or how three simultaneous supplier failures would ripple through your revenue model? Soon, there's a learning model finetuned exactly for that. These systems can give you a probabilistic readout, weighting outcomes based on thousands of interlocking assumptions, but they can't replace judgment. What they can do is inform it with far more breadth and depth than even the sharpest analyst team working around the clock.

These examples aren't theoretical; they're happening now. By the time you read this, most of the examples will seem quaint in comparison to whatever has just been launched from a lab in Silicon Valley or Singapore. And as these models improve, they'll grow more tightly integrated with the workflows around them. The machine doesn't replace your process; it

FIGURE 6.2 I knew we shouldn't have fed the toaster all of those McKinsey whitepapers.

becomes part of it. The trick, and this is the part MBAs must grasp, is knowing what questions to ask, what data to feed, and when to override the system when intuition tells you something is off.

The MBA and their learning machines

For all the power learning machines have given us, we need to remember where the limits lie. Models only know what they've seen. Biases, gaps, and structural inequities in training data will be reflected, sometimes amplified, in their outputs, and feedback loops can reinforce bad behavior. Explainability is still hard, especially for deep networks, and perhaps most worryingly, these systems are brittle in ways humans aren't. If we throw them into a domain they haven't seen before, their performance often degrades dramatically. Remember, even if the machine has mastered the art of learning, they are still tools. Powerful ones, yes, but still tools for you to wield.

One particularly important caveat to carry with you is that none of these systems actually *know* what they're doing. They're glorified function approximators, sensitive to the data they're fed and brittle to anything outside distribution. They don't reason as we do; they optimize. They don't know why "cat" means "cat" or what a cat actually *is*. All they know is that when pixels are arranged a certain way, the accompanying label is usually "cat." When the world throws them a hairless cat, or a chihuahua with suspiciously feline features, things can go sideways, until we backpropagate a new set of values that adjust for a broader concept of what a cat looks like. And then there's the noise, biases, errors, and blind spots. Just as children mirror their environments, machines mirror their datasets. And we've seen what happens when that mirror reflects too much of our flawed world.

So we've built powerful tools. But have we built trustworthy ones? The next frontier that our MBAs will need to guide our firms toward isn't building bigger models or faster chips for bigger and faster's sake, but to drive deeper alignment between humans and the silicon chips without losing sight on the value they are meant to drive. But before we get there, we need leaders who understand what we've already built, and how to use their capabilities in search of value. And that's where we now turn to, using our earlier archetypes as a guidepost.

Centaurs thrive on smart division of labor. They should treat the learning machine as an analyst that excels at pattern recognition, hypothesis generation, and draft-building but is weak at nuance, context, or abstraction. A Centaur MBA might use AI to test 100 strategic scenarios overnight based on a model they've finetuned to the client's exact use case, but they will choose which three to refine further, and which final result to present to leadership. They let the AI suggest M&A targets based on market signals that they've spent years studying the market for, but they alone gauge cultural fit or geopolitical risk that move too fast for any model to properly capture. Their workflow is deliberately hybrid where the first draft is by machine and the final judgment is by human.

Orchestrators operate at a higher abstraction layer. Their job is not to be the machine or use the machine; it's to manage many machines at once. The learning machine becomes both a cog and an ecosystem where separate agents for pricing, customer segmentation, demand forecasting, and creative generation learn away in the background. Orchestrators excel in system design and coordination, and they will intuit their way from one AI system that models consumer churn to another that runs targeted interventions while measuring impact with a third. They ensure these systems talk to each other cleanly, and intervene when outputs misalign with brand, ethics, or strategy. Their success depends on portfolio thinking where no single model is perfect, but a well-structured set of imperfect tools can deliver robust outcomes. They are curators of learning as much as authors of the final result.

Cyborgs blur the boundaries even further. They embed AI deeply into their iterative workflows, using learning machines as cognitive prosthetics, always on, always prompting, and most importantly, always learning. They co-edit documents with GPT, build product mockups with multimodal assistants, and swap ideas with AI as easily as with a junior team member while backpropagating their work to the models as the starting point for the next. Again, their challenge is discipline and using AI as a springboard, not a crutch. The Cyborg MBA must intentionally schedule offline thinking that is separate from their learning machines, and they should dedicate time to form opinions before seeing what the model says so that they can evaluate, not integrate its outputs. In performance reviews or deal memos, they should write down their reaction *before* asking the AI for an alternative, keeping their own cognitive machinery sharp. The key to thriving as a Cyborg is structured reliance where automation never goes on autopilot.

Artisans are the ones who say "Just because you can automate it, doesn't mean you should." They work slowly, sometimes inefficiently by design, in a world where everyone else is obsessed with speed. The Artisan doesn't reject AI; instead, they wield it like a hand-forged chisel, using machine learning to sift through mountains of data or prototype 20 product ideas overnight only after having refined the models, finetuned the workflows and given a clear template for the outputs. And when it's time to ship, they often choose the version that feels *crafted*, not just optimized.

Finally, a Client Whisperer might use unsupervised learning to detect shifts in sentiment before a customer calls to cancel or rely on generative tools to explore three different tones for a renewal email. But they know when to discard the automation entirely, pick up the phone, and ask the one question the algorithm could never frame: "What's not working for you right now?" They understand that value isn't always captured in a KPI, and the learning machine gives them reach while their empathy gives the model's results resonance. This archetype will be critical in high-stakes services like consulting, wealth management, and enterprise sales, anywhere the contract lives or dies on the client's felt sense of being understood.

Beyond the archetypes, MBAs must learn to navigate deeper conceptual shifts, none more vital than the long-awaited realization of the "learning organization." For decades, this idea has echoed through business literature like a yogic mantra. Everyone agreed companies should learn, adapt, and evolve. But most of the talk stayed metaphorical, even poetic. Yes, firms accumulate experience. Yes, they also adjust their behavior. But the reality is that none of them have truly become learning organizations as of yet. Large organizations, in particular, lacked the tools to systematically encode what they'd learned, let alone apply it at scale. That's now changing because for the first time, we have the technological means to turn that old ideal into something actually operational. A modern firm can learn things it never could before, and it can cover culture, deployment velocity, internal dynamics, brand salience like it did its production OKRs. We can extract insights and intent from unstructured Slack logs, quantify cultural cohesion through communication patterns, detect siloes before they cause breakdowns and, most importantly, learn from all of the mess before we sweep it under the rug. The MBA who once guessed at organizational health from surveys can now run models across org-wide behavioral telemetry. In a sense, we're only now gaining real access to the "dark matter" of the firm, and that means we're finally in a position to allow organizations to learn in ways they never could before.

The other shift MBAs must embody is taking the customer seriously, again. For all the AI strategy decks that promise "personalization at scale," too many still assume the customer is a fixed persona to be modeled once and optimized for once, after which the bucket sticks for the remainer of the deployment. No customer operates like that. They evolve, their preferences shift, and contexts change. The value of a recommendation engine or personalization model isn't in getting it right once, it's in getting better with every cycle and at consistently deeper levels. This means that no single model, no single campaign, will ever fully capture the customer, and that the learning loop must stay open. For an MBA, the implication is that your lessons on product-market fit are never finished, and your models are only as good as your feedback architecture. AI lets you serve the king, but it doesn't crown you for satisfying them once, or even twice in a row. You have to keep showing up and listening, and AI gives you better tools than ever to do exactly that.

And finally, the most overlooked opportunity of all is how the learning machine can be pointed inward. Why contain learning systems to improve your business when you could also use them to improve *yourself*. On the one hand, this can look like real-time coaching systems that reflect your communication blind spots and AI mentors that track your leadership patterns and highlight growth areas. On the other hand, you will find value from reflective journaling tools that learn from your decisions and that surface where you're leaning too hard on certain instincts or avoiding uncomfortable decisions. And on the topic of learning, there's much AI can help you accomplish that without learning a thing about yourself. Tools that fuel your curiosity and expand the scope of your reading will be critical for having wider and better perspectives. And if you use these tools right, they will help you grow not just as a manager or operator, but as a thinker.

In a sense, the MBA of tomorrow isn't someone who merely *deploys* machine learning. It's someone who *becomes* a learning machine themselves, which we'll get back to in Chapter 10.

Notes

1 The Electronic Text Corpus of Sumerian Literature. *The Dedication of an Axe to Nergal: Translation*, accessed June 1, 2025. https://etcsl.orinst.ox.ac.uk/section5/tr573.htm

2 Nappa, Antonio, Christopher Hobbs, and Andrea Lanzi. 2021. "Deja-Vu: A Glimpse on Radioactive Soft-Error Consequences on Classical and Quantum Computations." *arXiv e-prints*. May. arXiv:2105.05103. https://doi.org/10.48550/arXiv.2105.05103; https://ui.adsabs.harvard.edu/abs/2021arXiv210505103N/abstract

3 Rosenblatt, Frank. 1958. "The Perceptron: A Probabilistic Model for Information Storage and Organization in the Brain." *Psychological Review* 65, no. 6: 386–408. https://www.ling.upenn.edu/courses/cogs501/Rosenblatt1958.pdf

4 Rosenblatt, Frank. 1958. "The Perceptron: A Probabilistic Model for Information Storage and Organization in the Brain." *Psychological Review* 65, no. 6: 386–408. https://pmc.ncbi.nlm.nih.gov/articles/PMC9053657/#:~:text=In%20the%201950s%2C%20Frank%20Rosenblatt,human%20training%20or%20control.%E2%80%9D4

5 "New Navy Device Learns by Doing: Psychologist Shows Embryo of Computer Designed to Read and Grow Wiser." *The New York Times*. July 8, 1958, p. 25. https://www.nytimes.com/1958/07/08/archives/new-navy-device-learns-by-doing-psychologist-shows-embryo-of.html

6 Krizhevsky, Alex, Ilya Sutskever, and Geoffrey E. Hinton. 2012. "ImageNet Classification With Deep Convolutional Neural Networks." In *Proceedings of the 26th International Conference on Neural Information Processing Systems (NIPS'12)*, Lake Tahoe, NV, pp. 1097–1105. https://boundless.utoronto.ca/impact/can-machines-think-like-humans/

7 Sutton, Rich. 2019. "The Bitter Lesson." March 13, 2019. https://www.incompleteideas.net/IncIdeas/BitterLesson.html; https://www.cs.utexas.edu/~eunsol/courses/data/bitter_lesson.pdf

8 Netflix Research. "Recommendations: Figuring Out How to Bring Unique Joy to Each Member." *Netflix Research*, accessed June 1, 2025. https://research.netflix.com/research-area/recommendations

9 Zhou, Ren. 2024. "Understanding the Impact of TikTok's Recommendation Algorithm on User Engagement." *International Journal of Computer Science and Information Technology* 3, no. 2 (July): 201–208. https://doi.org/10.62051/ijcsit.v3n2.24; https://www.researchgate.net/publication/382423048_Understanding_the_Impact_of_TikTok's_Recommendation_Algorithm_on_User_Engagement#:~:text=Our%20findings%20indicate%20that%20TikTok's,the%20reinforcement%20of%20echo%20chambers

10 Amazon Science. "The History of Amazon's Forecasting Algorithm." *Amazon Science* (Staff Writer, August 9, 2021). https://www.amazon.science/latest-news/the-history-of-amazons-forecasting-algorithm

11 *UPS Deploys Purpose-Built Navigation For UPS Service Personnel.* Press Release. December 4, 2018, *UPS* (Atlanta, GA). https://about.ups.com/us/en/newsroom/press-releases/innovation-driven/ups-deploys-purpose-built-navigation-for-ups-service-personnel.html; https://www.productmonk.io/p/aws-success-secrets-from-startup-to-titan-473d04d0b889a9d0

12 Dastin, Jeffrey. 2018. "Insight – Amazon Scraps Secret AI Recruiting Tool That Showed Bias Against Women." *Reuters*. October 10, 2018. https://www.reuters.com/article/world/insight-amazon-scraps-secret-ai-recruiting-tool-that-showed-bias-against-women-idUSKCN1MK0AG/

7

MACHINA COGITANTIS—THE THINKING MACHINE

At the end of a long, nondescript corridor is an unmarked room. Inside it, a man sits alone. The room is windowless and silent, save for the occasional slip of paper that appears under the door. The paper is covered in strange symbols, elegant strokes he does not recognize, characters he cannot read. Next to him is a thick instruction manual and a neon yellow note with the rules of the game. When a piece of paper arrives, take it, examine the symbols one by one, find their matches in the manual, and write down the corresponding output symbols as instructed. When done, slide your response back under the door.

The man does as he's told. Over time, he gets faster. His responses become more fluid as he begins to recognize the symbols as a signpost, guiding him through instruction manual pages. Unbeknownst to him, he is a translation machine, taking Chinese symbols and converting them into Finnish. To a Chinese speaker, his answers are coherent and accurate as they are to those who evaluate his Finnish, but inside the room, the man remains entirely ignorant of what he's writing. To him, it's simply a mechanical exercise in manipulating symbols from one form to another.

This is the Chinese Room, a thought experiment posed by philosopher John Searle in 1980. Its question is as blunt as the dystopian view to the unwitting translator life is bleak: if the man inside understands nothing of what he is doing, yet the system as a whole appears to understand the outputs, what is the man in effect doing? Put in another way, if a machine, following a detailed enough rulebook, can produce intelligent-seeming responses, can we say it is *thinking*? Or are we simply watching a well-orchestrated illusion that simply happens to make sense to the reader?

The puzzle haunts us still, and if you had heard of it before, you know exactly what would follow from the first opening words of this chapter. Thankfully, we have no need to arrange our Chinese-to-Finnish translation services in this manner, but our machines are doing exactly that. They take in our language, parse it against trillions of patterns learned from the vast corpus of the internet, and return outputs that we deem not only appropriate but thoughtful. We ask them legal questions, and they summarize rulings. We ask for strategies, and they plan go-to-market campaigns. We ask for moral clarity, and they argue with ethical nuance. Like the man in the room, in our eyes, they pass for something intelligent.

But are they?

DOI: 10.4324/9781003508427-7

Here's what we'd expect a thinking human, especially one of our Descartes-certified MBAs, to be capable of in practice. Not that most of us could name even half of the categories philosophers and logicians have given the different types of reasoning. And yet, these are only some of the reasoning approaches that spontaneously arise from our neurons and how they are connected (Table 7.1).

This chapter begins with exploring the full depths of that question. When a machine appears to reason along one of the above categories, is it actually thinking? Or is it, like Searle's man locked behind a door at the end of the hallway, just shuffling symbols? And if machines can

TABLE 7.1 The methods of reasoning

Reasoning type	*Human origin*	*Machine approximation*	*Examples in use*	*Limitations*
Deductive reasoning	Applying general rules to reach a specific conclusion	Rule-based systems, symbolic logic, fine-tuned transformers	Legal contract analysis, tax code assistants	Rigid; fails with ambiguity or incomplete rules
Inductive reasoning	Inferring general patterns from examples	Supervised learning (neural nets, decision trees)	Fraud detection, churn prediction	Overfits if not generalized; lacks certainty guarantees
Abductive reasoning	Inferring the most likely explanation	Probabilistic models, Bayesian networks	Medical diagnosis tools, causal AI in supply chains	Requires well-structured priors; sensitive to noise
Analogical reasoning	Solving new problems by analogy to known ones	In-context learning, few-shot prompting	GPT completing prompts, transfer learning in robotics	Struggles without good analogues; prone to shallow matching
Causal reasoning	Understanding cause and effect	Structural causal models, do-calculus, counterfactual reasoning	Policy simulation, ad campaign optimization	Still early stage; most models conflate correlation with causation
Commonsense reasoning	Applying general knowledge about the world	Knowledge graphs, large language models (with RLHF)	Assistant tools answering general queries, open-ended dialogue	Can hallucinate; easily stumped by edge cases
Planning and goal pursuit	Structuring steps to achieve future outcomes	Reinforcement learning agents, Monte Carlo tree search	Game-playing agents (AlphaZero), logistics optimizers, code synthesis	Doesn't generalize well across domains; often brittle in new contexts
Reflective reasoning	Thinking about one's own thinking	Chain-of-thought prompting, tree-of-thought, self-refinement loops	GPT-4o solving logic puzzles, planning multi-step tasks with rationale	Can be verbose, repetitive, or misleading; not truly self-aware

FIGURE 7.1 Did I leave the stove on or was it I who was never even plugged in?

appear to think well enough to help us plan wars, draft laws, and coordinate global logistics, does it even matter whether there's "understanding" inside? In fact, what even counts as understanding when it comes to our Descrates-approved MBAs who are, and therefore hopefully also think?

If you're concerned that we're veering dangerously close into becoming a treatise on philosophy, don't worry. I have just the answer to all of the above that allows us to stay laser-focused on business. In fact, by the time we're done, you might even want to join me in arguing that most academic thinking on thinking machines are distractions. Adopting a consequentialist frame gets us where we need to go and guides us toward strategic, value-driving leadership. But before we get there, let's dig ourselves into an even deeper rabbit hole that most who enter, never find a way of getting out (Figure 7.1).

Let the Turing games begin

While our AI had barely learned to read, its proud parents were already prepping its college applications. Sure, the machine could now parse punchcards and calculate a few thousand digits of pi without breaking a sweat, but when will you become a board-certified doctor like your brother?

One of the first of these tiger-parents who was as well-meaning as he was wildly ahead of his time was Alan Turing. A tragic genius whose personal story still makes the heart ache, Turing gave us one of the most iconic frameworks for thinking about thinking machines. Long before Siri mangled your grocery list or GPT-4 made up a citation for you to add to your research paper, Turing offered us a test that most of their predecessors had great difficulties in overcoming.

Here's how it went. Put a machine and a human behind separate screens. Have a judge chat with both, back and forth, without knowing who's who. If the judge can't reliably tell the machine from the human, the machine passes. That's it. Turing imposed no equations, no circuit boards or Math Olympiad questions, just words passed back and forth. The idea at the core remains as elegant as it ever was. If the output feels human, who's to say it isn't? If we can't tell the difference, does the difference even matter?

Perception is reality after all, and when it comes to the Turing test, many have found that perception alone is more than enough to qualify machines as something more, something greater, than the sum of their parts if we perceive them to be one of us. What followed Turing's test was decades of computer scientists treating it like Mount Everest. First came ELIZA in the 1960s, a simple program mimicking a psychotherapist with canned questions and clever echoing. "Tell me more about your mother." It was parlor trick logic, sure, but enough people bought it. Some, somewhat disturbingly, even felt seen by it. Then came Kenneth Colby's PARRY, which played the role of a paranoid schizophrenic. That was a clever dodge, really, given how often even our human outputs make little sense.

Fast forward, and today we're surrounded by machines that routinely pass most variations of the Turing test, some by design, others by accident. The latest figures at the time of writing are 73% for the GPT-4.5 model and 23% for old ELIZA, which is an equal amount below chance as OpenAI's model is above it.[1] Unfortunately, the same study didn't bother to test actual humans, but based on what we know about our neighbors, colleagues, and your uncle who talks like reading from a podcast transcript, we can safely assume that humanity as a whole isn't batting 100%. Which brings us to the real problem: the bar was never very high to begin with. Thanks to Francis Galton we know that most traits, conversation skills included, follow a normal distribution, i.e., the notorious bell curve. That means half the population is, by definition, below average in their ability to hold a meaningful conversation. So when we cheer that an AI can keep up with "the average person," let's be honest, that's not exactly winning gold at the Olympics of cognition. That's the equivalent of winning a race at an airport when you're the only one on the moving walkway lane. The better question isn't whether machines can mimic our worst or even our middling selves to a point where others perceive them as one of us. It's this: when do they begin thinking about thinking like us, *without us in the room*? When do they start writing their own Descartes-style meditations in their own languages that we don't recognize, operating on logic we didn't teach them, spinning up questions we never asked? When do they begin their own internal dialogues on the meaning of life, unprompted, the moment we plug them in? But I digress.

Whatever you think of the Turing test of whether you think of it at all, you can call a customer service line this very moment, and you might spend five minutes chatting with a bot before realizing it doesn't have a pulse. 11Labs clones voices so convincingly and LLMs like GPT-4, Claude, and Gemini routinely pass the Turing tests we hand them. All that means is that a Turing test in 2025 isn't the achievement it used to be. We've collectively raised the bar, and then some. It's no longer enough for machines to sound smart or act helpful. Now we want to know if they're *conscious*. And worse, we've more or less decided on not taking *no* for an answer.

Every time an AI pulls off a new parlor trick, composes a racy poem, blurts out an unexpected insight, or catches us off guard in conversation, we nod like proud parents watching their kid say something weird and precocious. "See? She *gets* it." But a human's surprise is not proof of an AI's sentience.

In 2016, AlphaGo played Move 37,[2] an oddly placed stone that made the world blink. Lee Sedol, world champion and strategic savant, walked away from the board in response, not because the move cost him the game, which he would lose, but because what he saw genuinely rattled him. As expert commentators at the time remarked, the move was elegant, unorthodox, and disarmingly creative. It wasn't the brute-force search we had gotten used to, and the move felt like a spark of originality. "Surely, AlphaGo is creative," Lee would say after the fact. And yet, it was still a move born out of nothing but computation. What made it feel like something more was *us* and our expectations. The same thing happens now with large language models. ChatGPT refuses to answer your unethical question, or snitches on your prompt, or reminds you to check your sources, and suddenly, everyone is ready to proclaim that it's grown a conscience. But let's think clearly here for a moment. The model isn't making a moral decision. It's following a statistical path carved by human examples embedded into its training data. It has seen what humans say when they draw ethical boundaries, and it has learned to echo that tone, sometimes with eerie precision. It's modeling morality, not experiencing it. In fact, it is simply printing out words that it has learnt that its users associate with morality, doing little else than the man in the Chinese Room.

So why do we keep insisting that there's a ghost in the machine?

Maybe it's because we don't understand our *own* consciousness all that well. I probably don't need to convince you of the fact that we are ourselves desperate for answers to the enigma of *our* minds that we keep looking for a reflection in the silicon. If Ramon Llull were alive today, would he not climb Mount Randa to starve himself, contemplating over how we must ourselves become as gods so as to prove that our creator surely also exists? But zoom back in for a moment, and the truth is obvious. AI, as it stands today, is by measure conscious. Anyone who believes otherwise needs to spend a long, humbling afternoon with Michael Gazzaniga's work on the brain. Read it all. Map out the modular mess that is our cortex and study the split-brain experiments, the confabulating interpreter, the distinct circuits that compete and collaborate to construct that fragile thing we call a self. Then, and only then, compare that to a transformer model predicting the next token to the actual, real-life guaranteed to exist miracle, of our perception of a conscious experience.

If you're feeling the gravitational pull of the debate tugging you deeper and deeper into the abyss, you're not alone. And while you're down there, whatever you do, don't read Sapolsky's *Determined: A Science of Life Without Free Will* unless you're prepared to spiral into the possibility that there may not be anything all that special about the flavor of consciousness our brains whip out for us either. Let me toss you a ladder, because we don't have time for philosophical spelunking. There's money to be made, after all.

Here it comes: it doesn't matter how we perceive machines to think or whether AI is objectively conscious or not. What matters is the consequences of AI and how we use it. If some lonely soul wants to marry their GPT or swears their Alexa is more emotionally available than their spouse, let them. But if you're holding an MBA or running a business, the only thing you should be adopting Auguste Rodin's The Thinker's pose for is the question of whether this thing can solve a problem faster, cheaper, or better than you? We'll leave the Turing games for everyone else.

From *Learning* to *Cogitantis:* machines learning *versus* machines thinking

Let's begin by stating the obvious: learning is not thinking, nor is simply expressing what one has learned. In *Machina Discens*, we saw machines soak up patterns like sponges, digesting entire libraries of images, transcripts, spreadsheets, and clickstreams to perform uncanny feats of mimicry. The neural networks at the heart of this revolution don't know why a cat looks like a cat or what a customer *wanted;* they only learned to guess which rows of 0s and 1s make a human happy enough to keep their serves on. Given enough examples, they could write a convincing email or caption a photo with decent accuracy, but don't be fooled. They've learned curve-fitting at scale instead of thought. However, I'm here to tell you that for us who care about the business of creating and distributing value, that's good enough.

For most business applications, we don't *need* the AI to think, and we certainly don't need humans to think that AI thinks. We only need it to mimic our thinking well enough to unlock value by being a tool that does what tools do. If the pattern it spotted leads to better conversions or faster defect detection, no one's asking it to compose a philosophy thesis. Better yet, if a backoffice full of monkeys sent you the same investment deck, you'd say thank you may I have another.

But increasingly, we *are* asking for more than just monkeys typing out Shakespeare. We're asking these machines to advise a strategy, file a report, screen a loan, or decide who gets what. And suddenly the distinction between learning and thinking goes from philosophical to practical. Because a learner can tell you what *usually* happens next based on past data, when a thinker can ask whether *that's what should happen here too.*

To appreciate the nuance, it'll help us to break thinking down to parts. Experts like Nobel laureate Herbert Simon, who've thought about thinking deeper than most of us, identified three broad stages: intelligence and the initial phase of problem generation and data collection, design and where alternative solutions are developed and evaluated, and choice, the final act of selecting a course of action.[3] When you can't one up them, you *reword* them, and we'll use the terms of generation, evaluation, and decision-making instead, simply because of how they map more intuitively to both the AI conversation and what is really going in the heads of MBAs when they do what they do.

In this model, generation is the act of producing ideas, actions, or options, not from rote memory through summarization mind you, but through synthesis and abstraction. This is the realm of insight, imagination, creative exploration, and the "what if" spark that will surprise its audience. Evaluation is the act of assessing those ideas and options, judging them for relevance, feasibility, and identifying and weighing their consequences. This is where reasoning, logic, and value alignment come in. Finally, decision-making is the act of choosing between these ideas and options, often under uncertainty, and doing so in a way that reflects goals, constraints, and a sense of "why."

Another form of thinking that deserves a mention is rule application, lest we upset the entire career cadre of attorneys ready who are nothing if not happy about litigation. This is also an area where even the early AI systems like the first chess machines, excelled. They didn't learn from examples or extrapolate from datasets. Instead, they were told, explicitly in an if-this-then-that format, how to simulate human logic through hand-crafted rules. The next wave, dominated by deep learning, reversed the approach and machines stopped being told what to do and started figuring it out by example. No more explicit rules, only data from which to extrapolate. And as Richard Sutton noted, the fewer humans ruling the moves the better these systems could spot tumors in scans, transcribe speech in dozens of languages, and predict customer churn.[4]

TABLE 7.2 The cognitive styles of AI

Cognitive Stage	*Human equivalent*	*AI analogue*	*Maturity*
Generation	Brainstorming, imagining options	Language model outputs, tool use etc.	High
Evaluation	Logical reasoning, judging consequences	Chain-of-thought, world models, critics	Medium
Decision-Making	Choosing aligned to goals/values	Planning agents, multi-objective frameworks	Low-Med
Rule-following	Following an SoP, a blueprint, or a recipe	If-Then Deterministic algorithms	High

We can go even further and argue that for most of the above categories of human thinking, we have an AI equivalent that is outdoing its human peers. Just look at Table 7.2.

We can go even further and argue that for most of the above categories of human thinking, we now have an AI analogue that doesn't just keep up but actually outpaces, outlasts, and occasionally outwits us. Just look at the table again to see what I mean. The AI doesn't need to know *why* it's brainstorming or even know that it is. It just needs to produce options that make us raise an eyebrow and say "that's a great idea." It doesn't need to believe in logic when it's evaluating options; it only needs to walk through the reasoning steps better than we can. Sure, we feel squirmy at the thought of a machine making decisions. But how different is it, really, from the last dozen decisions you made based on a Google search where you clicked the first-ranked link? Ask ChatGPT for investment advice, and it will advise you. Now connect it to your E*TRADE account, and you've got skin in the game, and it will pull the trigger for you. The difference in outcomes of AI's thinking is all nuance about how it got there, while the outcomes are more often than not entirely human.

The point I am making is this. Whatever AI is doing, it's doing something functionally indistinguishable from human cognition in a growing set of contexts. If it walks like reasoning and talks like insight, then whether it actually is thinking and reasoning inside doesn't matter. For business, outcomes are the only currencies that count. What comes out of the pipe is more important than what's flowing inside it. And no, this doesn't let you off the hook on thinking. If anything, it should slap you awake. Because now the baseline for "smart" has shifted, and the bell curve has suddenly moved. The old trick of sitting around a whiteboard and feeling clever while inventing KPIs for your team is not going to cut it when your competitor's AI agent just simulated 10,000 market scenarios, generated 14 product pivots, and tested 8 landing pages at the press of a button.

So the question for our MBAs becomes painfully clear: how do we bring to bear the full weight of this new *Machina Cogitantis* on value creation and distribution?

The cognitive AI stack

We've spent the last few pages untangling the question of whether AI is really thinking, merely mimicking, or just faking it really well. But at some point, all that philosophical posturing needs to get off the couch and start paying rent. It's time to turn the spotlight from what it is to what it does. To unpack that properly, we're going to build up what I'll call the cognitive AI stack, which is your best answer to building a framework that comes as close as possible to having your machines think for you just like your humans would.

We start at the bottom, with the act of generating great ideas and options, which we can boil down to nothing more than a function of data, unique viewpoints, and a way to combine and iterate upon them. Here's how to get great at it with AI (Table 7.3).

First, you'll need access to whatever your competitor and their grandmother are already using. That means plugging into the same base models, GPT, Claude, Gemini, Mistral, take your pick, and harvesting what the entire internet has to offer from Stack Overflow answers to the Reddit rants and McKinsey white papers. This gives you fluency in the shared language, but it does not give you an edge. If you stop here, you're not generating differentiated ideas; you're mass-producing generic ones.

TABLE 7.3 The cognitive AI stack

Layer	*What it does*	*AI techniques*	*Human equivalent*	*Tools and examples*
1 Generation	Produces options, ideas, insights, or paths to explore	Base LLMs (GPT, Claude), Retrieval-Augmented Generation (RAG), fine-tuned SLMs	Brainstorming, research synthesis, lateral thinking	GPT + company data via RAG (e.g., Slack messages, support logs), Claude with proprietary prompts
2 Iteration	Enhances, mutates, or challenges initial outputs to stimulate novelty	Adversarial prompting, noise injection, multiple model runs, randomness seeding	Playing devil's advocate, divergent thinking, reframing	One model critiques another (e.g., "red team/blue team"), use of summarizers after provocation chains
3 Evaluation	Simulates scenarios, filters options, and prioritizes based on goal function	Chain-of-Thought prompting, World Models, Scenario Simulators	Strategic filtering, thought experiments, mental models	LangChain chains, Amazon's supply chain simulators, Bedrock agents
4 Decision-making	Makes choices or executes pre-defined actions based on scored or ranked options	API-triggered actions, human-in-the-loop pipelines, goal-based scoring engines	Judgment, risk-taking, gut-checking	Reinforcement Learning agents, algorithmic trading bots, automated task flows via Zapier or tools
5 Goal framing	Defines what "good" looks like; the objective function everything else optimizes toward	Objective definition models, constraint sets, outcome mapping	Business strategy, leadership direction, "north star" decision criteria	Custom metrics in evaluation stack, boardroom-level scenario modeling
6 Feedback & audit	Monitors outcomes, corrects errors, adjusts assumptions, improves the stack over time	Continuous learning loops, post-decision logging, model auditing frameworks	Learning from failure, post-mortems, iterative refinement	Evaluation dashboards, system observability tools (e.g., Weights & Biases, LangSmith)

To break out of that mushy middle, you need something proprietary. Your secret sauce, if you will. This is the stuff no one else has, or the data no one has figured out how to use yet. This could be your internal product telemetry, your closed-door customer feedback loops, your abandoned experiments folder, or the full transcript of how your sales team actually closes a deal. It might also simply be your founder's stream-of-consciousness voice memos, your HR exit interviews, or simply your past work which McKinsey is using to power its proprietary AI, Lilli. Whatever it is, make sure it captures the real, lived, messy texture of you and your organization. Once you've got it, your next job is to make it usable within the cognitive stack. That might mean fine-tuning a small language model (SLM) on your Slack messages, standing up a retrieval-augmented generation (RAG) pipeline to index your internal knowledge base, or building an internal tool that ingests every customer support transcript and lets your marketing team ask, "What did people hate about the onboarding flow last month?" You could go even further by inventing entirely new data by running micro-experiments that wouldn't have made sense before, simply because there was no way of effectively using the results at scale.

At this point, you're already ahead of 90% of the field. You've got access to broad foundational models, you've layered in your own differentiated context, and you've wired it all together in a way that makes it generative. But you're not done here. To make generation work, you need process and iteration. You can begin by breaking the generation process into smaller, modular steps, and then automate them. Don't just ask your model for one-shot answers; instead, build a system that assembles them step by step. Start with retrieval, and pull relevant snippets from your internal embeddings or knowledge bases. Then extrapolate, ask your model to imagine consequences, next steps, or outlier cases. For simulated creativity, add some noise and push it off-center. Use adversarial prompting where one model challenges the ideas of another. Summarize the resulting chaos and run it back through a filter seeded with randomness or injected weirdness for good measure. The goal is not to generate a perfect idea on the first try or even the second. The goal is to create a repeatable factory line of provocation, iteration, and surprise like with Move 37 that churns out enough structured novelty for you to grab hold of and refine.

Generation gives you the options, while evaluation is where you begin to figure out which ones might be worth doing. It's the part of the cognitive stack where the system stops asking *what could we do?* and begins asking, but not answering, *what should we do?* For the artisan who uses AI as a drafting tool, this might be where they exit the loop and take over. But for cyborgs, orchestrators, or any company trying to scale its decision-making, this layer is where they are just getting started.

To evaluate ideas effectively AI system, you will want to simulate outcomes, weigh their consequences, and compare them against your goal function. That function could be anything from "maximize profit" to "minimize carbon footprint" to "optimize for user trust," and in human cognition, we do this kind of thing all the time, entirely unconsciously. You think through scenarios where you imagine what will happen if you say yes to the offer, delay the launch, or hire that wildcard candidate. You run probabilistic chains in your head, informed by past experience and social context, and at the end, a verdict comes out, sometimes in the form of nothing but a gut feel. For AI to do this properly for you, it needs scaffolding to help it reason through the same chains. That's where chain-of-thought prompting and world models come in. Chain-of-thought prompting is exactly what it sounds like, i.e., guiding a model to explain its reasoning step by step. Instead of just giving an answer, you ask the model to work through every step that either you have set up or the system infers to be necessary. It's the AI version of "walk me through your thinking," and it helps root out hallucinations, surface assumptions, and create outputs that humans can actually audit.

This structure helps root out hallucinations, surface buried assumptions, and generate outputs that can be audited, explained, and improved. Now here's the important part: you don't need to build any of this from scratch. Major model providers like OpenAI, Anthropic, and Google are already embedding elements of this in their tools. GPT-4o's built-in system instructions, Anthropic's Claude's constitutional prompting framework, and Gemini's integration with tool use all hint at a future where reasoning chains will be baked into the model layer. But that still leaves you with reasoning exactly like your competition does, which is why we'll need to find a way of bringing in your context to the mix. At its simplest, you can simply chain prompts by yourself. For any meaningfully complex application, you'll want to use chaining frameworks and tools like LangChain and others that allow you to combine reasoning steps, tool calls, and more. You can go even further and create entire world models yourself. These models allow the AI to not just generate ideas, but test them against known dynamics and rules of, for example, the trading desk or the highway in front of the office, and even invent new strategies that work within those constraints. Amazon, for instance, uses agent-based simulations to evaluate thousands of supply chain decisions across weather patterns, consumer demand, port delays, and cost constraints.[5] Their internal systems generate options, and then simulate and weigh the trade-offs, optimizing for the goal functions of reliability, speed, and cost simultaneously. They accomplish this through a combination of proprietary data, scenario modeling, and goal-driven scoring, often using internal agent frameworks running on AWS. In cognitive stack terms, Amazon has built an industrial-grade layer for consequence analysis, one that any company can now start emulating with off-the-shelf tools like LangChain, Bedrock agents, or custom retrieval-augmented workflows. The secret isn't in the tools or having Jeff Bezos as your founder; it's in having your own sequences, your own metrics, and your own simulations running behind the scenes.

What's key to remember is that evaluation *needs* a defined objective. You can't simulate without knowing what success looks like. If your goal is fuzzy, "make it better," "grow faster," "be more innovative," then even the smartest AI will flail. Good evaluation stacks depend on good goal definition. This is where MBAs will find their final refuge once AI takes over everything else. Deciding whether the aim is to maximize revenue per customer, reduce churn, increase trust, or lower carbon impact requires clarity and judgment that is ultimately ours to make.

Which takes us to the final step in the cognitive stack: decision-making. Where evaluation hands off a ranked list of possible paths with their projected payoffs, decision-making is where the actual commitment happens. A Centaur might hand off the process to their human half, while the Artisan and Client Whisperer have long since powered down their cognitive stack and are now chiseling away at the narratives that will close the deal. Cyborgs and Orchestrators, on the other hand, might take things further, and if the conviction is there, and the parameters are clear, they can let the stack pull the trigger. This is precisely how algorithmic trading works by the way, where humans define the boundaries, build in the goal functions, and set the rules of engagement, but once the evaluation yields a winning option, the machine acts on it. In our cognitive stack terms, decision-making often amounts to one final pass. Is the top-ranked choice executable? At what cost? In what window? Once that's confirmed, action is only an API call away. And value, if all goes well, finally hits the board.

Now you might never build a cognitive AI stack for yourself or the company, and in most cases that may be fine enough as long as all of your competitors don't go ahead and do it. But that's the thing, isn't it? The minute even one does it well, the game changes for everyone else. Just like on the Serengeti, you don't need to outthink the world; you only need to not be the slowest zebra when the lion shows up. And if that lion happens to be an orchestrated cognitive stack fine-tuned on proprietary data and optimized for decision speed, good luck explaining to the board why your team is still manually syncing decks before every launch.

So, at a minimum, the MBA needs to update their internal firmware on what thinking actually is in the context of business. First, we need to drop the myth that there's something sacred about the human brain when it comes to creativity, insight, or even judgment. There's not. We aren't that special. When you deconstruct what's happening between your ears when you're thinking your hardest about business, you're still looking at a set of clearly defined processes that we can lump into a mixture of inputs, filters, comparisons, simulations, pattern-matching, narrative construction, risk assessment, and more. Today, there's an AI for that. For almost every one of those steps, there is now a tool, a chain, or a prompt setup that can perform the function, often faster, cheaper, and more scalably than your team of 20 MBAs ever could.

Second, they'll need to get uncomfortably comfortable with handing over the heavy lifting that they once prided themselves over. That includes idea generation, customer empathy modeling, risk simulations, and even early stage decision-making. Don't mistake this for obsolescence or take it as a cue to slack off. Treat it as a delegation of duties where you're not disappearing from the picture, you're upgrading to the corner office as you move up the abstraction ladder. The task of the MBA becomes setting up the right parameters, designing the right evaluation frames, and most critically, ensuring that the system is operating with the right goal function in mind. Garbage in, still garbage out. Now try well-structured ambiguity in with a dash of insider data and whimsy and see the magic happen.

Knowing where the AI faulters will be half the game here as well. The other half is giving it the best possible shot at being brilliant for you and with you. That's why we'll forever see the human stay in and on the loop, not because we're special, but because we're still wonderfully weird and surprising in ways that models just aren't. We've got our quirks and biases, sure, but we also have our hunches and gut-feelings. We leap when there's not enough data to justify it, and sometimes, we can notice things no one trained the model to look for. If nothing else, we can go fully PARRY on the system and show them what humans really can do when let loose. The reason I am bullish for the future of humans in the age of AI is that as long as the human brings something the system hasn't already been trained on a million times over, we're valuable to the system itself.

Which is exactly why the future-proof MBA must become a learning machine themselves. If your only edge is that you know what the HBR case study everyone else has read says, you're toast. You've got to ingest more than what's in the syllabus, and you're going to have to get comfortable reading outside your lane. Pull amply and widely from philosophy, biology, underground Reddit forums, and Sumerian tablets no one has bothered even looking at before. The more unorthodox the inputs, the more likely you are to show the system something it hasn't seen before, and the better chance of you actually generating a good idea worth evaluating and deploying once in a while. The way the MBA of the future ensures that they are creating value is by being the weirdest node in the network and the one that nudges the whole stack somewhere it wouldn't have gone on its own.

FIGURE 7.2

And most importantly, remember that none of this requires AI to be conscious, sentient, emotional, or even particularly elegant. It can be a mindless token-churning blob for all we care. None of the noise around consciousness matters. Regardless of how we define it, it is already the most powerful tool we've ever built to help us think better about value and how to get more of it. Whether it's faking it or not, it's helping us make better moves. And that, not its self-awareness, is the thing that's going to separate the next generation of business builders from the deck-polishers left behind.

That is, as long as they get off their models and start executing (Figure 7.2).

Notes

1 Jones, Cameron R., and Benjamin K. Bergen. 2025. "Large Language Models Pass the Turing Test." *arXiv preprint* arXiv:2503.23674. https://doi.org/10.48550/arXiv.2503.23674; https://arxiv.org/abs/2503.23674

2 DeepMind. "AlphaGo: AlphaGo Mastered the Ancient Game of Go, Defeated a Go World Champion, and Inspired a New Era of AI Systems." *DeepMind Research*, accessed June 1, 2026. https://deepmind.

google/research/alphago; https://deepmind.google/research/projects/alphago/#:~:text=,Surely%2C%20AlphaGo%20is%20creative

3 Simon, Herbert Alexander. 1960. *The New Science of Management Decision.* Harper & Brothers. https://doi.org/10.1037/13978-000

4 Sutton, Rich. 2019. "The Bitter Lesson." March 13, 2019. https://www.incompleteideas.net/IncIdeas/BitterLesson.html; https://www.cs.utexas.edu/~eunsol/courses/data/bitter_lesson.pdf

5 Veluchamy, Siva, Ilan Gleiser, Sam Bydlon, Jiyan Babaie-Harmon, and Justin Lyon. 2024. "An Agent-Based Simulation of Amazon's Inbound Supply Chain." *AWS HPC Blog*, June 19, 2024. https://aws.amazon.com/blogs/hpc/an-agent-based-simulation-of-amazons-inbound-supply-chain; https://aws.amazon.com/blogs/hpc/an-agent-based-simulation-of-amazons-inbound-supply-chain/?utm_source=chatgpt.com

8

MACHINA FACIENTIS—THE DOING MACHINE

It was never the learning or thinking that made business leaders really learn forward and open their purses in support of AI initiatives. For all the excitement about machine learning and big data, most executives and the big checks they are writing now stayed on the sidelines until AI started actually *doing* things. After all, ideas are cheap, and execution is everything.

If you are forced in pub trivia to name the number one driver behind the shift we're now living through, that is it. AI has moved from a bright student with untapped potential to a fully fleshed operator. One that sees, speaks, and acts on the basis of all that it has learnt over the decades. And in doing so, it is changing the very nature of work, including for MBAs.

This chapter chronicles the true beginning of AI's business revolution and how we got to where AI became capable of doing the work itself. Now, for the sake of clarity and ease of exposition, we'll temporarily suspend our disbelief that the underlying technological breakthroughs could be divided into seeing, talking, and doing. They can't, and in AI jargon, we're going to cover capabilities such as computer vision, natural language processing (NLP), generative AI, agentic execution, and much more, all of which have meaningful overlaps with each other. But don't get distracted by technicalities of it all. One key message of this book is that, for MBAs, all that matters is what these systems *enable* us to do. The chef isn't applauded for how the sausage is made, but what kind of meals they serve (Table 8.1).

In fact, by the end of this chapter, we'll argue that the inner workings of even the most complex agentic systems are becoming background noise to the people who matter most: the clients. For them, outcomes will always eclipse explanations, and the business value AI generates will trump specs, which is why MBAs will soon stop selling product features and start defining AI-enabled outcomes.

Before we get there, let's honor our agentic AI colleagues by running down the branches of their family tree one more time, first to learn when AI picked up its first pair of bifocals.

Tell me machine, do you see what I see?

The first time a machine ever captured a human view was, well, a bit underwhelming. You can see it for yourself below if you haven't already come across the *View from the Window at*

DOI: 10.4324/9781003508427-8

TABLE 8.1 The jargon to action map

What we're calling it	*What it includes in AI jargon*	*What it lets us do*
Seeing	Computer Vision, OCR, Image Recognition, Video Analysis, Sensor Fusion	Recognize products, track movement, process visual input, label inventory, detect fraud, assess damage
Talking	Natural Language Processing (NLP), Large Language Models (LLMs), Speech Recognition, Voice Synthesis	Draft emails, summarize meetings, translate in real time, generate customer replies, power chatbots
Doing	Agentic AI, Tool Use, Workflow Automation, Function Calling, API Chaining	Run processes, schedule tasks, update CRMs, automate reports, trigger alerts, make decisions
Thinking (emerging)	World Modeling, Chain-of-Thought Prompting, Goal Optimization, Simulation, Memory + Planning	Evaluate options, simulate outcomes, reason across steps, coordinate agents, optimize trade-offs

Le Gras, taken by Joseph Nicéphore Niépce in 1826 or 1827. This blurry, grainy, and yet entirely world-changing, snap is thought of as the first photograph even taken, and the ghostly rooftop scene was immortalized by Niépce via a process called "heliography." It took eight hours of exposure to burn the image into permanence, and with this accomplishment, Niépce and his heliograph marked something even more lasting: the first recorded collaboration between man and machine to witness the world together.

Now, the idea of a camera had been floating around for centuries. Arab scholars like Ibn al-Haytham were centuries ahead of their time and built pinhole contraptions that worked as rudimentary cameras, and a number of the brightest of European minds from Leibniz onward tinkered with optics, often in the name of national interest as much as scientific observation. It might not shock you that lenses were improved for the sake of surveillance and security long before the first closed-circuit camera came about. But Niépce's photograph was different from all that had come before. It was no longer making light pass through a hole to create an upside-down image projected onto a wall. This was a feat of processing and retention. Niépce's machine didn't simply help us see what he saw; it translated the view into a different medium for us to work with. It's hard not to see this as the prologue to everything AI is doing today given how it both captures the world and interprets it, whether it's by translating light, pixels, or symbols into action.

Soon after Niépce had fixed that first image to the wall, the machines didn't stop at seeing the world. They wanted to share it. In the 1860s, Giovanni Caselli unveiled the *pantelegraph*, a machine that could send images across telegraph wires, decades before anyone dreamed of a fax machine. To its early users, it must have felt like nothing short of sorcery. Press a stylus to paper in Paris, and moments later, the same mark reappears in Lyon. From this humble seed, entire industries like phototelegraphy, radio, and television blossomed. By the time the Dartmouth Conference convened in 1956, none of this would have felt magical anymore. The first color TV broadcast had already aired in the US in June 1951. The teenagers of the time would've looked at Niépce's rooftop ghost photo with the same "meh" of indifference they would have shown their parents' wedding album. While computer vision made the agenda in Dartmouth, it wasn't until a decade later at MIT's Summer Vision Project in 1966, helmed by Marvin Minsky and Seymour Papert, that the quest to give machines functional eyes began in earnest. The mission would turn out to be wildly successful, but only after decades of incremental achievements across a wide range of fields. Instead of a step-change by the 1970s as the MIT team might have hoped for, what followed was a slow, steady evolution that brought us concepts like edge detection, feature extraction, image segmentation, and compression algorithms.

In the 1980s, we finally began teaching computers to see and model the world in three dimensions like we did. But it wasn't until the early 2000s that computer vision finally started to *feel* like it was doing something worth business' time. By then, pattern recognition had finally matured, and human faces entered the frame. The Viola-Jones face detector was a landmark achievement, made possible by advances in learning algorithms that could classify visual data at scale.[1] Thanks to something called an *integral image*, it could compute these features almost instantly. Combined with a boosted learning algorithm, it was accurate *and* fast. That combo unlocked a whole new era for face detection that brought it to our cameras, webcams, photo libraries, and our iPhone where it remains a staple today. In a sense, this was the moment machine vision stopped being a science project and became a startup idea. Then deep learning hit, and everything kicked into an even higher gear.

By the mid-2000s, neural nets were learning fast enough to see what we saw, if not more. GPUs, graphical processing units originally designed for video games, became the engines of this revolution, and companies like Nvidia have become household names not because they made our video games run faster, but because they make all of our *machines* smarter. In short order, we went from detecting cats in grainy YouTube videos to self-supervised learning, vision transformers, and diffusion models that can today recreate entire worlds pixel by pixel. Cars navigate city streets with more precision than the average Uber driver because our machines see the world by anticipating how it will change around them. It's as if we gave them bifocals, binoculars, infrared vision, and a supercomputer and then told them to go build the future. And build they did.

Now that the machines have 20/20 vision, here's the next question: *What do they do with all that they are seeing?*

What's all that vision good for?

The *businessification* of machine vision is the perfect case study about Amara's law of humans' understating the long-term impacts of a technology, and how revolutionary tools can sometimes show up in the least revolutionary ways. While everyone's busy hyping up the age of agentic AI, most couldn't tell you a thing about the transformations that have already happened. Machines didn't wait for AGI to show up before getting to work. Simply giving computers the ability to see has already changed the game across the board. To really appreciate what happened, let's go back to the framework from our earlier chapter where we divided our tools into four categories: tools that help us do more work, tools that help us do better work, tools that do the work for us, and tools that open up entirely new kinds of work. Machine vision checks all four boxes with ease.

First, it lets us see *more* of the world, period. From surveillance cameras, to medical imaging, warehouse stock levels, and monitoring crop health in satellite feeds, the volume and velocity of what we can image have both gone the way of the hockeystick. There's simply more visual data than any human could parse thanks to computer vision, and now machines do the first pass, if not more. Second, it helps us *see better*. Forget telescopes, although your iPhone has more lensing power and post-processing software than Galileo could dream of. Computer vision scans the infra-red as natively as WiFi signals (yes, really), allowing us entirely new viewports to the world that none of Leibniz's lenses could have given us. The quality and accuracy with which we see, record, and transmit images of the world around us has grown exponentially thanks to machines picking up their Warby Parkers. Third, machine vision has already taken over whole workflows. AI systems now monitor industrial pipelines for leaks, scan shipping containers for damage, flag suspicious ATM behavior, detect fraud in insurance claims, and scan MRI films in radiology labs, often better than the human technicians they used to rely on. The cameras don't blink, and algorithms don't get tired. And fourth: vision AI has cracked open industries that didn't exist before. Maintaining and fine-tuning computer vision models is now a job that you will find difficult to explain to your average grandmother. Labeling training data is also a profession. Even Pokemon GO wouldn't exist without it, nor would self-checkout kiosks, cashierless Amazon stores, real-time visual search, or AI-powered fashion apps that tell you which jacket to buy based on your wardrobe.

And as computer vision has been on its relentless march of progress, we've seen humans pushed, showed, and augmented in exactly the ways we'd expect a revolutionary tool to do. Take medicine, for example. Fewer doctors read X-rays by eye than even five years ago. But those same doctors now spend more time making decisions based on richer, layered imaging models, guiding treatments, not just diagnosing symptoms. The low-level grunt work of inspection has been outsourced to machines, and humans have moved up the ladder of abstraction.

The whole multiverse of technological disruption is contained within the story of computer vision. People get displaced, others get promoted, and entirely new job categories emerge. And without fail, more value is created, and greater of it is distributed to those who value it more. And all of that comes from nothing else than machines having 20/20 vision. Now, imagine what happens when the machine starts to *speak*?

Hello world

Shifting through the record of the earliest instances of a machine "speaking" takes us back to an earlier hero of story. Hero of Alexandria would have clearly felt right at home in Silicon Valley given his knack for tinkering, and in the 1st century AD, he engineered a device that mimicked bird songs. His "singing bird" automaton chirped using air pressure and mechanical valves, and by all accounts, it was a marvel ahead of its time. But while that may have earned gasps from Greek theatre crowds, birdsong isn't exactly going to cut it in the boardroom. To really make an impact, machines would need to do more than make noise. They would have to learn how to speak, argue, and reason like *us*.

And so began the long, winding road to making machines that speak a reality. It took a millennium and a half before someone even came close to a machine that could speak words recognizably human. Enter Wolfgang von Kempelen, who in 1791 unveiled his "speaking machine," which was nothing less than a Frankenstein mix of bellows, pipes, and leather that could wheeze out simple syllables like "papa" and "mama." This time we don't need to imagine whether the contemporaries marveled at the invention or not. You can ask your own AI assistant to see the contraption in action right now, and then promptly rejoin me as I state for the record that no one in the entire history of mankind has been anything but traumatized by what he built. But it was a generative machine nevertheless, even if it barely squeaks past the definition.

What we wanted was something decidedly more human. We want machines that could navigate the messy jungle of human language with fluency, that could write, argue, and even persuade. For this part of the AI family tree to matter, it would need to give our thoughts form and structure faster than our fingers could type them. Although von Kempelen gets an A for effort, I would add to his gradebook a simple note: went for execution well before exhausting his opportunity to think about what he is about to do.

There's a cruel catch-22 baked into this part of tech history where every major breakthrough seemed to arrive a generation too early. Charles Babbage had designed a machine in the 1800s that, in theory, could compose music and generate text, but there was no way he and Ada Lovelace could do good on the theoretical promise of what they had built. Ramon Llull's Ars Magna was literally meant to combine concepts to uncover divine truth, a kind of logic-based text generator *avant la letter*, but without the theoretical frameworks and silicon scaffolding to support their visions, these pioneers remained prophets in the desert. And when it comes to tech, being too early *is* the same as being wrong.

Even as computing matured, we still kept running into a structural mismatch. Computers speak in the binary 0s and 1s. They need procedural instructions, while humans, on the other hand, thrive in context and ambiguity. We read between the lines where the computers read nothing but.

So, before we could teach machines to speak, we have to understand how we use speech to relay information. It would take up until Claude Shannon, working at Bell Labs in the 1940s, to crack open the idea of *information* itself. His "Mathematical Theory of Communication" gave us the foundational insight that language, like data, could be encoded, compressed, and transmitted.[2] Around the same time, Noam Chomsky began to map the invisible scaffolding of generative grammar and the deep structures that underlie our ability to obtain and produce language. Far from the first linguist, the distinction of which goes to scholars like Pāṇini who studied Sanskrit around the 4th century BCE, Chomsky was treading well-treated ground, but this time, he was asking entirely new questions. The same goes for Shannon. Information transmission was by no means a new field, as we've seen in how almost a hundred years earlier humans were transmitting rudimentary images with telegraph lines. What Shannon did was give the mathematical framework for quantifying, storing, and communicating information. Between them, Shannon and Chomsky gave us the twin poles of machine language: one focused on the bits and signals, the other on the meaning and syntax. And that allowed us to make progress.

We got better at organizing our shared workload with computers, largely because of how we got better at explaining their tasks to them. When the 0s and 1s proved too raw and cumbersome for humans to wrangle with, we wrapped them into more abstract symbolic languages. Out came LISP, COBOL, Fortran. Then C, C++, Java, Python, and whatever your Stanford University roommate has been building since they dropped out. The problem was, we were spending all of our energy in saying things that pleased the machine, instead of asking it to work with what we'd want to say instead. And for a while, the strategy worked. Computers got better at outputting exactly what we asked of them, as long as we placed the semi-colon *just right*. If-this-then-that logic flourished, and the engineers who mastered it would come to make fortunes.

When we ventured into the human side of language and chatbots like ELIZA and PARRY, their deterministic scripts were stitched together tightly enough to fool just enough people to keep the Turing Test mythos alive. We marveled when they responded to our non-deterministic blabbering in kind, even if the responses were the linguistic equivalent of a cardboard cutout nodding at whatever we said. In hindsight, it's clear we climbed the tree upside down. We had spent all this time teaching ourselves how to talk more like machines, when the real prize was always going to be in teaching machines to actually talk more like us.

To be clear, it's not that we hadn't tried to nail NLP. We tried *hard,* and we did so for decades. NLP was for long considered the holy grail of fusing human intuition with machine parsing, and it had been the carrot at the end of the stick for many since the very beginning of computer science. Early attempts at making it work relied on brute logic and rule-based systems that mapped input to output with an exhausting level of specificity. If the user says X, return Y, and regular expression chains that still give veteran coders PTSD when you simply mention the term. These early NLP systems were not too far from overworked junior receptionists that were capable of basic interactions when they were paying attention, but flummoxed by anything unexpected that their manual didn't cover. In the 1990s, the search for NLP shifted to statistical models. Instead of trying to understand language the way humans do, we began predicting it the way casinos predict behavior by betting on what's most likely to come next.

Just like at a casino, we became obsessed by tokens that capture anything from exclamation marks to entire words, and it is here where things started getting interesting. In another cruel example of the "too early = wrong" equation, we have IBM's Watson. It quickly became the poster child of this new probabilistic paradigm when it obliterated two human champions on *Jeopardy!* in 201 in a moment we all felt like we were on the brink of something transformational. The machine could parse clues, weigh context, and win our specie's greatest tributes ever to be sent to the hallowed halls of early evening game shows. And then, nothing really happened. Under the hood, it all still felt clunky and artificial. Businesses, including IBM itself, struggled to find real-life applications for what it had built, and the MBAs sat on the sidelines, waiting for something even to come about. The problem was that while Watson was powerful indeed, the conversation was still one-sided. The machines could now answer questions, sometimes better than us, but they couldn't really understand us when we talked to them, neither could they talk to you. Not in a way that we cared about, anyway.

That is, until the real breakthrough came in November 2022.

When ChatGPT 3.5 went live, suddenly we all had machines in our pockets that conversed as well as computed. It felt like our browsers were suddenly reasoning with us. Most importantly, suddenly we all saw a future where our computers no longer asked us to speak in 0s and 1s anymore. Instead, our machines now listened to us.

To call this an unexpected inflection point is tantamount to acknowledging that one hasn't been paying attention. See the technologist had seen it coming for years. They had been building up to this moment for their entire careers, and Sam Altman and his board members knew exactly what they were doing when they pressed the big red launch button at OpenAI's HQ. But for the MBAs, the consultants, the strategists, the middle managers, and brand whisperers of the world, this was when their ears first perked up.

And just like MBAs should, they haven't shut about a thing they know they can make money from ever since.

Generation Generative AI reporting to duty

This is where we ditch the history books for a moment, not out of irreverence mind you, but simply because there's no history yet to read. We're still living and breathing the moment itself, and it is all difficult speak with confidence about what this moment will look like to external observers once they ultimately take stock of it all.

And yet, we *do* have perspective, just that it requires us to zoom out and take the bird's eye view of what exactly happened when ChatGPT launched in November 2022 and kicked off what will be remembered as the most significant tech cascade since the birth of the Internet. In what feels like a matter of days, we had not one, but an entire alphabet soup of chatbots and language models to choose from, Claude, Gemini, Grok, DeepSeek, and their off-brand open-source cousins over at Hugging Face who'll do what the big ones do for half the price. Each week seemed to bring a new model with new capabilities into the world, etching a record not far from that of the Cambrian explosion (Table 8.2).

If you don't mind me waxing poetic for a paragraph, the moment was one of pure *synthesis*. Everything we've traced up to now from punch cards to transformers, from Turing and Shannon, had quietly built toward this moment. And just like you need Homo Sapiens to give meaning to 400 million years of vertebrate evolution, you needed this generation of AI to give meaning to the long, slow march of machines learning how to think, speak, and see. This is the payoff that Hero of Alexandria was denied. This is what Llull, von Kempelen, Leibnitz, Turing, and the Dartmouth trio were all aspiring toward. Here, all the individual breadcrumbs of history suddenly turn into the main course. Dinner is now well and truly served.

A few things happened that made this inflection point hit as hard as it did. For the first time in the history of computing, the machines stopped asking us to speak *their* language and finally learned ours. No more "computer says no." Now even your grandmother can talk to a computer the way she talks to the pharmacist or the postman and get a SaaS product in return. She doesn't need to know how to code or understand SQL. All she needs is a few words typed, a handful of buttons clicked and a monthly swipe of a credit card and boom, she's in business. You can call it democratization, accessibility, or even old-fashioned anarchy. Whatever you call it, the outcome is undeniable: the cost of creating things with our machines has collapsed.

The second inflection point that stems from November 2022 is that AI has started to build itself. Once machines became able of generating the next iteration of their own codebase and the tools used to build them, we've been in the grasps of a feedback loop so fierce it broke our ability to chart the curve. Each wave of innovation builds the next, turning recursion into an industrial machine. This self-propelling engine has started reshaping the very way we make software, conduct research, write copy, build products, analyze strategy, and spark creativity. It's also the reason why, in a very real sense, if you blink, you'll miss the next breakthrough. Now only imagine how it feels to write a book about AI for MBAs amidst all of this, and have mercy on whomever foolhardy enough to take on the task.

The term we now use to bottle this absolute ball of lightning is *Generative AI*. Only a few years ago, getting machines to understand our words felt like trying to teach a pigeon to play chess. Today, they write better than most of us. And they certainly don't stop there. In the span of just a handful of quarters, we've gone from capturing a landscape to animating it in 3D and layering it with spatial audio. Soon enough every marketing agency on Earth will be running campaigns stuffed with words and visuals first ideated by a machine, and already today most of the thought leadership that you encounter on LinkedIn is thought up by whatever GPT the CEO's team gave them access to.

TABLE 8.2 The generative revolution

Category	*Key models/examples*	*Core capabilities*	*Key characteristics/ nuance*
Large Language Models (LLMs)	ChatGPT (OpenAI), Claude (Anthropic), Gemini (Google), Grok (xAI), LLaMA (Meta), Mistral (Mistral AI), DeepSeek	Generate and understand human-like text; answer questions, summarize, translate, write code, write essays, simulate agents	Trained on massive corpora; capabilities vary by parameter size, training data, instruction fine-tuning, and alignment method (RLHF, constitutional AI, etc.)
Image Generation	DALL·E (OpenAI), Midjourney, Stable Diffusion (Stability AI), Imagen (Google)	Generate novel images from text prompts, inpainting, outpainting, style transfer	Uses diffusion or transformer models; quality and control vary; open-source options like SD popular for custom training and fine-tuning
Code Generation	GitHub Copilot (OpenAI/Microsoft), AlphaCode (DeepMind), Code LLaMA (Meta), StarCoder (Hugging Face/ServiceNow)	Write code, complete functions, debug, translate languages, comment code	Specialized LLMs trained on code (e.g., GitHub, Stack Overflow); often embedded in IDEs; great for boilerplate, not logic-heavy innovation
Multimodal Models	GPT-4o (OpenAI), Gemini (Google), Claude 3 (Anthropic), Kosmos-2 (Microsoft), Gato (DeepMind)	Understand and generate across text, image, audio, within a single model	Enables richer user interactions; essential for robotics, video QA, and unified interfaces
Audio and Music Generation	Google Magenta, OpenAI Jukebox, Suno, ElevenLabs, Stability AI's Harmonai	Generate music, songs, sound effects, realistic speech (TTS), voice cloning, soundscapes	Combines waveform and symbolic generation; Jukebox works end-to-end while others rely on diffusion/ synthesis; strong IP & copyright concerns
Video Generation	Sora (OpenAI), Runway ML, Pika, Synthesia	Create short video clips from text prompts or edit existing ones	Still emerging; frame consistency and long-form coherence are hard; great for synthetic b-roll and advertising
Agents and Agentic Frameworks	AutoGPT, BabyAGI, LangGraph, MetaGPT, CrewAI, Devin (Cognition)	Chain reasoning steps, call tools/APIs, plan multi-step tasks autonomously	These are frameworks built on top of foundation models to simulate autonomous workflows and decision-making chains

In a paradigm shift as radical as this one, a little bit of perspective goes a very long way. First of all, what we're witnessing isn't some unhinged avalanche of technology consuming the world although it might feel like it. Instead, what we're seeing is a handful of trajectories reaching their logical conclusion, only far faster than any of us expected. Computer vision, NLP, and image generation, all of it dreamt up centuries ago, are now coming from the lab to the production floor, all at once. Generative AI might feel limitless, but it's not. It still answers to one ceiling: the breadth of human creativity, not at the level of the individual, but of the species. Before AI, only one of us could paint the Sistine Chapel. Before AI, only one of us could write *1984*. But soon, all of us will be able to conjure something indistinguishably similar, should we only desire to do so. Whatever domain humans have excelled in before, and that we have dutifully enough captured and digitized is now something AI will inevitably learn to do, and eventually, outperform most of us in.

If that sounds like a career death sentence, it's worth remembering something every teacher knows: there's *always* someone better than you in the room. There always has been. Most of us live our lives close to the bell curve's belly, modestly competent in most, occasionally insightful in some and, rarely if ever, transcendent in any particular field. For all of the centuries during which we've labored under capitalistic societies, that's been enough. Civilization was built not on pure genius, but on accumulated adequacy that we have collectively sharpened over time. The difference now is that what once was occasional brilliance can now be distilled onto a microchip. The bleeding edge has become the average, and your personal genius bestie now travels with you in your pocket. If you'd like to see a Wes Anderson movie, why not create one of your own. All you need to do is ask. The problem is, most of us never even have the idea to begin with.

Now, if you've ever found yourself useful in a field where someone was better than you somewhere else, or even close by, then congratulations. You already know how to live in the AI era. The next step is not to try to outperform it, but to orchestrate it to do our bidding. And that's what we'll turn to next.

You have exactly three wishes, use them well

The robot overlords sci-fi promised us didn't turn out quite like the original storyboarders imagined. Instead of Rosie from *The Jetsons* marching down the hallway with perfect posture and a steaming cup of coffee in one hand or the Centennial Man feeding us quarterly reports while adjusting your thermostat, we got magic lamps. What we got is almost as powerful as Aladdin's omnipotent blue friend, and just like in the story, we only get three wishes that we must be careful not to waste. Ok, maybe you get 100 if you're on the enterprise plan, but after that it's time to swipe your card and feed the token counter again.

One of the most powerful use cases for the tokens we have is burning them on something that resides toward the upper echelons of the agentic spectrum. Here's what one impression of the spectrum looks like (Table 8.3).

No matter what levels you envision or what terms you affix to them, thinking about the *Machina Faciendis* on a spectrum that blends agency with capabilities is useful for at least two reasons. First, it reminds us that this isn't a zero-sum race to full autonomy where everything is handed off to the most powerful model that can do everything. Even if we had Artificial General Intelligence (AGI) in our backpockets, we'd still have plenty of reason to keep niche models in the mix. That is because there will always be a need for specialization in our toolkits. We'll want a healthy mix of co-pilots, reactive agents, niche expertise assistants, and stripped-down

TABLE 8.3 The agent's role

Level	*Agent capability*	*Human role*	*Example*
1 The respondent	No independent action. Waits for input. Delivers knowledge on demand.	Human asks, AI answers	Using ChatGPT for Q&A, searching Google, retrieving data from a dashboard
2 The assistant	Performs tasks with explicit instruction. No autonomy.	*Human in the loop*	AI writes a draft email for you to edit, or flags suspicious transactions for approval
3 The operator	Executes pre-defined actions. Informs human but doesn't need constant direction.	*Human on the loop*	AI manages calendar invites, triages customer support tickets, or adjusts pricing automatically
4 The autonomous agent	Acts autonomously to achieve objectives. Makes decisions within scope.	Human steps out of the loop	AI handles sales outreach end-to-end, optimizes supply chain routing, or reorders inventory
5 The autonomous ecosystem	Coordinates with other agents. Multi-agent systems solve tasks collaboratively.	Human architect or observer	Multiple AI agents negotiating energy trades; autonomous customer journeys across SaaS tools

models that do one thing and do it well. The world will never be run by a single large model, but it might be orchestrated by one that has an ensemble of actors playing different roles at different levels of initiative at its disposal.

Second, the spectrum allows us to place the human with greater precision. You'll hear people talk about humans being "in the loop," "on the loop," or "off the loop" with growing frequency, referring to a sliding scale of oversight and intervention. The differences might seem semantic, but they matter a great deal in practice. Being in the loop means directing every step, while being on the loop means watching and jumping in only when needed. Off the loop means letting go entirely, which sounds exactly like what our Cyborg archetypes would do. The spectrum also allows us to ground our MBA archetypes in something concrete, with Artisans firmly in the loop, Centaurs operating on and off it, and the Whisperers, well, they co-design the loop itself with their clients.

We've already seen the full agentic spectrum blossom into dozens of real-world use cases. Technologies like Retrieval-Augmented Generation (RAG) now combine in-house knowledge with external sources on demand. Agents are running outreach campaigns on Salesforce, pulling market data, generating reports, and even iterating on creative copy in real time. Tools like MCP (model context protocol) and A2A (Agent2Agent Protocol) are stitching together workflows where one agent requests, another executes, and a third evaluates, all without a human in the room. This is why it is not at all outlandish to wager that the first one-person unicorn has already been founded. This is why the hype cycle has taken us to the heights that it has. Truly, in the history of doing machines, we have never had anything quite as capable as we have built for ourselves today.

TABLE 8.4 The MBA's agent-orchestration workflow

Stage	*What it means*	*Example*
1. Ideate tasks	Define high-leverage, automatable steps where agents can add value	Brainstorm with GPT to break a product launch into tasks
2. Delegate across models	Choose the right models or tools for the job and route the tasks accordingly	Assign research to Claude, visuals to Midjourney, and slides to Gamma
3. Evaluate outputs	Review, edit, and apply quality filters based on context and constraints	Use RAG to fact-check, re-prompt for clarity, or run A/B variants
4. Package with purpose	Shape agent output into polished, human-friendly formats	Turn bullet points into a pitch deck, summary into a press release
5. Wrap in narrative	Infuse the final product with story, vision, and emotional logic	Add customer anecdotes and mission-aligned messaging
6. Sell and ship	Present or distribute the output for stakeholder buy-in and operational rollout	Pitch to clients, share with execs, launch campaign on Notion
7. Iterate	Capture feedback and refine with looped agent workflows	Fine-tune with prompt changes, retrain custom models, update RAG sources

This is as good a moment as any to bring our MBA protagonist back into the frame and ask: what exactly will the future workplace demand of them? In an environment increasingly run by AI co-workers, the MBA of tomorrow must become part strategist, part creative director, and part conductor of autonomous agents. Managing people will still matter—but so will managing models, tools, and synthetic workflows. That means mastering a new operational cadence: one that spans ideation, delegation, evaluation, and execution. Below is a streamlined version of that workflow (Table 8.4).

And before you call me out and say "There's an AI for that" for each of the above, hear me out. Yes, AI can cold-call leads. Yes, it can prototype a product and spin up the go-to-market plan before your second espresso. It can even invent an entire brand from visual identity, voice, domain name, and all by the time you're done reading this paragraph. But the doing machine will never take the place of the MBA where it counts. Think of it this way. Even today, a machine can give you a massage without ever getting tired, if not something entirely more intimate. And yet, most people I have ever met still prefer a human touch. The moment something matters to us, we turn to someone we trust instead of something. We're sufficiently parochial and xenophobic enough with each other for anyone to think that we'd ever let Blade Runner's android run our businesses for us, even if they could do it better. And should the above statement be proven wrong, we'd still need humans to buy from them, govern them, and own them, all of which are tasks that practically call out for an MBA to take hold of it. Silicon Valley sometimes tends to forget this. They think GPUs and lines of code are the future, simply because it's more efficient. But the business of business will always be human. AI may do the heavy lifting, but the reason why it boots up in the first place will be because a human somewhere sees value in it doing so.

The future of business belongs to those who learn to work with their genie the smartest. That is what we turn to next (Figure 8.1).

FIGURE 8.1 "The genie is out, we ran out of tokens."

Notes

1 Cen, Kaiqi. 2016. *Study of Viola-Jones Real Time Face Detector*. CS231A Final Project Report. Stanford University. https://web.stanford.edu/class/cs231a/prev_projects_2016/cs231a_final_report.pdf

2 Shannon, Claude E. 1948. "A Mathematical Theory of Communication." *Bell System Technical Journal* 27 (July): 379–423; (October): 623–656. https://people.math.harvard.edu/~ctm/home/text/others/shannon/entropy/entropy.pdf

9

KEEPING THE TOOL IN ITS PLACE

If there is a sport that turns accountants into philosophers and salespeople into monks, it is golf. Few games capture the tension between control and chaos as precisely, and even fewer have drawn in as many MBAs and their clients under the promise that discipline can outsmart chance.

Everything about the game seems designed to humble even the most confident player, and much of that humility comes from the tools themselves.

In 1955, during the US Open, a journeyman golfer named Jack Fleck stepped onto the fairway with what many considered the wrong club in hand. He was chasing Ben Hogan, the undisputed titan of golf at the time. Whether his caddy handed him a seven iron by mistake or Fleck insisted on the unconventional choice, he took the shot everyone thought called for an eight. The ball arced across the fairway in what *The New York Times* later called a "rainbow shot," landed softly on the green, and stopped seven feet from the cup.

Against every expectation, Fleck went on to beat Hogan in a playoff and win one of the greatest upsets in golf history. Sportswriters called it divine luck, and Fleck himself eventually agreed. Yet the moment became something more enduring, a parable about mastery over one's tools. The wrong instrument can still deliver the right outcome if the swing is true and the intention is clear.

That is what this chapter is about. For every Jack Fleck, there are thousands who have buried their careers in sand traps of their own making, swinging the right club at the wrong time with the misplaced confidence that they had made the right choice.

If there is one thing artificial intelligence is teaching us, it is this. Knowing how to swing is no longer enough. You have to know which club you are holding and be willing to swing it proudly even when everyone else thinks you are crazy.

Know yourself, and know your tools

Throughout history, our progress has been defined by our ability to match the right tool to the right problem.

Fire was not useful until someone learned how to keep it from burning down the village. The wheel only made sense once the ground beneath it was made smooth enough to roll. The

DOI: 10.4324/9781003508427-9

compass, the transistor, and even the distributed ledger each found their moment only after humanity discovered their proper place in the order of things.

Artificial intelligence now sits at the same crossroads. It's the most versatile tool ever made, yet its power also tempts us to use it everywhere, for everything. Even for things where it clearly doesn't belong.

That is exactly what we are seeing today. In the earliest wave of generative AI adoption, only about 5% of deployments delivered measurable value, according to a study by MIT.[1] For comparison, conventional wisdom based on now decades of surveys on digital transformations holds that 70 to 80% of traditional digital transformations succeed, which makes the downgrade hard to ignore.

Much of this gap comes down to how new the technology still is and how entirely human our instincts about AI remain. Our first impulse with any new tool is to stick it into whatever it is that we have at hand and see what happens. If you have ever watched a toddler explore the world, you have seen the same process in miniature. The curiosity is pure just as the experimentation is constant, but the results remain almost entirely unproductive.

From that perspective, even the 5% is a sign of success. Innovation never begins with efficiency. Progress starts as a dance between a waste of time and discovery, and results often arrive disguised as a mess that someone else makes sense of much later. Seeing even modest gains at this stage is not a failure of the tool but proof that it is behaving as early innovations always do.

The real danger in the long run is not that AI fails, but that it works too well in the wrong places. A powerful system can optimize the wrong outcome, automate a broken process, or amplify an error until it looks like excellence. The machine can execute perfectly, and we can still be worse off as a result.

The story of NASA's ballpoint pen has become cliché for a reason. Engineers designed it to write in zero gravity, spending time and money to overcome a problem that the Soviets solved by simply using a pencil. The lesson endures, because complexity has a way of seducing us into proving our cleverness when judgment would have done the job better.

The temptation to apply AI as a universal bandage is growing by the day. We plug it into workflows, departments, and decisions simply because we can, hoping something magical will emerge. What the MBA of tomorrow requires instead is a rare mixture of forward-deployed vision and restraint, combined with a clear sense of where intelligence, human or artificial, actually adds value.

To succeed in the world ahead of you, you'll need epistemic judgment, the ability to sense where certainty ends, and creativity begins.

The first step is not to reach for the most intelligent tool but to properly understand the nature of the task itself so that we can put the tools in their place.

Some tasks demand deterministic precision, others benefit for generative exploration, and many simply need to be completed reliably with whatever means possible. Good leadership begins by matching the level of intelligence to the level of uncertainty in the work, which is, if you think about it, all a project leader at a consulting firm is paid to do.

Once the fit between task and approach is clear, the next question concerns quality. If a simpler tool can produce results of equal or higher quality than a more advanced one, the wiser choice is the simpler one. Occam's razor has stood the test of time for a reason, and more intelligence does not always mean better outcomes.

And once the fit produces the quality we need, the real test is whether the value created exceeds the total cost of achieving it. Sometimes the juice is simply not worth the squeeze, and the smarter move is to step back, simplify, or let a lighter tool do the work.

TABLE 9.1 The task, quality, and value mapping

Dimension	*Guiding question*	*AI fit*	*Example*
Nature of the task	Is the problem structured or open-ended	Match tool intelligence to uncertainty	Forecasting demand versus designing a new product
Required quality	What level of precision or creativity does success require	Compare human, simple algorithmic, and AI-driven options	Rule-based contract review versus generative drafting
Cost and value	Does the improvement justify the added complexity and expense	Assess return and risk tolerance	Automating pricing versus deploying predictive systems

This is the practical logic of leading with AI that you are called to embody as MBAs. Understand the kind of problem you are solving, the standard of output it demands, and the price you are willing to pay to meet it. Rinse, repeat, and retire after a long and happy career.

Progress often comes not from choosing the smartest tool but from choosing the tool that is most proportionate to the value of what we're solving. The goal is alignment between problem, intelligence, and purpose, and when that alignment holds, both efficiency and creativity tend to follow.

Understanding the nature of the beast

Work processes broadly align themselves with two categories, deterministic and non-deterministic, with most real-world cases living somewhere in between.

Start with the classical deterministic example of accounts payable. An invoice comes in, money goes out, and everyone goes home happy is what you'd write on the product specs note. And somewhere in the details is the implicit requirement that there is simply no room for interpretation or imagination. We invented double-entry bookkeeping, three-way matching, and audit trails precisely to make sure that what we pay is what we owe.

This is work that must run on rails. Any deviation can be either a firing offence or the start of a scandal. Deterministic processes are built on logic, not taste, and a well-run accounts payable function does not surprise anyone, which is exactly the point.

Now contrast that with product design, one of the more non-deterministic workflows out there. Here, structure gives way to exploration, and the whole process can be delightfully off the rails for much of the time. In fact, it might benefit from it. Regulations may set boundaries, and consumers add pressure, but the space in between is a field of possibility. There is no single right answer to what the next iPhone should look like, nor does anyone know what ultimately comes along and finally kills it, as headlines have trumpeted for ages.

A new product can take a dozen viable paths to market, and teams can start their exploration from data or simple chance encounters. Once the product is made, marketing can test through guerilla campaigns, influencer outreach, traditional media, or some hybrid mix that builds on an audience no one has tapped into yet.

Whereas in payroll, knowing how the most efficient team runs its process teaches you almost everything, in design, knowing how Pixar made *Up* teaches you nothing about how to make your own hit. Even if you followed every documented step, you would not recreate the same spark. You would simply produce a well-made imitation that arrives too late to matter.

TABLE 9.2 Is it deterministic?

Dimension	*Deterministic AI*	*Non-deterministic AI*
Nature	Rules-based, repeatable outcomes	Probabilistic, adaptive, exploratory
Examples	Forecasting models, robotic process automation, pricing algorithms	Creative generation, strategy synthesis, scenario design
Risk profile	Low variance, high reliability	High variance, higher potential upside
Human role	Supervisor, auditor	Partner, interpreter, sense-maker
Typical domains	Finance, logistics, compliance	Marketing, innovation, leadership

Most of what we do in business falls between these two poles. Some parts of a process must be followed exactly, while others invite interpretation, improvisation, and human flair. The challenge for leaders is not to locate which pole they are at, but to know where to place their hands on the bar in between.

Here is one way to think through it.

Excelling in the deterministic domain

Finding a deterministic process is cause for celebration, especially for MBAs looking to drive efficiency and bring costs down. Stumbling on determinism means you have discovered something that can be automated safely, reliably, and often all too profitably, which is a topic we'll return to shortly.

Simply put, deterministic processes are automation potential at its best.

We have already seen what happens when determinism reaches maturity. Take the telephone operator. For much of the 20th century, entire halls were filled with people connecting calls by hand, patching wires from one line to another. Their task had no room for creativity, only precision and patience. No one wanted their phone call to be routed to a surprise recipient.

Those once-bustling operator floors have since been distilled to the size of matchboxes and buried inside network switches and software. The tasks still exist, but the hands performing them are now silicon and lines of code. Just like the ice trade, the industry now employs more people than there ever were operators in those vast halls. And just like the ice trade, we can see that when any single process becomes fully automatable, a machine will eventually take it over, leaving the humans to find other tasks to fulfill.

The fact that something is automatable does not mean that it should be given to artificial intelligence. If you take nothing else away from this chapter, it's that many deterministic processes are better handled by simpler forms of automation.

A generative language model is an entirely overqualified and unreliable choice for something that a two-line regular expression could execute perfectly every time. When the task involves pattern recognition without nuance, logic will always beat language.

Consider a simple example. Imagine you need to clean customer email addresses in a database. You could fire up a prompt to an LLM and ask it to "Find a string that has some text, then an @ sign, then some more text, then a dot, then some more text." Or, you could save yourself millions of upcoming API calls by writing a simple line of regular expression code such as [^@]+@[^@]+\.[^@]+ will catch invalid entries with perfect consistency. Using a large language model to do the same work would be like hiring a world-class novelist to fold laundry. The job would get done, but at unnecessary cost and with entirely unpredictable results.

In the deterministic domain, the right mindset here is orchestration rather than inspiration. The MBA's task is to define the rules, monitor the exceptions, and adjust the system to keep performance stable. The most effective leaders of deterministic domains are not the ones who write code but the ones who understand the cost of error and the value of precision.

When you find a process that can be turned fully deterministic, rejoice. It means you can free people from repetition, reduce risk, and direct attention to the parts of work that still require judgment.

And remember, the best solution is often the simplest one that meets the need. ELIZA already taught us this lesson decades ago. With only a few kilobytes of pattern-matching rules, it managed to convince people they were speaking to a real person. If the goal had been to persuade half the population of its humanity, ELIZA would have succeeded at a fraction of the cost and complexity of today's systems. The lesson still holds. More parameters do not equal more intelligent results. A handful of well-designed rules, guided by a clear purpose, will often outperform the most advanced model. True intelligence lies in knowing when you do not need any more of it.

The way to excel in the deterministic domain is to rely on the simplest solution that meets the required quality at the lowest possible cost. Here, efficiency follows from restraint instead of sophistication. There is no bonus for sending ACH transfers with creative flair, and many of the early failures in AI adoption stem from the fundamental misunderstanding of applying non-deterministic systems to deterministic problems that never called for imagination in the first place.

The story of the telephone operator captures this perfectly.

Imagine if, instead of replacing the operator's mechanical labor, we had simply added a generative layer on top of it by deploying an AI that could chat politely while it routed the call to the right recipient. The result would have been a clever patch on an inefficient system, not a true leap forward. Much of the failed AI deployments fall for exactly this mistake, replacing workers by tools instead of redesigning the steps entirely. We shouldn't automate fragments of old workflows with AI when we should be than asking whether the workflow still deserves to exist to begin with.

Once the tools arise that can automate a fully deterministic process, our job is to automate it at the lowest level of complexity and cost, after which we move on to the frontier that still resists such certainty.

And that frontier is the realm of the non-deterministic, the world of problems that not only demand judgment and creativity but outright reward them.

The probabilistic frontier

If deterministic systems reward the kind of low-variance automation that simply gets the job done, the probabilistic frontier is where intelligence, both artificial and organic, begins to show its worth.

This is the world of interpretation, adaptation, and generative reasoning, and it is also where generative AI in particular begins to shine.

Consider the process of managing customer experience or handling a company's inbox. There is still a deeply deterministic foundation lying underneath. Messages arrive, responses are sent, and cases are closed, ideally within a tightly framed timeline and a further set of key performance indicators.

Yet unlike payroll or invoice matching, this process is not a fixed sequence of steps; instead, it's a flow. Every client's message arrives within a slightly different context and carries different intent. One might demand a refund, another might need reassurance about an order, and a third could be exploring a potential partnership that no one has a good answer to in the whole organization.

No static set of rules can account for all these variations. Context changes constantly, the language clients use evolves, and each situation demands a response that balances a seemingly unbalanceable load of requirements. Humans are naturally good at exactly these kinds of load-bearing functions within an organization. We interpret meaning and find understanding even when information is incomplete, and some of us are preternaturally drawn to tasks such as this.

Yet the question remains whether we are the most efficient way to do it.

There is a limit to how far people can go in terms of answering emails and resolving tickets while maintaining quality over long stretches of time. AI, on the other hand, has none of the all too human limitations. As a result, it is not surprising that customer experience has become the first large-scale home of applied generative AI.

Even so, this is not an area for full automation. Leaving a company inbox entirely to a general-purpose model would be careless to the point of malfeasance. Every organization has its own rules, tone, regulatory boundaries, and sources of knowledge that must guide responses. This is where the hybrid approach we discussed earlier comes in. Probabilistic reasoning can handle the variation and nuance, while deterministic control ensures that the output aligns with policy, brand, and common sense.

A single customer interaction helps illuminate the point.

Not all of this is artificial intelligence, nor should it be. Some parts of the process belong to simple algorithms that handle repetitive pattern recognition. Others call for generative systems capable of reasoning through ambiguous inputs. And there are still moments where only a human in the loop, or even on the loop, can ensure the process works as intended. The tool must find its rightful place at every stage, and it is the MBA's task to guide it there. The work of leadership is to decide what belongs to logic, what belongs to learning, and what must stay human.

Determinism provides structure and reliability, while non-determinism fills the gaps with creativity and judgment. The strength of a hybrid workflow lies in knowing when to use each. Some moments call for the precision of logic, others for the flexibility of language.

The ability to separate work into deterministic and probabilistic layers is becoming a key leadership skill. The task is not to choose between human and machine, but to match each part of the process to the form of intelligence it requires. The aim is to achieve the right level of quality at the right cost so that value is maximized without unnecessary complexity.

TABLE 9.3 A worked example of a client interaction

Step in client request process	*Deterministic component*	*Non-deterministic component*
Identify whether this is a new or existing case	Lookup against CRM records	Interpret ambiguous customer input
Understand the issue	Extract key terms and entities	Infer tone, intent, and emotional state
Draft response	Apply template or rule-based steps	Generate adaptive language and reasoning
Decide on action	Approve refund, escalate, or close ticket	Evaluate fairness, persuasion, or opportunity
Confirm resolution	Log case closure, update metrics	Gauge satisfaction and suggest process improvements

That calibration and the art of balancing simplicity against sophistication and cost against value is where we turn next.

The lazy river principle for managing AI as a tool: balancing quality and cost with value

The lazy river principle offers a simple guide for using AI wisely. Do as little as necessary to enjoy as much of the ride as possible. The goal is not to build complexity for its own sake, but to reach the destination with the least resistance and the best return.

Nowhere in business does this matter more than with artificial intelligence. Every model, workflow, and integration carries a cost in design, computation, and oversight. The art is to know when enough is enough. If a simpler tool produces the required quality, use it. The best system is often the one that quietly works without demanding constant attention.

To keep the tool in its proper place, start by understanding what kind of problem you are solving. Not every task belongs in the realm of AI. If it is deterministic and rule-based, it probably does not need intelligence at all. A script or algorithm can often do the job faster, cheaper, and more reliably. But when the work requires coordination, reasoning across systems, or orchestrating multiple layers of input, that is where AI begins to earn its keep.

If quality matters and what defines that quality changes with context, then a non-deterministic approach may be appropriate. Even then, apply the lazy river principle. Begin with small steps. Test outcomes, compare alternatives, and see what level of quality the situation truly demands before scaling up. Perfection is rarely worth the price; what we're aiming for is maximum value for the price of admission.

Which means that at each stage, you need to take the cost of the ticket into account. The value produced by an AI-augmented process must outweigh not only the cost of running it but also the cost of its next-best alternative. Sometimes that alternative is a simpler tool or a less sophisticated AI overlay, and sometimes it is a human doing the work with care and focus.

Tools exist to deliver results, not to prove how advanced we are.

And results require vigilance. Every system, no matter how well designed, drifts from its original purpose if left unattended. To manage AI well, we need to keep the swing true, which brings us to the practice of evaluation and drift.

Keeping the swing true: evaluation and drift

Even the best clubs change with time. The shaft bends, the grooves wear smooth, and the grip loses its hold just enough for the swing we knew was going to hit to miss its mark entirely. The same happens to artificial intelligence systems, although it might be much harder to see the process in action.

What begins perfectly tuned can drift off course until the model that once hit every fairway starts slicing into the trees. Evaluation is how we keep that swing true. In technical terms, it is the process of measuring whether a model continues to perform as expected, both during training and long after deployment. It involves comparing predictions to reality, checking for errors, and adjusting parameters or data when the two begin to diverge. It is the discipline that separates experimentation from engineering.

Without regular evaluation, drift creeps in quietly. Not only that, but the inputs we also used to build our systems on move as customer behavior changes and entire markets shift. Before long, the elegant model you built to predict yesterday's world is optimizing for a future that no longer exists.

This is why good evaluation is both continuous and structured. Engineers can measure accuracy, precision, recall, and bias in the lab, but once the model is deployed, the focus shifts to stability and impact. The most sophisticated AI systems now run in perpetual feedback loops where new data flows back into retraining pipelines, and human checks confirm that outcomes remain consistent with the organization's goals.

This table captures the different lenses through which evaluation occurs today. Deterministic systems require precision checks, repeatability, and control. Non-deterministic systems demand more interpretive evaluation where we measure coherence and relevance rather than strict correctness. In both cases, the aim is not to make the model perfect but to make it proportionate so that we match the cost of oversight to the client value at stake.

If you are anything like my MBA students, your eyes are already glazing over.

But the risks of leaving evaluation to the engineers who optimize for precision instead of purpose are far too great for us to stop here. You see, calibrating accuracy and loss functions are important, yet they are only stand-ins for what truly matters, which is whether the client, user, or organization receives more value as a result.

TABLE 9.4 Keeping our AI in check

Stage of lifecycle	*Purpose of evaluation*	*Deterministic systems*	*Non-deterministic systems*	*Calibration to client value and cost*
Training and Validation	Measure baseline performance and identify sources of error	Use fixed datasets and benchmark tests to confirm repeatable outputs	Use probabilistic scoring and scenario testing to assess variance and creativity	Focus on ROI of improvement: whether extra accuracy justifies longer training and higher cost
Pre-Deployment Testing	Confirm readiness for production	Test edge cases, compliance, and exception handling	Evaluate adaptability to new or unseen data	Balance speed of deployment against potential risk of misalignment
Deployment and Monitoring	Detect drift and ensure stability over time	Automated rule checks, threshold alerts, and error logs	Continuous performance tracking, sentiment or context drift analysis	Set alert levels relative to value at risk; adjust oversight accordingly
Post-Deployment Review	Audit impact on users, systems, and strategy	Verify deterministic logic remains correct	Ensure probabilistic outputs continue to align with intent and tone	Link evaluation cycles to business outcomes and client satisfaction metrics
Retraining and Governance	Restore accuracy, update to new conditions	Replace or patch outdated rules and data sources	Retrain on new data, add human feedback, refine prompts	Decide when retraining costs exceed marginal value gains; recalibrate cadence

This is where the MBA stands up in attention again. A model that improves accuracy by 1% at a cost of one hundred million dollars while delivering ten might be a heroic engineering milestone, but it should have never left a government-funded institution.

Having business leaders involved in designing, or at a minimum understanding, even the most technical parts of evaluation, ensures that engineering progress stays connected to economic reality. Drift and performance decay only matter when they reduce what clients care about. If a system's accuracy drifts slightly but client value remains constant, retraining might not be the answer. Recalibrating thresholds or adjusting expectations may serve the purpose better.

MBAs bring the language of trade-offs into rooms that too often prize perfection over practicality. They ask the question that keeps projects grounded: not "How accurate is the model?" but "How much value does this level of accuracy create, and at what cost?"

Only when evaluation aligns with value does an AI system stay both useful and sustainable. Otherwise, organizations end up chasing numbers that look impressive on paper but make little difference in the real world.

And so we come back to golf, and how this stage of putting the tool in its place is ultimately all about keeping the swing true, where we neither overcorrect nor let the system wander. And that begins with understanding how far the tool can take us, and when accuracy itself stops being enough.

Understanding probabilities—when 99% isn't enough

Most people hear "99% accurate" and exhale. But any leader who's lived through a system failure knows that the last 1% is where catastrophe hides.

A model that is 99% accurate at approving loans still means one in a hundred people is wrongly rejected or granted credit they cannot repay. In healthcare, one in a hundred wrong diagnoses could mean a hundred patients suffering each day. In aviation, 1% off course is the difference between a safe landing and a tragedy.

The value of an error is rarely linear; instead, it grows with its consequences often in an exponential fashion. A single failure in a high-stakes context can wipe out the gains from thousands of perfect predictions, which is exactly why value thinking must replace considerations of raw accuracy.

The numbers AI engineers bring mean little until they are tied back to what the client experiences, and what happens to the company as a result. A 1% increase in accuracy only matters if it delivers a measurable improvement in the outcome that counts. Sometimes that might be fewer errors, higher trust, or smoother experiences. Other times, it could simply mean faster service at lower cost. And often, the trade-off is not between right and wrong, but between efficiency and opportunity.

It is reasonable to seek 100% accuracy in deterministic systems where perfection is the point. But in non-deterministic work, where decisions are based on probabilities and interpretations, the goal shifts to finding balance and the point where added precision no longer adds value.

And this is where MBAs belong in the room without question. Their role is to connect the throughlines between quality, cost, and value, all the while keeping the client front and center. Their task is to translate percentages into impact and to see not only what has improved but what has been lost in the process as Table 9.5 invites us to do.

TABLE 9.5 Getting to value

Scenario	*Reported improvement*	*Hidden trade-off*	*Real value consideration*
Customer service chatbot reduces incoming calls by 10%	Lower staffing costs	Missed upselling or retention opportunities in human conversations	Determine whether cost savings outweigh the loss in customer engagement
Automated email system increases response rate by 10%	Faster throughput	One percent of replies contain serious pricing or product errors	Assess financial and reputational risk relative to speed gains
Generative AI improves marketing content volume by 20%	Greater reach	Inconsistent tone or diluted brand messaging	Measure whether added content drives genuine conversions
Predictive maintenance reduces machine downtime by 5%	Improved efficiency	Over-servicing low-risk assets	Compare operational savings to maintenance costs
AI hiring filter reduces screening time by 30%	Faster recruitment	Risk of excluding qualified candidates due to bias	Balance efficiency with fairness and compliance

Each of these examples shows that the brightest ideas can often carry a long shadow with it. MBA mindset is designed to make these trade-offs visible and measurable and to bring judgment to the table where metrics alone fall short.

We've spent the past decade teaching machines to think faster, and the next one will be about teaching humans to think slower and to apply more of their judgment because that is what cannot be automated.

When your teams ask whether a model "works," your job is to ask *for what kind of work* does it work in.

When your company asks what AI can do, your job is to ask what it *should* do.

And when everyone else is busy automating their swing, your advantage will come from knowing which club to pick, when to trust your instincts, and when to let the tool do what it was designed to do.

That is the heart of strategy in the age of AI, not knowing everything but knowing the right place for everything.

So before you swing at the future, take a moment to study the terrain. Feel the wind, understand the course, and ask what kind of game you are really playing. Then reach for the right tool and use it where it belongs, even if everyone around you thinks you have lost your mind.

Note

1 MIT Nanda, Aditya Challapally, Chris Pease, Ramesh Raskar, and Pradyumna Chari. 2025. *The GenAI Divide: State of AI in Business 2025*. July 2025. https://mlq.ai/media/quarterly_decks/v0.1_State_of_AI_in_Business_2025_Report.pdf

10

BUILDING AN IRONCLAD BUSINESS MODEL

Some business models simply aren't built to last. We won't drag the ice trade through the slush again because by now you know the story and the moral behind a once-booming industry that was made obsolete by something colder, cheaper, and closer to home. And sure, we could pick from the usual graveyard of once-proud industries now reduced to footnotes and Wikipedia nostalgia pages like switchboard operators and Blockbuster, but instead, let me take you back even further.

Two thousand years ago, give or take a few lunch breaks, someone in ancient Rome was hungry. Not just hungry of the generic "anything will go" sort, but craving a chicken leg or two. And lucky for them, all they needed was a quick stroll through the forum, not far from the temple of Apollo. There, among the marble columns and the gossip of the day, they'd find themselves passing through a row of food stalls, each sizzling with either sin or sustenance. From snails to quail eggs and amphorae full of wine, the economics of the whole affair were simple: cook the food, serve the food, collect the coin, and repeat. Feeding people has always been a solid business. If someone hadn't already claimed "the world's oldest profession" for something a bit more risqué, I'd put my denarius on the humble food vendor. It was as viable of a business model in the 1st century as it is today, and yet, on that day, our hungry fellow navigated their way to their go-to stall, its operator couldn't have been making a bigger mistake than keeping it running.

Had our entrepreneurial chicken-slinger known what was coming on August 24th, 79 AD in Pompeii, they would've packed up early. Maybe closed the stall the night before, said a prayer to Vesta, and went to visit family far, far away from Mount Vesuvius. But they didn't, because how would they have known. Sure, the whole town knew that the mountain behind their backs wasn't there only so tourists could send envy-inspiring wax tables back home. But nothing would have given them reason to the illusion of continuity that a long streak of volcanoes decidedly not erupting had created. Sometimes, you just might be doing the right kind of business in the wrong place and time.

That example is, of course, entirely unfair, but you get the point. Most of today's business models are perfectly reasonable, rational choices even, until you notice they're being run at the foot of a volcano. Many of them are tested, proven, cash-generating machines, built to do exactly what they were meant to do, and the magiststratus has been crying over the dangers of

DOI: 10.4324/9781003508427-10

the volcano for ages without a puff of smoke to show for himself. But what most businesses haven't been built for is everything we've covered thus far. Generative AI, autonomous agents, open source deep learning models, and every other cousin under their family tree necessitate a long hard look at how we run our business, and what we choose to build for tomorrow. Try as we might to prepare ourselves and warn others, the truth is that most companies still won't see it the coming. Not because they're blind to the smoke and ashes, mind you, but simply because what they'll be seeing won't necessarily even look like destruction. It might all look like business as usual. Meanwhile, the stall next door moved their kitchen into a cart that can be moved to the town further downhill, and their neighbor replaced their entire marketing team's output with a $20/month subscription and a prompt. Today, we're all in Pompeii stuck with a chicken leg in our hands that might turn out to be the last one we'll ever sell.

These final two chapters are about making sure that doesn't happen to you. The MBA of the future will need to know how to build the kind of business that won't end up excavated by someone 2000 years later just for them to say "huh, didn't know they also liked chicken nuggets." We want you thriving in the disruption, not simply surviving. We want you making money as well as making out with your lives and the business once the landscape shifts beneath your feet. In short, we're going to talk about what it means to run an ironclad business in the age of a flood of lava.

Why most companies don't make it

There are only a handful of reasons why companies fail, and it usually has something to do with the idea, its execution, or the timing (Table 10.1).

That's the basic anatomy of success as well. In fact, most of what we think of as "strategy" is simply a crew of MBAs trying to climb their way up this table by tweaking their timing, reworking their idea, or hiring someone with the right experience to fix their execution. Now let's make this table dance by adding a bit of dynamism to it. Imagine someone closer to the bottom suddenly has a genuinely great idea. Suddenly, they land closer to the top of the able, and others start to take notice. Someone in Palo Alto spots the idea it from their glass office, swirls their oat milk latte, and mutters the five most dangerous words in modern capitalism: I could do that better. And after they've executed and optimized every square inch of the idea, our table suddenly looks like this for everyone else (Table 10.2).

As more players rush in, the bell curve fills out and so does our table. We get decent ideas with good timing and okay execution as well as bad ideas propped up by too much capital. Now and then you get brilliant ideas, ruined by teams who think "scrum" is something you have for breakfast. The table fills up, and most companies hover in that mushy middle where "fine" lives. And right before our Palo Alto corporate ranger gets to cash in their vested shares, the table is dancing again. Somewhere down below, another company nails the next generation of ideas and matches it with spotless execution. Maybe it's vertical integration, maybe it's an AI agent that cuts costs by 70% or maybe it's a better experience for the users that the previous incumbents have forgotten. The best players at the top push the boundary, the camera zooms in and suddenly a bunch of companies that were inside the frame yesterday are now offscreen, dropped to the bottom row next to the skulls of their brave ancestors.

Over time, this dance repeats, again and again, and while for each individual company the outcome feels binary as they either pivot or perish. For the economy, however, this dance creates a visible rhythm we've come to learn with many other names like Kondratiev waves, market

TABLE 10.1 Great ideas need great timing

Idea quality	*Timing*	*Execution*	*Outcome*
Brilliant	Perfect	Perfect	Breaks the curve and raises the bar
Brilliant	Perfect	Sloppy	A waste of resources at best
Brilliant	Too early	Doesn't matter	Dies waiting for the world to catch up
Brilliant	Too late	Perfect	Gets ignored
Terrible	Doesn't matter	Doesn't matter	Straight to the corporate graveyard
Good enough	Good enough	Good enough	Becomes the mediocre middle (added here because who doesn't think being average is just as good as failing)

TABLE 10.2 Even great ideas can age like milk

Idea quality	*Timing*	*Execution*	*Outcome*
Is brilliant	Perfect	Perfect	Pushes the bar even higher
Was brilliant	Perfect	Perfect	Plays the second fiddle and manages legacy systems
Was brilliant	Perfect	Sloppy	Shrinks or entirely shuts down
Was brilliant	Too early	Doesn't matter	Writes book about their idea and how they coined the term others are making money off of
Was brilliant	Too late	Perfect	Teaches the topic at your local university after failing their own startup
Still is terrible	Doesn't matter	Doesn't matter	Now serves as an example of how we should never spend our money
Is no longer good enough	Good enough	Good enough	Does its best to catch up with whomever is in the lead this time
☠☠☠	☠☠☠	☠☠☠	Here lie the hopes and dreams of many a founder

TABLE 10.3 The MBA's response

Vulnerability	*AI amplification effect*	*MBA response*
Point solutions becoming commodities	AI makes standalone products easy to replicate or outperform	Focus on bundling, outcomes, and brand/ecosystemmoats
Human-only workflows	Automated agents reduce headcount needs in rote tasks	Upskill toward orchestration and oversight
Monolithic platforms	AI-native competition is modular, API-driven, and nimble	Re-architect for plug-and-play flexibility

momentum, and cycles of Schumpeter's creative destruction. What looks like a wave from above is often nothing but the messy, misaligned timelines of companies living and dying at different speeds as better ideas and more efficient ways of executing them arise. We could continue Table 10.3 ad infinitum and never run out of relevant vulnerability-response pairs, simply because of how they circle and wave through the economy.

The lesson for our MBAs is painfully clear. Never rest on your laurels. Just ask a Finn how it feels to once have had Nokia contribute 4% to our GDP only for it to become a shorthand for what happens when you snooze at the top. Put another way, the first rule of building an ironclad business is that when you think you have one, you don't. We're all playing quantum physics, really. As soon as someone observes you succeeding, your waveform is about to collapse. The only way to make sure you rise to the top and stay there is to move faster than the frame that's shrinking around you. Here's a few ways to get started.

How you too could be one of the lucky few

If it seems to you that the secret to having an ironclad business model is simply a matter of finding a great idea, pairing it with great execution, and never stopping iterating on either, you're not wrong. In fact, we've arrived at the ELI5[1] equivalent of an MBA degree right here. The real problem at hand, obviously, is how to get either one of these done once, let alone consistently over time. And to be clear, it is a devilishly hard problem for even the smartest people on this planet. Most startups don't make it to their third birthday, let alone their Bar Mitzvah. And only a rare few like Apple, Crayola, Coca-Cola, or Salesforce are old enough to drink, vote, and remember when the world ran on dial-up.

So what are they doing right, and what could we learn from them?

As our table above made clear, timing matters. You might have a sharper idea than the original or come up with an execution engineered to be perfect and none of it will matter. If you're too early, the market shrugs. If you're too late, the market yawns. Either way, it is you who is wrong, not the market. Timing makes fools of geniuses and geniuses of the merely lucky. And once you do get timing right, another lever kicks in, one that often determines who gets to stick around, and that lever is scale. Companies that nail their product portfolios and then build deep, defensible layers around them tend to linger. It's not that they've found a way to always do things better at each step as much as the the walled gardens and sticky ecosystems they've built are ensuring that even if one part of the machine breaks, something else keeps paying the bills. For Google, it's search, for Apple, the iPhone, and for Amazon, it's AWS. When you've got that kind of architecture, you only need one part to be firing on all cylinders for the whole machine to lumber ahead. But scale cuts both ways. It breeds blind spots, and it tempts leaders into an unearned sense of complacency. And that's where the door of opportunity cracks open. Smaller more agile companies suddenly can wedge themselves into a niche, and suddenly we have Figma and Canva that first felt like toys until they started poaching entire design teams from Adobe and sending creative agencies into existential crisis therapy.

And here's a little secret that many venture capitalist often forget as they obsess over their moats. Most markets aren't winner-takes-all, they're winner-takes-enough. Most MBAs fight for a chance to work for one of the big ones, be it in finance or consulting, and none are looking at Bain or JP Morgan in fear of them failing lest someone copies a page or two from their playbook. The real issue is that when you're expecting multiples of 5–10× or more on your investments, winning a little feels quite a lot like losing. And for founders, the same is true when the startup next door is throwing rooftop parties after their Series A raised more than you'll clear in revenue in a decade. And yet. The market doesn't care. It's perfectly happy to make room for all of you, as long as you're solving real problems and doing it better than someone who used to matter. Obviously, you're going to be the one throwing the rooftop parties here, which is why we'll get back on track and start sharpening our formula for an ironclad business model by examining where it all begins: the idea.

And no, you can't teleport back in time and start Apple before Steve Jobs. That window's closed, as are many other ones that could have been terrific fits for you and your team. Instead, you're going to have to come up with something new. But here's M. Night Shyamalan with his twist: no one said your idea has to be original.

Great business ideas don't have to be invented. They can be stolen, inherited, borrowed, re-skinned, or even accidentally misapplied from another domain to great success. Instead of thinking of business ideas as a result of originality or creativity, think of them as a recipe for creating and distributing value. You don't have to be the first to put hot coals and chicken wings together; you have to make something people want to eat, ideally somewhere far away from active volcanoes. Sure, we celebrate the visionaries, but some of the best founders aren't creative souls. They're remix artists that found some dusty concept in another industry and applied it somewhere else in search of pockets value others hadn't tapped into yet. Salesforce took enterprise software and turned it into a subscription. Uber didn't invent taxis; it unbundled the dispatch and rebundled them into their app. Canva made Photoshop usable by people who don't use the word "kerning" in everyday conversation. The hall of fame of business is all Picassos the whole way down.

And how do you know if your idea is any good?

You sell it. You don't need to trademark the logos or finesse the decks. You simply ask someone to pay you for it, and their response will be a measure of whether they see value in what your offering. Build and they will come works if you're coding an application portal for the DMV, but the rest of us mortals have to make sure what we're doing actually adds value. Payment, or the promise thereof, is the only signal that matters. In the early days, think of pricing as feedback instead of as revenue, and if you can sell it once, you might have a business. If you can sell it twice, you're already ahead of most.

AI already excels in both generating ideas and evaluating them. You can point it at a competitor's website and ask for a go-to-market that needs nothing but a few API keys to get going. Use this power at every step of the way. Be a Centaur or a Cyborg and entangle your neurons with the GPU connector pins and become a monster when it comes to developing ideas. Or become an Artisan who chisels perfection out of the chunks of marble AI delivers for you. Whatever way you use AI to your advantage, never lose sight of the fact that the real measure of any business idea is how it produces value to the client.

The value validation loop of the future

One of the more persistent misconceptions in business that is held with equal fervor by fresh founders as well as seasoned executives is that what a company sells is what its customer is actually buying. In fact, harboring the idea that the beautifully branded widget or Swiss-architected SaaS solution is the value veers on delusion.

Let me show you what I mean. Picture this as a table, or better yet, another ladder where each step takes us a tad closer to the thing the client actually wants (Table 10.4).

Congratulations. You've just made yourself the Maslow of the Margins. Whatever you want to call this process, the point of it is simple. No one really wants your tool or your service. They want the outcome it delivers. Even if you're at the bottom of that stack today, selling the point-solution of all point-solutions, you're still involved in the client's mission at the very top. The old story about JFK and the janitor at NASA might be apocryphal, but it bears repeating. When asked what his job was, the janitor didn't say "cleaning floors." Instead replied, "I'm helping put a man on the moon."

TABLE 10.4 Getting to the bottom of it

What they buy	*What they actually want*
A license to JIRA...	To get the IT team to provision email faster
...email access for sales...	For the sales team to move faster
...sales team efficiency...	To close more deals
...more deals closed...	To grow revenue
...**higher revenue**	**To win in the game of business**

The smartest firms in the world build their entire engagement model around this logic. McKinsey, BCG, and the rest don't pitch their ability to optimize your JIRA tickets even though they are well and truly capable of that. They start their thought process at the top of the ladder, target a goal like shareholder value, market leadership, category dominance, and then work their way backwards. They map every intermediate step, every lever, every metric that can be influenced and in doing so, they position themselves not as problem-solvers, but as co-architects of your eventual triumph.

I invite you to begin doing the exact same, but with AI as your junior analysts.

No matter how small your product or service may seem, your narrative should begin at the highest level of value you can credibly anchor to. Airbnb doesn't rent lumpy couches with questionable sheets anymore; they sell experiences. During COVID-19, Peloton didn't sell exercise bikes; they sold community and endorphins on demand. Your job is to identify that top-level value, obsess over it, and then iterate around it. Don't get into the habit of making a better mousetrap but ask why the client wants to catch mice in the first place. And if the answer is that they want peace of mind in their home, then maybe the next iteration of your business isn't a trap at all, it's running a cat café next door that solves your client's problem and gets a few extra dollars out of them via lattes and cuddles. Value always transcends the product, and once you find that source of value, validate it, and when you're sure it's real, don't get comfortable.

What the history of technological shifts teaches us is that long-term winners don't descend the value chain; they climb it. Simon Sinek said to start with why, and I'll add only this: don't stop there. Once you understand why your client pays you today, ask yourself how you can deliver more of that value better, faster, and with less friction at the highest level possible. Even if it means torching your current offering and licensing predator-grade cats on a SaaS model. Because if you don't, someone else will.

MVPs are dead, long live the MVP

Nowhere is the fact that AI is rewiring how we build companies more obvious than in the world of startup execution. Now, don't get me wrong, I love Frank Robinson and Steve Blank as much as everyone. Their frameworks were a godsend in a world where speed to market was a proxy for survival, and capital was too precious to waste on polished failures that wouldn't see. But now, in the era of AI, I am here to tell you that the minimum viable product (MVP) as we knew it is obsolete.

To begin with, in hardware, the MVP never even really had a fair shot. No one wants to beta-test a blender that barely blends or a self-driving scooter that turns left when it feels like it. You needed to overshoot the "minimum" to make a safe and effective sale, and the idea stuck around mostly out of romanticism for garage-built prototypes that got the founders barely far enough to land their first VC check. In software, the concept has flourished for a reason. But now, even at its home stadium, AI has blown it wide open, and what replaces it is a more thoughtful evolution that re-centers us on value. We can even keep the acronym as long as we gently push the meaning. Here goes: enter the age of the *Monetizable Version of the Product*.

This shift in thinking is necessary first and foremost because of how AI compresses the entire build–test–iterate cycle into something that looks like a weekend hobby, not a year-long grind. You can ideate, prototype, and launch ten versions of your product in the time it used to take to wireframe one. And when the marginal cost of launching is close to zero, the old MVP logic of fail fast, learn faster to protect the runway starts to feel like overcautious advice for a slower world. The new game isn't to get to what's viable, simply because of how easy it is to ideate and execute on something that is. You need to build something that someone pays for faster than others. The only MVP that matters now is the one someone will swipe a card for. The Monetizable Version of the Product, aren't we right?

This subtle shift changes everything you aim for while changing very little of what you'll actually do. Because now, you don't waste a week building one MVP, you build one a day. You throw them into the world, one per trial customer, and you see what sticks not based on feedback or engagement, but on revenue or the promise thereof. Technical viability still matters, but it's the entrance fee that allows you to chase validation of your idea actually delivering value. Real validation in terms of dollars in, proof of value out.

In essence, we're simply frontloading your product–market fit to the nose of your development cycle instead of the tail of it. In that sense, it's no longer a matter of fit at all. It's all about gravity, and whether you've built something that can create enough gravitational pull that people orbit it with their wallets. We've also arrived at one of the reasons why people think of MBAs the way they do. If price is proxy for validation, then the higher the revenue, the better the idea. Humanities majors might still wince at the idea, but if someone's paying for it, it's valuable. That's the only metric you need to hit when getting started. With AI, the founder's playbook shifts from painstaking craftsmanship to industrial cultivation. You don't build one thing and hope it sings. You build ten, sort them by revenue per user, lifetime value, retention, and you start businesses around what rakes it in the most.

Now, for the lucky few MBAs who land a role in a pre-existing business, one with real products and services already in-market, your job isn't that much different. You're running the same concepts, this time on a bigger playing field. You'll also find that the AI revolution will increase the pressure that comes at you from three directions at once. First, new entrants, like you just a paragraph ago or slightly more caffeinated, are spinning up AI-native challengers in a fraction of the time it takes you to schedule your board together for an alignment call. Second, while AI helps your peers run leaner, it also enables them to scale into adjacent spaces and ascend the value stack in search of higher-margin outcomes. Third, and most dangerous of all, your customers will be changing as well. They'll be expecting more from you because they're using AI themselves. They're internally deploying the same capabilities you once used to differentiate, which means your edge is melting faster than you think. Also, everyone else you're competing with has already shown your clients what their new AI features can do. So whether you're bootstrapping your way to relevance or safeguarding a throne you didn't build, the rule holds: the viability of a product, service, or an entire business model is no longer enough. Only what monetizes survives, and that which monetizes at a higher level of the value ladder wins.

We can recap the MVP doctrine by exhorting you to test fast and sell faster. Build in loops, not lines, and whenever in doubt, follow the money. The best product or service isn't the prettiest or even the smartest; it's the one someone pays for today, and again tomorrow.

Three inevitable consequences of AI and what they mean for strategy

Let's build our last section of this chapter up from first principles, like we would in our classroom. Remember that AI, at its core, is a tool. It's a tool that can see, write, learn, reason, and act faster than you, cheaper than you, and eventually, more accurately than you or anyone you know. Second, access to this tool is democratizing at an incredible rate, making past niches of knowledge and expertise publicly available with an API call. Third, your clients have really never cared about what value you bring to the table, not what you sold them. And fourth, everyone wanting to keep their seat at the table will be aiming to capture more of that value for themselves and their clients.

From these facts, three particularly important consequences arise.

First, we're going to see the great servicification shift pick up steam, and this time, it's going to move like a freight train with rocket boosters. Developed economies already left the factory floor behind when they moved up the global value chain, and this time we're not only going to see more services, we'll see more granular ones. Think about your friendly neighborhood marketing agency. Back in the day, they'd bill you top dollar for building a website, and if they were feeling spicy, maybe they would toss in some banner ads while they were at it. Today, that same agency is likely running your entire ecommerce operation, your influencer strategy, your content calendar, your TikTok and probably ghostwriting your founder's LinkedIn too, all in the name of revenue growth. Just ask Intel, which quietly handed over its entire global marketing team to Accenture in a move that is nothing if not contract theory manifest. With AI, it becomes not only possible but absolutely *irresistible* to turn fragmented functions into unified outcomes that deliver more value by definition. And once someone starts promising outcomes, you can bet nobody's going back to buying features. Once you've been chauffeured, you don't want to go back to learning stick shift for twice the price and 24-month contracts. This is what happens when the top of the value ladder becomes your new baseline, and the smart firms are already positioning themselves to sell the win directly in addition to the steps thereto.

The other major trend we'll see is a growing amount of bundling. On the one hand, it follows from the above. To create great services, you'll want to cover as much ground as possible under whatever prong of the value ladder you are standing. Jira licenses, AI ticketing agents, and managed IT services all delivered together bring more value than any of them alone, and now bundling them is easier than ever. Another reason is how sticky scale and bundled offerings can be. It's harder for clients to say pull out a bundle than a point solution. And on the producer side, the cost of delivery drops when the portfolio is scaled correctly. In an increasingly competitive landscape where any one feature can be MVP'd away by an entrant in an instant, the best way to add defensibility is to expand the walled garden and offer tighter integration with broader coverage. The AI-native firms will figure this out early and fast. They'll start by offering narrow solutions to earn their right-to-play, and once they sniff out the next prong on the value ladder, they'll keep on expanding into adjacent services until they're hitting the limits of what can be bundled. And because they can deliver it all with agents, their margins won't even blink.

Finally, we'll see that the surviving point solutions will get even pointier. It's tempting to take the above to predictions and call out the slow death of the individual product and the product-led-growth motions that fuel many of the most successful ones. Sure, most clients will gravitate toward service providers that don't hassle them with products to begin with, or then to bundled offerings that do everything in one category under the sun. But there will always be killer apps. It's just that this time, they'll find it worth their while to become even pointier by becoming more fungible and embeddable. Think of these like Stripe, a hyper-focused and hyper-scalable product that can be easily slotted into bigger workflows. Those building their walled gardens and bundles will still want someone to do the heavy lifting for them, and in the niches where expertise, proprietary data, and knowledge matter, like finance, you'll find plenty of space for being a point solution that enables the servicification and bundling of others to continue. However, there's always the temptation for the Stripes of this world to build their banks, particularly now that doing so is a lighter lift than ever before.

So what makes a business model ironclad in the age of AI? Patents, superior distribution channels, or a genius founder aren't going to cut it this time around. What you'll need to bank on is the compound effect of custom processes, unique data, and people enabled by AI to do more of what matters to the client. It's knowing when to bundle, when to strip things down, and when to orchestrate with agents instead of employees. It's mastering the cognitive stack to generate better options, evaluate them faster, and make moves before the market even realizes a shift is happening. It's building loops where insight inevitably leads to action, and action can't help but lead to more value being created and distributed.

In short, the most defensible businesses of this era won't be the ones that *have* AI or even a better, more unique version of it, because just like the electric motor, AI will soon disappear into the fabric of every process and will be treated as a *given*. What will remain visible are the outcomes and the time to value. The real edge belongs to those who *use* AI to unlock what only their people, their data, and their timing can do. Ironclad strategies are the ones that turn AI into invisible infrastructure for delivering more client value than anyone else, no matter what mix of tools, tactics, or workflows it takes (Table 10.5).

What does all of this mean for you, the strategic mastermind in training, the MBA who knows just enough about the inner workings of AI enough to be dangerous, peering out over the foggy horizon and wondering how to build something that actually lasts? Simple. Be nothing if not relentless in your pursuit of value.

And no, I don't mean your own value or the product's proposition of value, but the real value. Seek out the thing your client is actually paying for, whether or not they've figured out how to put it into words yet, and latch onto it for dear life. Your job is to get as close to that value source as possible, park yourself there like a hawk, and never stop inching closer. Use the cognitive stack we built in the past chapters as your own internal innovation engine and ask it to aim for the new kind of MVPs. Iterate upon them like it's your job, because from now onwards, it is. And when you think you've got the business model nailed down to a T, do something radical and try to blow it all up. Hire a Skunkworks team of misfits, weirdos, and perennial troublemakers who see around corners and don't care about your org chart. Give them one mission and one mission only, to figure out how to get to the same core customer value at one-tenth the cost, one-twentieth the bureaucracy, and don't expect any of them to ask permission. Let them treat your business model like a starting point, and see how they orient it all around value in ways the rest of the organization couldn't.

With AI, nothing is safe. Not even a business model that's been working since Pompeii. Even selling fried chicken might require you to slap some wheels on your stall and start moving again.

TABLE 10.5 Makings of an ironclad business model

Pillar	*What it is*	*Why it matters in the AI age*	*What MBAs must master*
Proprietary data loops	Internal telemetry, user behavior, unstructured insights, micro-experiments	AI is only as good as the data it sees, owning unique signals drives better decisions	Curate, clean, and activate your own datasets
Custom processes	AI-native workflows built on your org's knowledge and goals	Plug-and-play tools create parity; custom chains create edge	Build internal stacks that reflect your context
Agentic orchestration	Delegating tasks to AI agents with clear triggers and goals	Scales execution without scaling headcount, faster, cheaper, sharper	Design and supervise agent workflows
Human judgment layer	Strategic use of cognitive stack, idea gen, evaluation, decision-making	Keeps AI outputs aligned with brand, ethics, and impact	Use chain-of-thought, goal functions, world modeling
Timing and tempo	Ability to act not just fast, but at the right moment	Speed is useless if it misses the window; advantage favors the time-smart	Map your market's rhythm and act with calibrated urgency
Bundled value creation	Integrated offerings solving multiple user jobs at once	Reduces churn, raises switching costs, boosts perceived value	Design bundles where 1 + 1 > 2
Platform + Distribution power	Unique access to attention, networks, or platforms	Even perfect products die without distribution; AI can amplify both	Build inroads and ecosystems around your core
Mission and meaning	A strategic purpose that resonates and guides	Keeps human talent loyal, customer trust high, and AI aligned with intent	Translate purpose into metrics, actions, and stories
Client-centricity	Structured obsession with value delivered *to the client*	AI lets you automate inward-facing work, so you can focus outward	Define and measure client-perceived value constantly

Note

1 "Explain like I am 5," one of the most powerful prompts in the age of AI for learning a new concept.

11

THE UNSTOPPABLE MBA AND THEIR AI STACK

By now, I hope I've given you reason to believe that the workplace of the future will need you more than ever. The MBA has always been a shape-shifter, showing up in different roles, with different titles, but always in service of the same fundamental task: creating value. There will be plenty of roles like that to play. More importantly, there are ways to ensure that whichever path you take, you become inevitable.

But before we explore what that actually looks like in practice, let's play a game. Your task is simple: pick a profession from 2000 years ago that you could've worked in the longest, earning the most, without losing it all when the tides turned. You can go unemployed for decades, even centuries, but you can't hide your wealth. If a revolution comes, if a new empire rises, if the crowd turns, your fortune and your head are gone.

So, what job do you pick?

If you're like most people who dig into the economic structures of the ancients, you'll probably find yourself surprised about how rich and recognizable their world really was. Strip away the Wi-Fi and the froth of modernity, and the people who walked this earth two millennia ago were shockingly like us. Ambitious, smart, and as status-seeking as the modern Homo Sapiens. As you comb through the ranks, you'll find scribes, the literate class of Egypt who controlled knowledge like a currency. You'll come across agronomists like Cato the Elder, who wrote the oldest surviving Latin prose, which reads like an MBA's operations manual for Roman landowners, complete with advice on acquisitions, supply chains, and heavily enslaved labor force. There were bakers, cobblers, masseurs, and merchants hawking goods along the Silk Road and in the bazaars of Antioch. You could choose to be a king, sure, but that was a short-term gig, typically ending with poison, betrayal, or a knife mixed with the bathwater. Succession lines have a habit of not surviving much further than you could throw the crown jewels.

Peasants did survive all the way to today, but they did so as cogs embedded into the operating system, not the executive suite. They worked the land then, and they work the land now. Safe, sure. Lucrative? Don't even get Marx started. Whatever job you settle on, pause for a moment and think back to one of the central messages of this book: business is, and always has been, a decidedly *human* thing. Every enduring profession is tied to the fulfillment of deep human needs one way or another just like every winning pick will fundamentally be linked to

DOI: 10.4324/9781003508427-11

the creation of distribution of value. Choose right, and you'll find yourself solving for something that's lasted millennia, be it shelter, belief, nourishment, desire, certainty, or identity.

Now, let's make the game a bit harder and fast-forward to today. Which role, right now, will still exist 2000 years from now and would give you the greatest ROI?

Software engineers are already under siege, and who doesn't hope that TikTok influencers to be a thing of the past. Chicken stall vendors are still around, but that's hardly a high-income play. Let me tell you the role I would pick: the advisor.

Consider Niccolò di Bernardo dei Machiavelli. He wasn't a general nor was he a noble. Pushing the limits of the word, he was *only* a diplomat, a civil servant, and later, as we know him today, a writer. In the chaos of warring Italian city-states, as the Holy Roman Empire thundered through and the Medici family rose and fell, Machiavelli built his career by getting close to power not by wielding it himself, but by *interpreting* it. He advised Florence's leaders, negotiated with popes and kings, and when exiled, wrote *The Prince* to win his way back in. His equivalent of a McKinsey whitepaper on CEO's most effective habits worked, and he was reinstated. In the end, his ideas would far outlive the state he served.

Advisors have persisted since time immemorial. They exist behind every throne, inside every boardroom, and today we find them on every podcast where everyone with a microphone, including myself, is pretending to be one. Marcus Aurelius had them, before he himself became one to the point that his Meditations influence more people than he himself ever ruled over. And whether you love or loathe advisors, everyone in business you care about has one, even if they themselves have had to become their own guiding lights.

FIGURE 11.1 Turns out, they still needed someone to run the offsite even after the AI apocalypse.

Sure, you could try your luck as a founder, an operator, a manager, or a landlord, which are solid bets in this game. But now you've got to pick an industry or a location, and that's where survivability plummets. Disruption, regulation, taste, geopolitics, among a plethora of other minefields await, while the humble advisor gets to play the entire board.

Before you assume I'm trying to convert you into a career consultant at BCG, let me be clear. I'm not. I'm inviting you to adopt a mindset instead. Taking a page from the advisor's playbook is one of the easiest ways to future-proof your career in the age of AI. Not least because it means becoming someone whose insight and way of framing problems and designing action earns trust from people who run the systems that shape our world. That might mean founding something yourself. It might mean teaching, writing, or leading the change with your own force of will. But the posture of the advisor is what endures, and it is one where MBAs have excelled for as long as we've had them.

Over the coming years, when AI will accelerate the chaotic, flatten the predictable, and reward the adaptable, your first task as an advisor is to learn three things deeply if you intend to differentiate yourself: Know the business. Know the tool. Know thyself (Figure 11.1).

Know the business

There are two levels to knowing the business, and with AI around, you'll need to be intimately familiar with both. The first level is as simple as knowing what your company actually does. Here, I mean the actual steps the business takes as it lives its life vicariously through the intern fielding support tickets or the ops person duct-taping five systems together to get invoices out by EOD. Your task is to know exactly what steps each of the employees takes in service of their customers and internal operations. AI rewards those who understand operations at the granular level because only then can you start reverse-engineering which parts of the process AI can augment or take over entirely. In fact, it's impossible to effectively automate a task you don't understand to begin with. This is why companies that have never bothered to create SOPs, Visio maps, or simply write down how work gets done will fall behind, fast. Sure, exposing the internal plumbing of an organization might not be sexy. More than that, it can be extremely ungrateful work. But as every management consultant knows, this is where the magic starts. The internal plumbing is also where inefficiencies hide and where AI is practically begging to be pointed at them like a laser beam.

As you're laying out the plumbing, here's what you'll be keeping an eye out for. First, take note of value-destroying steps just like John Snow took note of cholera-filled wells in the town square. These are the tasks no one should be doing, and most often than not, no one really wants to do them to begin with. You might find some of these wrapped in legal risk-aversion or HR folklore, and some stick around like the appendix that has long since outlived its evolutionary adaptation. If removing the step doesn't make the end product or process worse, and if nothing compensates for it existing naturally, chances are it's bureaucratic sludge and your task is to kill it. If it must stay, redesign it. This is the realm where AI excels by taking over redundant form-filling, unnecessary handoffs, rules-based gates that were put in place "just in case." Let my people go, indeed.

The second thing your keen advisor-eyes should be trained on like a hawk are value-adding steps that are under-leveraged. It is not at all uncommon for a junior staffer to fix something elegantly while the senior staffers suffer through various stages of Seligman's learned helplessness. You'll often find solutions hiding in the cracks in the form of routines or fixes someone built quietly for themselves, while others have adapted to dysfunction. Uncover them, broadcast them, and incentivize more of them by turning bottom-up innovation into a cultural norm. Today, you can point AI to do much of this for you. Deploy tools like Gong, Fireflies, or internal GPT-powered team meeting transcribers to comb through meeting transcripts, task comments, and internal messages for patterns of "local optimizations" buried in offhand remarks. "We use a shared sheet for that now" or "Sarah figured out a faster way last month" is the gold vein you are looking to strike. And when you find them, make heroes out of the hackers. AI-powered tools like Glean or enterprise-grade knowledge bases can spotlight and auto-summarize bottom-up fixes worth evangelizing. But they won't get traction unless the organization sees and rewards them. Use AI to find a source of value first, and then amplify it. And while you're at it, why not turn all of this into a loop. AI thrives on feedback exactly like humans do. Set up workflows where good local solutions get documented, rated, and fed back into the system so that the next time someone faces a similar problem, the AI suggests, "Here's what worked for a teammate last quarter." Suddenly, the quiet fix becomes institutional memory, and your MBA degree just paid for itself.

If an advisor really wants to earn their keep, they'll also surface value-adding steps that don't yet exist within the organization. These are the blind spots that no one's looked into yet, but which competitors, insurgents, or smarter teams are already capitalizing on. When you encounter one, steal like Picasso and borrow like a strategist. Use AI to detect whitespace and model what a new value-creating action could look like based on what everyone else already knows. You would be surprised how often even the most sophisticated companies leave better ways of working on the table, simply because they haven't thought of them, or someone high up didn't believe in them. And finally, avoid like the pox any task or process that isn't done today that would destroy more value. Why fix something that isn't broken, and why break something that doesn't need fixing.

As you're mapping out the inner workings of the organization, use the following tested and tried methods. Start by sticking with a task all the way through like a post-it note attached to it. Live the task and follow it from the moment it begins to the moment it ends, tracing every hand-off, delay, and undocumented detour along the way. You'll be amazed by how few organizations can actually describe how their work gets done at the task-by-task level. All most can muster are org charts and job descriptions. This is the same project Frederick Taylor began alongside Henry Ford, stopwatch in hand, measuring every movement down to the second. But we're not here to police the factory floor or micromanage our knowledge workers. We're here to finish what Ford and Taylor started by mapping task flows so that we can discover where AI can take over and scale, releasing the humans to climb up to the next ladder of value above. Next, talk to people and ask them what they think they are doing, and how does that make them feel. Instead of the managers who usually either hear only problems or are told about none of them, depending on their leadership style, start with the people closest to the tasks themselves. Interview them like you're conducting a therapy session, not extracting a report. Your goal is to surface the absurd, the broken, the "we've always done it this way" rituals that everyone has stopped questioning. Each such story is breadcrumb pointing toward either hidden value or institutional entropy that you and your cognitive AI stack can have a field day with. And finally, lift your gaze beyond the walls and benchmark obsessively. Look at how others do things and what results they achieve. From there, begin to draft your own internal ontology of work and what is worthwhile doing. Create a structured, living map of how things *should* operate as according to you. Use that as your reference frame to identify the gap between how things are and how they could be. That delta is where new tools enter the scene to both streamline and to transform.

Which is why through all of this, *think in AI*. Every task you see performed is typically made of dozens of subtasks hiding underneath. And somewhere in that decomposition, there's a moment that's *AI-fiable*. Maybe it's the summarization after a meeting, maybe it's the manual routing, scheduling, or extraction of information from invoices. Your job is to lay out that pipework, find the pieces ripe for AI integration, and get the right tools into place whether it's an API call, a LangChain agent, or nothing but fine-tuned prompts embedded in someone's daily flow.

But don't be fooled, none of this will be as easy as Sam Altman and Jensen Huang make it seem like. In large, aging orgs, the temptation to blow it all up and rebuild from scratch can sometimes be strong. Sometimes, that's the right call, and sometimes it's a recipe for disaster and endless management consultant fees. Remember, most corporate transformation programs fail today even *without* AI. And while AI is a powerful lever, it hasn't made change management any easier, not least because we still understand astonishingly little about how humans work with machines, especially when they're smarter than us at narrow tasks. Instead, you may need to think like a systems architect. Bring AI not to full processes, but to *fragments* of steps. Or perhaps invent new AI-mediated micro-steps that link together what were previously silos. You'll find providers like Glean, EMA, or Zapier starting to do exactly that, stitching knowledge work into AI-ready workflows without replacing the whole system.

In the MBA's modern toolkit, knowing the business is the rarest and most undervalued skill that they can have. But it's also the one that separates those who can survive AI disruption from those who will drive it. You see, if you know the business better than the owner, you will always have a role to play as an advisor, an operator, or a future buyer who simply understands the risks better than anyone else. This is why I invite you to make it your business to know the business and then make it better.

I promised you a second level of knowing the business, and here it is. In addition to knowing what the business does on the surface level, you'll need to also know what it actually does on the value creation and distribution level.

Most businesses aren't in the business they think they're in, at least not if you know how to ask the right questions from the right person. Sure, the driver for a logistics company might think they move boxes but ask their clients about why they pay for them over their competitors, and you'll learn that the company in fact monetizes trust and just-in-time certainty. The media companies may say they create content, but what they really sell is audience access to executives and a fleeting hit of dopamine for the consumers. The consultancy tells itself it provides insight, but its real asset is confidence on the decision-making, rented by the hour. Every industry and every company carries this duality where the thing it says it does is rarely the real source of value that it gets paid for.

This is your job now, to see both perspectives on the business of the business itself. As an MBA, your task is to understand the symbolic business as deeply as the actual business and to see how the public narrative and the internal plumbing joint drive the value exchange that is going on under the hood. Because AI won't be of much help to you until you do.

If you bring a GPT into the room aiming to automate influencer outreach or speed up invoice approvals, you'll find no shortage of wins on the surface. But unless you widen your aperture to ask *why* those tasks exist in the first place, you'll miss the far greater opportunity of reimagining the system that made those tasks necessary at all. This is how companies find killer ideas like Figma or Canva. Had they stuck on the transactional task level, they could have just as well optimized what existing software was doing like a plug-in. But the founders saw things differently

TABLE 11.1 The levels of knowing the business

Level 1: Understanding what the business *actually* does (the internal plumbing)		
Approach	*Purpose*	*How to do it*
Shadow a task end-to-end	See how work really flows vs. how it's documented	Stick with a task from start to finish. Be the post-it note no one peels off.
Map internal workflows	Spot redundancies, bottlenecks, and AI-ready steps	Use Miro/Lucidchart + interviews to diagram workflows as they actually unfold
Interview frontline employees	Uncover pain points and process absurdities	Talk like a therapist, not a manager, ask what's broken and why it hasn't been fixed
Use AI to find local optimizations	Surface bottom-up hacks and smart workarounds	Analyze meeting transcripts or Slack with Fireflies/Gong/GPT
Trace how decisions really happen	Detect unofficial power dynamics and approval chaos	Map decision paths backwards who slowed it down, who actually decided
Shed light on the shadow systems	Reveal the real systems that run the business beneath the surface	Ask "what spreadsheet/tool could you not do your job without?"
Level 2: Understanding what the business *really* delivers (value creation and perception)		
Approach	*Purpose*	*How to do it*
Ask: what would clients miss if we disappeared? What would they do instead	Find the *emotional and functional value* you actually provide	Run structured interviews focused on outcomes, not features
Conduct value interviews with clients	Clarify the real reasons customers stay and pay	Use GPT/Claude to summarize interviews for patterns and emotional keywords
Analyze sales vs. delivery promises	Spot dissonance between the dream sold and the service delivered	Compare sales decks and pitch calls with onboarding reports
Benchmark competitors' narratives	Discover your differentiation gaps or underleveraged strengths	Tear down their messaging, web copy, sales motions, compare side-by-side
Run a reverse contract theory exercise	Pinpoint the transaction under the transaction (what clients *think* they buy)	Ask "If you were paying us 10x, what would you expect? If 10%, what would you still need?"

and understood what the end users were actually paying for, and optimized for that instead. This is where thought frameworks like Contract Theory, the Value Ladder, and Outcome over Output become your compass. They're analytical lenses to spot the difference between work that *feels* productive and work that actually moves the needle because it gets closer to the actual source of value. No AI can tell the difference unless you do, which is exactly where the MBA's edge sharpens. Because most agents, no matter how advanced, still lack context, and even when they have it, they only know how your company makes money today. They can generate outputs, but they can't infer which rung of the value ladder to hit instead. That's still your job.

This is why I ask you to make it your habit to ask: where is value really being created here? Where is it captured and where is it leaking? If you can answer that, AI becomes an amplifier that will allow you to shout over the noise of your competitors. If you can't, you're building castles in the sand that can be faster to build and flashier than the kid's next door, but no more real or sustainable.

It's easy to romanticize knowing the business, and I know that much of the above sounds noble on paper, but difficult to even imagine how to bring to practice. But for the MBA who wants to stay relevant, there's no shortcut: you've got to get under the hood. To help you get started, I've compiled a set of practical, high-yield ways to understand your business at both levels: what it *actually does* internally, and what your *clients think* you do for them. Each is paired with a clear purpose and a concrete tool or method to make it actionable (Table 11.1).

Know the tool

Like Cato the Elder's reminds us in what amounted to the first instruction manual for MBAs in agricultural productivity, a farmer must know the tools they're using. This means not only understanding what the tools can do on a practical level but also what impact they'll have on the business and the farmer. In the same way, the real impact of AI will be transmitted to you by what others can do with theirs. To do this, you need to know the tool family and what kinds of problems each of them were designed to solve, where they excel, where they fail, and how to stack them in creative ways. To give you a sense of what kind of a task you are up against, here's a well and truly simplified list of recent developments across the AI family tree (Table 11.2).

The way AI has evolved tells a clear story that MBAs must pay attention to. The tools we use are getting more powerful, more wide in the application, and more embedded into workflows with each cycle. Worse yet, each cycle is compressed as the pace of evolution picks up. Your job is to learn how to ride each wave without letting the ocean swallow you up. So how do you actually learn to get a grasp of these tools? Start getting your hands dirty. No amount of theorizing can replace actually playing with toys that our friends in Silicon Valley have given us. Each AI family tree branch deserves your time and respect, and each deserves to get their operating models embedded into your intuition.

Here's your personal syllabus to help you get started with six weeks devoted to lightweight yet tangible projects that cover every aspect of the tool tree, giving you an idea of where and how to apply AI as your ambition grows.

Week 1: automate your calendar (it's time)

Project goal: Create a fully AI-driven calendar that optimizes for both your professional priorities and personal habits (deep work blocks, commutes, family time) and automates scheduling.

KPI: By end of week 1, your calendar should auto-schedule 80% of your meetings, auto-reschedule on conflicts, and protect your flow state.

If there is one domain where AI is begging to be invited in, it's your calendar. Modern tools like Google Calendar and Calendly now embed smart suggestions, automatic buffer zones, and conflict detection as well as scheduling tools, but that's only scratching the surface. Pair these with intelligent orchestration layers like Reclaim.ai, Motion, or Clockwise, and your calendar stops being a bottleneck and becomes a dynamic productivity engine. These tools use classical machine learning to learn your habits and priorities, and autonomous workflow models to make

TABLE 11.2 A short history of a revolution

AI family	*1990*	*2000*	*2020*	*2022*	*2023*	*2024*	*2025*	*2030*
Machina Discens (Learning Machine)	MYCIN, decision trees	Weka, SVMs, scikit-learn	TensorFlow, PyTorch	Self-supervised learning (BERT)	Gemini 1, Mixtral, LLaMA 2	Mixtral + Claude fine-tuned agents	Fully trained models as co-pilots (e.g., in Notion, Salesforce)	Agentic lifelong learning
Machina Cogitantis (Thinking Machine)	Rule-based systems	Bayesian networks, Hidden Markov Models	AlphaZero, GPT-2 reasoning	Chain-of-thought prompting (PaLM, GPT-3.5)	Claude 2+ (more aligned), Toolformer	Auto reasoning stacks (e.g., AutoChain, E2B)	Multi-agent coordination logic (e.g., Sweep, Cognosys)	Hybrid neuro-symbolic
Machina Loquens (Talking Machine)	Early NLP tools (ELIZA etc.)	IBM Watson's NLP models	GPT-2, BERT	GPT-3, Whisper, CodeGen	GPT-4, Claude, Gemini, voice + text chat	Multimodal Chat (voice, code, image)	Embedded assistants on Slack or Glean	Custom voice-first agents
Machina Videns (Seeing Machine)	Optical character recognition	Viola-Jones Face Detection	YOLOv3, OpenCV	CLIP, DALL·E 2	Midjourney, Gemini vision, Stable Diffusion XL	Sora, Meta V-JEPA, VEO3	Integrated video+image+ context models	Real-time scene interpreters
Machina Facientis (Doing Machine)	Basic robotics (e.g., Honda ASIMO)	Robotic process automation (RPA)	Boston Dynamics Spot	AutoGPT prototypes	Devin (Cognition), Meta Open Agents	Devin the first Coding agent	Agentic AI, MCP, A2A	Agentic AI ecosystems

scheduling decisions on your behalf. They parse natural language in your invites, understand task dependencies, and adjust in real time when conflicts arise or your day unravels.

Start by plugging in your calendar and letting the tools run on your recurring meetings, commute windows, focus blocks, and daily wind-down time. Then invite even more of AI into the mix. By the end of week 1, aim to have 80% of your scheduling and reshuffling happen without you lifting a finger. The goal is a calendar that adapts to you, not the other way around.

Week 2: generate a video for your loved ones of their loved ones

Goal: Bring a still photo to life with a narrated message in the voice of a lost loved one. Add music and subtitle using AI.

KPI: Create an emotionally resonant 30-second tribute using two or more AI tools by combining models across modalities.

Start with a photo that means something who means something to you. Maybe it's a decades-old portrait of your grandmother in her youth, a wedding snapshot of your parents, or that one faded image of your cousin who left too soon. Feed this image into a model like D-ID, which specializes in photo animation, or give it to most foundational models that can handle picture-to-video transformations. Then comes the voice. If you have even a short clip, an old voicemail, a birthday message tucked away in a Google Drive folder, or a cassette that you could digitize, you can use tools like ElevenLabs or Descript to clone the voice and create a new narration. Next, write the message. You can use ChatGPT or Claude to help you draft something that walks the line between poetic and precise. Then generate the narration in the cloned voice. Pair the audio and animation in a tool like Runway or Veo 3. Add gentle background music, something AI-generated via Soundraw or AIVA if you want a truly unique composition. Within an afternoon, you've taken a still photo and given it life, voice, and emotion. You've also taken a grand tour around some of the greatest AI accomplishments in learning, vision, talking, and doing.

Week 3: connect two pieces of AI together for a productivity hack

Starter task:

Use Zapier or IFTTT to connect a weather API with your Google Calendar or phone notifications to remind you to bring an umbrella.

Advanced task:

Use LangChain or Flowise to monitor your inbox for new subscriptions or bills, auto-extract data that gets written to Google Sheets, which then triggers an email reminder when a threshold is crossed.

KPI: Create a three-step automation chain that triggers without you needing to click a button.

The superpower we're unlocking here is connection. Think of each AI tool as a sharp but solitary mind. Alone, they're clever, but when you link them together like neurons, you've got something that counts for real intelligence and autonomy.

Let's begin small. You live in a city, and weather matters. Set up a simple automation using Zapier or IFTTT: connect a weather API (like OpenWeather) to your Google Calendar or phone's Reminders app. If rain's forecast in the next 12 hours, you get pinged at 7:30 a.m. with an "Hey, grab the umbrella." You'll never curse at the sky again for drenching your white sneakers.

Once you're done, let's get tape together a more productive pipeline of tools. You've probably got a dozen subscriptions, a few recurring bills, and at least one service you forgot you were paying for. Build a pipeline to make sure you cancel what needs canceling and pay what needs paying. Use LangChain, Flowise, or Zapier AI Actions to monitor your inbox for keywords like "invoice," "receipt," "subscription," "thanks for your payment." When an email with the trigger words lands, AI parses it, extracts the amount and other details, and adds them to your Google Sheets. Once a threshold is crossed, say, over $200 in a week, send yourself an email reminder with suggestions on what to monitor or cancel for maximum impact.

Week 4: let an agent take over excel

Goal:

Send a messy Excel task to an AI agent that performs multi-step reasoning, from cleaning to charting and trend commentary.

KPI:

Pick a recurring spreadsheet task (reporting, KPI, invoice summary), delegate it entirely, and use it to create reports.

Think of all the time you've spent nudging Excel cells into place, fixing typos, aligning columns, building charts, and then writing up a summary your boss will never read. Now imagine handing that entire loop off to an AI agent and what you could have done with your time instead. Now multiple this by every colleague you've ever had, and you're starting to get why the AI hypesters are so hyped up.

This week, pick one messy, recurring spreadsheet job at work, something you usually dread. Maybe it's your team's weekly KPI tracker, or that client invoice summary you pretend takes more time than it does. If your company doesn't give you permission too work on real data, ask your favored GPT to create an Excel file with dummy data instead. Now, instead of opening Excel and firing up your formulas, upload the file to an AI agent powered by tools like OpenAI's Code Interpreter, Microsoft's Copilot for Excel, or tie together more advanced frameworks like AutoGPT, LangChain, or ChatGPT Custom GPTs with file-reading abilities. Give the agent a clear goal: it should clean the data, fill in missing values, reformat dates, and detect any outliers. Then it should auto-generate a chart or two to show performance at a glance. Finally, ask it to draft a short executive summary of what it is seeing in the form of: "Revenue up 8.4% MoM. Conversion dipped slightly, possibly due to the mid-month campaign shift. Recommend monitoring next week." This is how reports should be done today, where you get to drive the insights, not handcraft them into existence.

Week 5: use agentic research to generate and evaluation business improvement ideas

Goal:

Run a multi-step deep dive into a pain point in your work, generating ideas and evaluating them for impact and feasibility.

KPI:

Produce a brief presentation with a target action list, evaluation of each for feasibility, and suggested next steps.

Week 5 is where your inner consultant gets an AI upgrade.

Every organization has a few pain points that linger like background noise that are too routine to escalate, yet too costly to ignore once the competition comes knocking. This week, you'll bring in an AI research agent into existence first to describe the problem, and then to help you figure out how to solve it end-to-end and make the case for the change. Start with clarity of purpose. Pick a single persistent pain point and describe it, in your words, as thoroughly as you can. It could be an internal inefficiency, a workflow mess, or an external choke point. Describe it in plain language, include who's affected, when it tends to flare up, and what workarounds currently exist, if any. Then activate your agentic research stack to start finding ways out of the mess. This can be as simple as passing a prompt to ChatGPT's Deep Research with browsing, or a more layered approach using tools like Phind, Perplexity, and Consensus. Frame your ask like a strategist:

> Here's a common pain point in [industry/department]. What do best-in-class companies do about this? What improvements have been piloted and shown to work? Give me 10 different angles of attack ranked by impact and feasibility.

Ask for examples of each idea in action and request variations tailored to your company size or tech maturity. Use the early answers of one model as input for your next round of questions with another. This type of recursive AI thinking is how you generate more diverse insights even when everyone is using the same tools.

Now it's time to make it visual. Use Beautiful.ai, Gamma, or Tome to turn your research into a high-impact visual presentation. Import the best insights into slide format. Ask the AI inside these tools to group your top 3–5 ideas into a "Now, Next, Later" framework or a two-axis matrix with feasibility and value. Ask them to automatically generate illustrations or graphs that map the opportunity size, pain point intensity, or customer impact.

Finally, build your own GPT agent to help you continue the brainstorming. Use OpenAI's custom GPT builder to train a lightweight agent on your project's context and current ideas by feeding it your findings and goals. Going forward, this becomes your sparring partner for iterating on these and future challenges. It remembers what you've explored, where you've hesitated, and what kinds of solutions match your context. By the end of the week, your deliverable will be more than equipped to make you a much more dangerous advisor and trouble shooter than you've ever been.

Week 6: create your own teacher

Goal: Never pay me or anyone else again to teach you what you can do with AI. Become the Machina Discens.

KPI:

Build a self-paced curriculum on one AI topic and create a process for learning how to deploy any AI tool in your organization.

You've automated your calendar. You've conjured loved ones into digital motion. You've even linked workflows across clouds, handed Excel over to agents, and used AI to diagnose organizational pain points. Now it's time for the final, most important act: replacing me and this book.

Seriously. If this bootcamp has worked, you won't need me or any other teacher to give you the 101 of AI in business ever again. I want you to create your own auto-didactic machine that teaches you not what AI does today as fluently as it helps you adjust to what it could world around you continues to change.

Your task is nothing simpler than building an auto-didactic AI stack that can take you from zero to dangerous in any AI topic you choose. Want to master diffusion models for creative work? Curious how Retrieval-Augmented Generation (RAG) is changing enterprise search? Or maybe you want to finally learn how vector embeddings power recommendations? Perfect. Pick one and make that your case study. For me, I'm learning AI-enabled game design, because what else would someone who has spent too much time with their computer since age 8 being interested in doing.

Let's begin with the syllabus. Use any system, perhaps even the one you set up in Week 5, to map out what someone needs to know to understand and apply this concept. Ask it to include everything from key concepts and definitions to must-read papers and books, a glossary of confusing terms, real-world business cases, and to create quizzes and checkpoints along the way. Ask GPT to tailor this to your background. If you've never coded, it should include no-code tools and analogies (remember the ELI5). If you've built AI pipelines before, it should challenge you with architecture patterns and implementation details in addition to mastering the concepts. In the next step, is where tools like NotebookLM come in. Upload your PDFs and transcripts and let the AI become your tutor. You can ask it to summarize complex readings, explain them in simpler terms, generate quiz questions, and even link concepts across documents. It turns passive files into active dialogue. Pair that with Khan Academy's Khanmigo, especially if you're covering math-heavy or technical concepts. It connects you with the vast archive of Khan Academy's YouTube videos and adds interactivity to it, allowing you to ask follow-up questions, dig deeper, or slow things down without judgment. Combine this with YouTube's newer auto-captioning and transcript features, and suddenly, every video becomes recursive inputs to your learning machines. Next, quiz yourself with tools like Typeforms Quiz builder or simply within your GPT stack. Don't take a fail for an answer, and lean into what's hard because that signals where the most learning opportunity is. The next step is to apply what you've learned as soon as you can. Learning is only really cemented when it changes what you do. Pick a real problem where your new skill could help, continue with a real project you could take to the bank, and learn everything around it. For example, if you were learning about image generation with diffusion models for a post-apocalyptic game set in New York that you're building, try automating the path from a prompt to concept art entirely. Or if you dug into multi-agent systems to automate FP&A processes, simulate a multi-role meeting where AI agents take different parts of the process while working on the same sheets.

Finally, use everything you learn to build a compoundable meta-process. Refine the process of learning itself, codify the steps you're taking, and bring more and more AI to help you expand your reach and to expedite your learning. This is how you, the MBA, keep one step ahead of the competition that's still busy telling everyone AI can't even count the letters "r" in strawberry.

And that, dear Machina Discens, is the last technical skill I could ever hope to teach you.

Know thyself

Imagine I could take you back to 1999 and grant you two hours a day with your favorite AI tool. Two hours with ChatGPT, Midjourney, the spreadsheet agent you've trained on your own workflow, or your NLP stock picker that you pulled off of Github. What kind of havoc would you have unleashed on your industry within those moments? What shortcuts would you have taken to run rings around your peers and competitors?

Now ask yourself, how much would you have paid to be the only one with that advantage?

Whatever number comes to mind is proof that you already understand, intuitively, how AI acts as both a great equalizer and a ruthless leveler of competence. It doesn't care that you've logged Gladwell's 10,000 hours mastering Excel shortcuts and formulas, because now no one needs to. The same outputs are just a prompt away. AI strips away your hard-earned edge without blinking, and in doing so, it upends the entire career path that once rewarded burrowing into a snug little rabbit hole and staying there until retirement. What's left now to differentiate you is simply you. What doesn't matter is your skills or your raw technical prowess, and what does is what you know, how you think, how you choose to learn, and where you draw from. The safest moat is no longer your mastery of tools, but your ability to recombine knowledge, draw novel insight, and move across domains with fluidity and intuition. This is why I picked the advisor at the top of the chapter.

As you peer ahead to the future, you have two paths. You can go deep, or you can go wide.

If you're pushing the frontiers of foundational models with in the lab or serving clients in a niche that AI simply can't grasp no matter how hard it tries, go deep. You'll earn your edge by knowing *more about less* than anyone else. But if you're operating anywhere else, and let's be honest, most of us are, you'll need to go broader. I don't mean shallow, mind you, but wide. The world needs another prompt engineer as desperately as it needs another generic MBA. What it truly demands is an one who studied jazz improvisation, supply chain logistics, and fluid mechanics history and who can use all three to solve today's problems with fresh eyes.

The point isn't to be everything to everyone. The point is to be the one thing that no one else is. The only combination of curiosity, memory, instinct, scar tissue, and story that hasn't yet been scraped into the training set is you, and whatever you choose to do with your degree, the existence of AI incentives you to lean into yourself as the differentiating factor. Even if you find yourself in an industry that rewards even deeper niches and rabbit holes, you'll find the cultivation of range a potent differentiator even there. There's a reason why the ability for lateral thinking is mythized the way it is.

To future-proof yourself, cultivate a version of you that is able to think in diagonals as well as straight lines. You don't need to compete with machines on recall, speed, or optimization because you can never win. What you need to become is the unpredictable variable thrown into the machine. As long as you bring something your AI stack hasn't already conquered, there's always marginal value for adding you along. And if you accept as your task to maximize the marginal value of you on the loop, here's what I'd recommend you busy yourself with.

First, let's find you a stomping ground. Instead of chasing a passion manufactured for a college essay, we'll begin your grand differentiation process by beginning to notice what genuinely pulls at you. Life doesn't hand out sorting hats, and passion doesn't come from a job posting, which means we'll have to do the hard work ourselves. What we're looking for are those moments that sometimes veer on the obsessive, when your brain won't let go of a particular problem or puzzle. Do you find yourself chasing unsolved problems that bounce between industries like a pinball, never quite settling into one? Are you the type who loses sleep optimizing a spreadsheet that no one asked you to touch after hours? Do you draw energy from a crowded room and shared moments, or does your brain only light up when the last meeting ends and no one's breathing down your neck anymore? Whatever it is that tucks at your cranium and won't let go, start paying attention today. And whatever you do, don't start with personality tests. Instead, begin taking note of what pulls you in like a ball of yarn calls to a kitten, and start pulling on those threads as hard as you can. Your differentiation in the age of AI will come from knowing what everyone else knows and using what they use while also being deeply, whole-heartedly and entirely irrationally, *you*. Even if that means becoming the global thought leader in competitive crocheting powered by templates created by diffusion models.

Second, give yourself permission to explore. The corporate world isn't known for rewarding curiosity, at least not on company time. Your manager won't hand out promotions for the side quest you went on to learn about large language model tokenization or how Pixar storyboarding (ugly babies!) could improve your pitch decks. Don't wait for applause to begin, because then you never will. Instead, know ever so smugly that each thing you learn outside your lane is building a strategic luck surface for new opportunities to stick to. Curiosity is not a distraction when you weaponize it for your personal growth. On the contrary, it is how you upgrade operating system.

Third, build on everything we've covered about turning AI into your co-pilot for learning. Replace your Monkey OS that is nothing but a glorified status quo preservation system with a future-forward, curiosity-maximizing Learning OS and turn every "might this work" question into a lesson plan. Ask GPT to teach you vector embeddings like you're five, and then see if you can't spin one up on Supabase yourself. Summon Claude to explain economic incentive structures through the plot of *Dune* if you must. Your job is to turn AI from a passive answer machine into a self-directive compass. You are what you explore, and you become what you give yourself permission to.

Fourth, find mirrors to help you grow. Find the people, or yes, even AI coaches, who can reflect you back to yourself more clearly. Sometimes we can't see what makes us different because we're too close to it and can only see the mess, not the clear edges. Other times, the world gets it wrong and doesn't see in us what we know to carry within us. Maybe you've been cast as the odd one out for being a generalist in a world obsessed with specialists. Good, embrace it as your unfair advantage. Trust your inner compass as long as it's calibrated to find what pulls you toward productive differentiation and pressure test the results, even when it means seeing if what you've learned can be monetized. Some of the world's most extraordinary careers started with someone realizing they were the ugly duckling only because they hadn't found their right pond yet.

And finally, build the habit of pivoting on purpose, because soon enough you might need to do so because you have no other choice. Most people meet disruption with resistance and rejection. They grieve, stall, and hope the old path returns. But that won't be you. When Salesforce wipes your go-to-market plans, or Gemini automates your role, I want you to bravely default to the second-best option you've already been secretly cultivating. If you play your cards right, you'll always have a curios string you've been pulling on that's now ready to reveal the whole sweater.

In fact, I want you to be exactly like the humble slime mold. It's not much to look at, just a single-celled organism with no brain, no central nervous system, and no plan for the future. But when placed in a maze or set loose on a forest floor, it does something remarkable. It fans out slowly in all directions, feeling its way forward. It doesn't guess or rush; it simply explores its surroundings. When it finds dead ends, it retreats. When it finds food, it strengthens the paths that led there and never gives up on what it's gotten its unicellular mitts on. Over time, its messy-looking sprawl becomes an elegant, optimized map, one that can mirror the most efficient routes human engineers can design.

If that's what curiosity can do to a unicellular organism that has survived uncertainty for hundreds of millions of years, imagine what it can do to you. It makes you explore widely, tentatively, with no promise of immediate payoff but with a deep knowing that eventually, something

FIGURE 11.2 Congratulations, you're now ready to educate yourself.

connects. When the world shifts, you don't panic because you've already mapped your options and know exactly where to stretch to in order to grow forward.

When the internet arrived, the best MBAs didn't panic. They learned to use it before the rest of the world had even figured out how to boot up AOL. When automation hit supply chains, the smartest operators didn't resist it; they used it to streamline and scale what others hadn't even mapped to a dashboard yet. And now, when AI came for the MBAs' jobs, they welcomed it as a co-founder instead of a competitor.

That's what the unstoppable MBA does. You're not here to be the last of the old model; you're here to become the prototype of the next. What AI gives you is what no one else can: a chance to become *more*. More curious. More capable. More radically, dangerously, *you*.

And that, my friend, is how you win the age of the machine. Not by outworking it, because you can't. But by out-*humaning* it at everything you care about (Figure 11.2).

12

IT'S NEVER OVER FOR MBAS

There's one more lesson I have to share, which is to never promise to write a book about a revolution while it is still unfolding.

Capturing the contours of the concentric waves of AI adoption is like sketching a storm from the eye of it. The edges keep changing, the pressure is intense, and whatever felt certain on Monday becomes obsolete by Thursday.

Every time you think you have found solid ground, another tremor hits the landscape, and it's back to the drawing board. Writing about artificial intelligence while it is still being built has been both a privilege and an exercise in humility, and it segues us beautifully to the closing chapter.

Dealing with AI while building a company with it, teaching it, and writing about it has forced me to strip business, technology, and leadership down to their most basic questions, now laid bare in the nine chapters before you.

What exactly do we create in our economics, and why do we do it? What do technologies and tools have to do with it all, and what is the role of the MBA when the very foundations of management are being rewritten in real time?

Whatever AI certification or course you've taken is most likely already out of date. The moment the ink dries on a syllabus, a new architecture or paradigm shift in application appears. Models are expanding by the day, and the frontier moves faster than any textbook can keep up with. This is not a failure of education or the student in keeping up; it's simply the nature of living systems.

That is why our focus in these pages has not been on specific models or technologies, but on frameworks for thinking more clearly about them. The only sustainable advantage in a world of self-improving systems is the ability to learn and unlearn faster than the environment changes, which is why we've spent the whole book thinking about building a cognitive learning stack that teaches you how to think, not what to memorize.

The MBA, for all its flaws, remains uniquely suited to this challenge.

While other disciplines might chase tools and perfect them, the core of business focuses on the value it all creates and distributes. It teaches how to connect effort to outcome, and it forces us to reconcile intelligence with impact. That instinct, the fixation on value and how to distribute

DOI: 10.4324/9781003508427-12

it, makes the MBA mindset immortal, while the tools themselves can have a shelf life measured in days or weeks.

An MBA can operate on the surface of the moon with nothing but robots for company just as well as it can operate in the boardrooms of New York, Lagos, or Mumbai without losing a step in translation. And it can certainly operate in the age of AI.

That is, as long as it never stops learning. The next chapter of this story is being written as we speak, and it will test everything we think we know about business, economics, and power. Three major shifts are already underway, and while none of them are fully ready for a book like this, they are close enough on the horizon to see their shape forming. You would do well to be at the forefront of each of the below changes, even if it means creating the frontier yourself.

The business logic itself will become engineerable

Until now, business logic has lived in the minds of managers and the manuals of operations. It has been human, implicit, and context-dependent. That is about to change. Increasingly, we are moving this logic into the machines themselves.

AI agents are beginning to automate not just discrete tasks but the reasoning behind them. We are engineering workflows that no longer stop at "if X, then Y," but continue into "why X, and what happens if Y fails." This means the business logic of pricing, procurement, logistics, and strategy is being written as code.

For MBAs with a taste for systems thinking, this is a turning point. The language of spreadsheets and Gantt charts is evolving into code that connects directly to APIs, CRMs, and payment networks. Agent-to-agent (A2A) protocols are replacing email threads. Machine coordination protocols (MCP) are linking entire corporate systems into shared reasoning layers.

Imagine a future CFO who can debug a pricing model as easily as a developer debugs a program. Imagine a strategist who no longer needs to simulate market entry in Excel but can deploy a reasoning agent that runs millions of scenarios overnight. This is not science fiction in any sense other than the timing. For this future is coming, and it is certain to be the next iteration of business practice.

The MBAs who thrive here will be those who bridge business logic and computational logic. They will not just manage workflows; they will design them. The more engineering-oriented among them will find their place not in IT departments but in the heart of strategy, orchestrating human and artificial actors as parts of one integrated system.

The search for full automation

The second trend is the pursuit of complete determinism and the limits thereof.

Every generation of technology dreams of removing friction. Now that dream extends to the possibility of fully automating entire business functions.

Can an ordering process be made completely autonomous without reducing value? Can a zero-person hedge fund deliver sustainable returns? Could an entirely self-operating logistics company outperform one that still employs people? These questions are moving from philosophy to prototype, and a future MBA somewhere is already pushing the boundaries as we exchange thoughts on this page.

On one level, the answer to all is an obvious yes.

When processes are rule-based, structured, and measurable, machines already outperform humans. A well-trained model can trade faster, allocate capital more efficiently, and execute without emotion. But that is not the whole story. The real question is whether this kind of perfection creates or destroys value, and whether humanity wants this future to exist over the alternatives.

The drive for full automation risks erasing the very friction that gives business meaning. Human judgment, with all its flaws, introduces creativity, ethics, and empathy into decision-making. Strip that away, and what remains might be efficient but hollow. A hedge fund without a human will make money until it breaks the system it was designed to exploit.

The question then becomes one of limits.

How far should we push automation before the value it creates begins to erode? When does determinism become a liability? These are not technical debates, they are strategic and moral ones, and MBAs must come to own their seat at the table where these topics are discussed, because these discussions will define the next decade of management.

The geopolitics of intelligence

The third and perhaps most consequential trend is geopolitical.

Artificial intelligence is no longer confined to the domains of commerce and creativity, and it has found its place in the fields of warfare and statecraft, which makes the field laden with tripwires lying in ambush.

When Francis Fukuyama declared the "end of history," he imagined a world where liberal democracy and market capitalism had triumphed. What he could not have predicted was a new kind of competition, one fought not over ideology but over computation.

The next great power struggle will not be about who owns the oil but who owns the chips. The unit of labor is shifting from the human hand to the silicon wafer, and the capacity to manufacture, program, and secure those wafers will define global influence. AI has become both a weapon and a marketplace.

In this landscape, MBAs will once again find themselves near the center. The negotiation tables of the future will not only discuss trade or policy, but the regulation of intelligence itself. The leaders who understand the economic, ethical, and strategic implications of AI will shape the next global order.

They will have to answer new questions. How do you price data sovereignty? What happens when an algorithm, not a person, triggers a conflict? How do you tax labor when it is executed by machines? The consequences are immense, and the decisions we make now will echo for generations. It would behoove each MBA to find a way to lead these discussions, instead of following them.

GLOSSARY

Action orchestration The coordinated sequencing of steps an AI system or agent takes to accomplish a goal. It decides not just *what* to do but *when* and *in what order*, often across multiple tools or systems.

Action space The set of all possible actions an agent can take within its environment. A well-designed action space determines how flexible or constrained the agent's behavior can be.

Agent A system capable of perceiving a goal, planning steps toward it, using tools, and adjusting its behavior based on outcomes. It is more than software, because it can act, not only compute.

Agent loop The continuous cycle in which an agent observes the environment, plans a step, takes an action, evaluates the result, and begins again. This loop is what gives agents their sense of momentum.

Agent-to-agent (A2A) The interaction, negotiation, or collaboration between multiple agents. It allows machine systems to divide tasks, exchange information, or coordinate like miniature departments inside a company.

Agentic system A collection of interconnected agents that handle complex workflows together. When designed well, they behave like a digital organization with roles, memory, and shared objectives.

API (Application Programming Interface) A structured method that allows software systems to communicate or exchange functionality. APIs are what make it possible for an agent to direct external tools as if they were extensions of itself.

API call A specific request sent by one system to another, asking it to perform an action or return information. For agents, API calls are the primary way they interact with the outside world.

Automation The delegation of human tasks to machines, typically following predefined rules. It increases speed and consistency but depends on the task being stable and predictable.

Autonomy levels A spectrum describing how independently an AI system can operate, ranging from requiring constant human supervision to functioning entirely on its own. Higher autonomy raises both capability and risk.

Batch processing Executing work in large grouped segments rather than in real time. It is efficient for high-volume tasks but slow for workflows requiring immediate feedback.

Behavior policy The internal logic that guides how an agent decides its next action. It determines whether the agent behaves cautiously, aggressively, or strategically in pursuit of its goal.

BPMN flow (Business Process Model and Notation) A standardized visual map of a business process. It translates complex workflows into diagrams that can be automated or handed off to agents more cleanly.

Business logic The rules, decisions, calculations, and constraints that define how a company functions operationally. Encoded business logic is what allows agents to operate inside real businesses rather than toy examples.

Chain-of-thought The reasoning trail an AI model follows to reach its answer. While usually hidden, exposing it can help diagnose errors or improve reliability.

Cognitive load The mental effort required to process or complete a task. Automation and agents reduce cognitive load by absorbing repetitive or structurally complex steps.

Context window The amount of information an AI model can consider simultaneously. Larger context windows allow for longer reasoning chains, deeper recall, and richer planning.

Control plane The management layer that coordinates multiple agents, tools, and workflows. It is the digital equivalent of a command center, ensuring that agents don't work at cross-purposes.

Cost function The mathematical measure a model uses to judge whether its predictions are correct or desirable. Training is essentially the art of minimizing this cost.

Data governance The practices and rules ensuring that data is accurate, secure, and used responsibly. Strong data governance is a prerequisite for trustworthy automation and AI.

Data ingestion The process of collecting, cleaning, and preparing data for analysis or model training. It is the first and often most difficult step in building reliable AI workflows.

Data leakage When unintended information influences a model during training or prediction, often inflating performance artificially. It is one of the easiest ways to accidentally build an unreliable system.

Data pipeline The full journey through which data flows, from initial capture to transformation and storage. A robust pipeline ensures agents operate on timely and trustworthy information.

Deterministic system A system that produces the same output every time given the same input. Rule-based automation depends on determinism, which is why it thrives in stable environments.

Divergence When an agent's behavior drifts from the intended pattern, often due to compounding errors or unexpected environmental changes. It signals that oversight or recalibration is needed.

Embedding A numerical representation of text, images or other data that captures semantic meaning. Embeddings let models "understand" similarity and context in a mathematical form.

Error propagation The phenomenon where small mistakes at one step cascade into larger failures downstream. Agents require guardrails specifically to prevent this effect.

Exception handling The logic a system uses when a workflow encounters unexpected or invalid inputs. Strong exception handling is what separates robust automation from brittle automation.

Fine-tuning The process of adjusting a model using a smaller, domain-specific dataset to improve its performance on a particular task. It makes generic models behave like specialists.

Few-shot learning A model's ability to learn a new task from only a handful of examples. This is what allows modern systems to take on workflows they were not explicitly trained for.

Function calling When an AI model triggers an external software function, turning language instructions into real actions. Function calling is one of the foundational skills of agentic systems.

Generalization A model's ability to perform well on new, unseen data. High generalization is what differentiates genuinely intelligent systems from brittle ones.

Generative model A model that creates new content—text, images, audio, or code—rather than selecting from predefined options. Generative models are the creative engines of the AI ecosystem.

Governance layer The systems and rules that oversee how agents behave, ensuring safety, compliance and ethical alignment. It is the AI equivalent of corporate oversight.

Hallucination When an AI system produces outputs that are incorrect, invented, or logically inconsistent. Understanding and managing hallucination is central to enterprise adoption.

Heuristic A simplified rule or shortcut a system uses to make decisions quickly. Humans rely on heuristics constantly, and agents often do the same.

Hyperparameter A model setting chosen by designers rather than learned from data. Hyperparameters shape the model's behavior and performance characteristics.

Inference The process by which a trained model generates predictions or outputs. Inference is where the model's "knowledge" becomes visible.

Intent The underlying purpose behind a user's instruction. Effective AI systems must infer intent even when phrased imperfectly.

Iteration loop The cycle through which a system improves itself by repeatedly trying, evaluating, and refining. Continuous iteration is what makes agentic systems resilient and adaptive.

Knowledge base A structured repository of facts and rules that an AI system or agent can draw upon. It gives the agent something akin to institutional memory.

Latency The delay between a request and the system's response. Lower latency creates smoother user experiences and more responsive agents.

LLM (Large Language Model) A model trained on massive amounts of text that can reason, generate text, summarize information and interact through natural language. LLMs are the backbone of modern AI.

Memory architecture The design of how an agent stores, retrieves, and uses information from past interactions. Good memory design allows agents to behave coherently across long tasks.

Decision table A structured representation of conditions and corresponding actions used in deterministic systems. It allows complex rule sets to be automated cleanly without ambiguity about which branch to follow.

Decision threshold The cutoff point a model uses to decide between outcomes, such as classifying something as fraud or not. Adjusting the threshold changes the balance between accuracy and risk.

Deterministic automation Automation that follows fixed rules and always produces the same result from the same inputs. It is the foundation of traditional enterprise software and the easiest domain for agents to absorb.

Diffusion model A generative model that creates images or other media by iteratively denoising random noise. It has become one of the most powerful tools for synthetic visual content.

Distributed system A system in which computation or storage is spread across multiple machines rather than a single server. Most large-scale AI architectures rely on distributed systems for speed and resilience.

Domain adaptation A method for adjusting a model trained in one environment to perform well in another. It is crucial when the training data differs from real-world conditions.

Edge case A rare or unusual scenario that falls outside normal system behavior. Good automation anticipates edge cases; good agents learn to avoid or correct them.

Embedding space The multidimensional mathematical environment in which embeddings live. Distance in this space reflects semantic similarity, which enables search, clustering, and reasoning.

Emergent behavior Unexpected capabilities that arise in large models even though they were not explicitly trained to perform those tasks. These behaviors often feel surprising but signal scale-driven complexity.

Environment (agent context) The digital or physical world an agent interacts with, including available tools, data sources and constraints. A well-defined environment determines how effective an agent can be.

Error correction loop A cycle in which an agent identifies a mistake, revises its approach and attempts the task again. It is essential for agents to operate reliably at scale.

Event trigger A signal that starts or modifies a workflow. Modern enterprises use triggers to automate everything from notifications to multi-step processes.

Explainability The ability to understand why a model made a particular decision. As AI moves into regulated sectors, explainability becomes a competitive advantage rather than a luxury.

Feature extraction The process of identifying meaningful components of raw data so that a model can use them effectively. Even in end-to-end deep learning, feature quality still strongly influences performance.

Feedback loop The circular mechanism where outputs influence future inputs, leading to improvement or degradation over time. Feedback loops determine whether an agent becomes more effective or drifts into error.

Flow state (workflow context) The uninterrupted span in which an agent or automation completes a task without human intervention. Higher flow states correlate with greater efficiency and lower operational drag.

Function registry A catalog of all the tools, APIs, and functions an agent is allowed to use. It defines the agent's "hands" and determines the scope of actions it can perform.

General-purpose agent An agent designed to pursue many kinds of goals across domains rather than a narrow, specialized one. These systems are flexible but require strong guardrails and structure.

Generative workflow A process in which part of the output is produced by a generative model and then passed to other steps or tools. Many creative and analytical tasks now follow this pattern by default.

Guardrail A restriction or safety rule that prevents an AI system from taking harmful or undesired actions. Guardrails are essential for making agentic systems enterprise-safe.

Hallucination suppression Techniques used to reduce incorrect outputs, such as retrieval grounding, confidence scoring, or verification loops. It is one of the central engineering challenges in deploying LLMs.

Hardware accelerator Specialized chips such as GPUs or TPUs designed to train or run AI models efficiently. The availability of accelerators often determines the practical speed and scale of AI adoption.

Heuristic search A search method guided by heuristics rather than brute force. It allows agents to find solutions more quickly in complex spaces.

Human-in-the-loop A system that requires human oversight or intervention for critical steps. It balances autonomy with accountability and is often a transitional stage in automation.

Hybrid agent An agent that blends deterministic logic with probabilistic reasoning, switching modes depending on task structure. Most real-world enterprise agents will fit this category rather than purely deterministic or purely generative ones.

Inference latency The time it takes for a model to process an input and return an output. Low latency is crucial for real-time agents and any workflow where speed shapes user experience or profitability.

Inference pipeline The chain of steps a model runs during prediction, including retrieval, reasoning, tool calls, and post-processing. A well-designed pipeline determines whether an AI system feels instant or sluggish.

Inference server The infrastructure that hosts and runs AI models in production. Its design affects scalability, cost, reliability, and the practical ceiling of what your agents can do.

Information gain The value an agent receives from acquiring new data that reduces uncertainty. Agents use information gain implicitly to decide when to look something up versus when to act.

Input modality The format of data a model can understand—text, images, audio, video, or structured fields. Modern multimodal systems can operate across several modalities simultaneously.

Instruction following A model's capacity to interpret and execute user commands accurately. It is the backbone of enterprise reliability and determines how easily non-technical teams can work with AI.

Intent classification The process of identifying what a user is *actually* trying to achieve with a prompt. Strong intent detection ensures that agents choose the correct workflow instead of performing something adjacent but wrong.

Iteration horizon The maximum number of cycles an agent will attempt before stopping. A carefully chosen horizon prevents runaway loops and excessive cost.

Knowledge distillation A technique where a large model trains a smaller one to replicate its behavior. It produces lightweight models that preserve key abilities while reducing compute demands.

Knowledge graph A structured representation of entities and their relationships, allowing models to reason over explicit connections. It acts as a map of institutional or domain-specific knowledge.

Knowledge grounding Anchoring a model's responses in external, verified information rather than relying solely on internal patterns. It is one of the most effective methods for reducing hallucination.

Learning rate The parameter that controls how quickly a model updates its weights during training. Too high and learning becomes unstable; too low and learning becomes unbearably slow.

Memory retrieval The mechanism by which an agent pulls relevant past information into its working context. Good retrieval design allows long, multi-step tasks to feel coherent.

Meta-prompt A prompt that guides *how* a system should think, not just what to produce. Meta-prompts shape an agent's behavior, tone, and reasoning style.

Model checkpoint A saved snapshot of a model at a particular stage of training. Checkpoints allow developers to roll back, test variants or resume training without starting over.

Model compression Techniques that shrink a large model into a smaller one while preserving performance. Compression makes it feasible to deploy AI on edge devices or cost-sensitive environments.

Model interpretability The degree to which humans can understand why a model behaved the way it did. Interpretability becomes vital in finance, healthcare, and any regulated sector.

Model inversion A vulnerability where attackers reconstruct training data from a model's outputs. It highlights why privacy-preserving training is necessary for sensitive domains.

Model serving The act of deploying a model so it can handle live requests. Good serving infrastructure separates consumer-grade AI from enterprise-grade AI.

Multimodal model A model that understands and generates across several data types—text, images, audio, video or code. Multimodality expands agents into domains previously inaccessible to LLMs.

Natural language interface An interface that allows users to interact with software purely through text or conversation. This is the key reason AI systems have become accessible to non-technical workers.

Observation space The information an agent can "see" at any given time. A richer observation space gives agents more context but also requires more sophisticated planning.

Onboarding workflow The series of steps required to integrate a new user, customer, or employee into a system. It is one of the workflows most likely to be fully agentic within the next decade.

On-policy learning A reinforcement learning method where the agent learns from data generated by its own current behavior. It encourages consistency but can trap the agent in narrow behaviors.

On the loop A human supervises an autonomous system, ready to intervene if needed. It is the middle ground between manual operation and full autonomy.

Orchestration layer The layer that coordinates tools, models, data, and agents to perform workflow-level tasks. It is emerging as the most strategically important layer in enterprise AI.

Output token The smallest chunk of output a model generates, typically a fragment of a word. Token limitations shape how long or detailed a model's reasoning can be.

Overfitting When a model learns patterns that apply only to its training data and fails to generalize. Overfitting produces systems that appear brilliant in testing and brittle in reality.

Override logic Rules that allow humans or systems to stop or redirect an agent's actions. Override mechanisms provide a final safeguard against harmful or runaway behavior.

Ownership boundary The dividing line between what is controlled by humans and what is controlled by agents. Designing this boundary well determines the safety and efficiency of AI deployment.

Parameter A numerical value inside a model that shapes how it processes information. Modern frontier models contain trillions of parameters, giving them the flexibility to generalize across domains.

Parsing engine The component that structures unstructured input into something a model or workflow can use. Strong parsing determines whether an agent understands a request or misfires entirely.

Payload The content passed into or out of a tool, API or model call. Payload design influences reliability, cost and downstream reasoning.

Performance drift The gradual decline in a model's accuracy as real-world conditions shift away from its training data. Drift forces organizations to monitor, retrain or adapt their systems continuously.

Planning module The part of an agent that breaks a goal into steps, evaluates its options, and sequences actions. Strong planning is what separates tool callers from genuinely capable agents.

Post-processing The clean-up phase after a model produces an output, such as formatting, validation or applying business rules. It ensures that generative outputs are usable inside enterprise workflows.

Pre-training The initial phase in which a model learns general patterns from massive datasets. Pre-training creates the broad intelligence that fine-tuning later sharpens for specific tasks.

Prompt engineering The craft of designing instructions that guide a model's behavior. As agents rise, prompting evolves from tinkering to encoding business logic.

Prompt template A reusable structure that standardizes how models receive instructions. Templates bring consistency across teams and workflows.

Query expansion Techniques that broaden a search request so retrieval surfaces more relevant information. Expansion helps agents avoid missing critical context.

RAG (retrieval-augmented generation) A method where a model retrieves external information before generating an answer. RAG reduces hallucination and increases factual reliability.

Reasoning trace The model's intermediate chain of thoughts, hidden or visible, that leads to its final answer. In inspection mode, traces help diagnose errors or evaluate trustworthiness.

Reinforcement loop A sequence in which an agent learns from rewards or corrections over time. Reinforcement loops underpin autonomous improvement.

Reliability score A confidence measure assigned to a model's output. Scores help enterprise systems decide when to trust, verify, or escalate.

Reproducibility The ability to produce the same result consistently given the same conditions. Essential for debugging, regulation and credibility.

Resource allocation agent An agent designed to distribute time, money, or compute to competing priorities. It transforms budgeting and planning into dynamic, data-driven processes.

Retrieval corpus The database or document set that retrieval-augmented agents draw from. The corpus becomes the agent's practical memory of the enterprise.

Reward function The signal that tells an agent whether its actions are desirable. Designing this well prevents misaligned or unintended behaviors.

Routing layer The logic that decides which model, tool or agent should handle a given request. Routing layers become critical as enterprises run dozens of AI systems simultaneously.

Runbook A structured guide that outlines how to perform a complex process. When encoded into agents, runbooks become executable workflows.

Scaling law The predictable relationship between model size, compute, and performance. Scaling laws explain why larger models often gain emergent abilities.

Self-correction A model or agent's ability to critique and revise its own output. This capability dramatically improves reliability in ambiguous tasks.

Self-supervision A training method where a model learns patterns from raw data without human labels. It is one of the breakthroughs that enabled modern LLM performance.

Semantic search A search method that uses meaning rather than keywords. Semantic search allows agents to retrieve contextually relevant information even when phrasing varies.

Session memory Temporary memory that persists across interactions within a workflow. It lets agents maintain context throughout multi-step tasks.

Shadow mode A testing state where an agent runs alongside humans without taking real action. Shadow mode lets organizations evaluate readiness and safety before full deployment.

Simulation engine A system that allows agents to rehearse actions in a controlled environment. Simulation reduces errors before agents operate on real data or customers.

Slippage The divergence between what a user asked for and what an AI system actually did. Reducing slippage is one of the core challenges of agent design.

State machine A deterministic model describing all possible states of a system and the transitions between them. State machines are the backbone of rule-based automation.

Synthetic data Data generated by models rather than collected from the real world. Synthetic data accelerates training and protects privacy when real samples are limited.

Task decomposition Breaking a goal into smaller, solvable steps. Decomposition is what gives agents the illusion of strategic intelligence.

Task horizon The maximum distance into the future a model or agent can reliably plan. Short horizons require tight supervision; longer horizons allow autonomous workflows.

Telemetry Operational data emitted by models or agents, such as timing, errors or success rates. Telemetry enables monitoring, debugging, and compliance.

Temperature (model hyperparameter) A setting that controls randomness in model outputs. Low temperature produces predictable answers; high temperature encourages creativity.

Tool affinity The tendency of an agent to prefer certain tools or functions when uncertain. Tuning tool affinity helps eliminate bias toward suboptimal actions.

Tool call schema The structure that defines how an agent communicates with an external tool. Clean schema design determines reliability and interoperability.

Tool orchestration Coordinating multiple tools across a workflow so they operate in sequence or parallel. Orchestration is the practical backbone of agentic systems.

Traceability The ability to track how an output was produced, including data sources, model versions, and steps taken. Traceability is mandatory for regulated enterprises.

Training corpus The dataset on which a model learns its initial patterns. The corpus shapes what the model knows, what it misunderstands and where it generalizes.

Transformers The neural architecture underlying modern LLMs, known for efficient attention mechanisms. Transformers unlocked long-context reasoning and scalable learning.

Validation logic Rules that check whether inputs or outputs meet required standards. Validation prevents cascading errors inside automated workflows.

Vector database A database optimized for storing and searching embeddings. It allows semantic reasoning across millions of documents in milliseconds.

Vector search A method of retrieving information by measuring similarity between embeddings. It is foundational to modern RAG systems.

Versioning Maintaining labeled versions of models, prompts or agents so they can be audited or rolled back. Good versioning separates experimentation from production.

Window size (context window) The maximum amount of text or data a model can consider at once. Larger windows let agents reason over entire workflows, documents, or histories.

Workflow compiler A layer that turns high-level instructions into executable agent actions. It makes agent design more like programming without code.

Workflow orchestration Coordinating multiple steps, tools, and agents to achieve a business outcome. Orchestration turns isolated automations into end-to-end systems.

Zero-shot learning A model's ability to perform tasks it was never explicitly trained on. Zero-shot capabilities underpin the generality of modern LLMs.

Zero-touch operation A system that runs end-to-end without human intervention. Zero-touch workflows foreshadow the shift from automated enterprises to autonomous ones.

INDEX